GRAPHIC
DESIGN
THEORY

graphic design in context

GRAPHIC
DESIGN
THEORY

Meredith Davis

WITH 260 ILLUSTRATIONS, 188 IN COLOR

Thames & Hudson

First published in 2012 in paperback in the United States of America by Thames & Hudson Inc., 500 Fifth Avenue, New York, New York 10110

thamesandhudsonusa.com

Library of Congress Catalog Card Number 2012932515

ISBN 978-0-500-28980-8

Designed by Deborah Littlejohn

Printed and bound in China by 1010 Printing International Ltd

CONTENTS

This is a textbook and I am a teacher of design. I decided to write this book, not because I intended to undertake original research in theories of design, but because I found it difficult to inform my students about the conceptual underpinnings of their discipline through the dense philosophical and scientific writings of theorists. How could they make sense of Roland Barthes's essay "From Work to Text" with no background in semiotics or post-structuralist theory? And how could they make the leap from reading the original essay to their critique of typographic experiments from the 1980s or their current problem-solving task in the studio? What did it mean to teach them the Gestalt principles of design if they did not also understand the historical effort to frame issues of human perception as a science? And how could they play a future role in the developing practice of interaction design if they had no critical perspective on the issue of designer control versus user participation in the design process?

In searching for a textbook that could support studio instruction, I found many in which design was a footnote to the larger discussion of art or business, but none that addressed ideas from both the humanities and the social sciences. My strategy for helping students to unpack complicated theory had for many years been based on an assembly of readings on the reserve shelf of the college library. This approach suffered from an almost total lack of context for the students' interpretations—for either the making of design or for the larger historical trajectory of ideas. It therefore led me to develop a lecture course on design theory through which to frame an introduction to concepts. But not all students have access to such coursework, and many young teachers are not prepared by their own design education to slog through the literature in an effort to cull design-relevant sources from the overwhelming body of knowledge.

The aim of this book is therefore to survey a range of theories about graphic design for students who are beginning their studies, and to

introduction

introduce a collection of ideas and sources for later scholarly investigation. It also sets out to inform the development of students' visual work. For this reason, I include only those theoretical frameworks for which I could find direct and obvious links to form and its outcomes with the audiences for design. In editing down a larger list of theories, I chose only those for which I could describe a visual example in application.

I also debated the extent to which business and the economic context for design should be addressed. My final decision was to focus on the more general issues of representation rather than on implementation strategies within commerce. There is a great need in the professional education of students for theories about the value of human-centered design in business. And although I lament the fact that very few texts have been written from a designer's perspective, it was simply too daunting to address those particular concerns in a first effort to compile a survey of theory.

The decision to limit scope also meant forgoing not only in-depth discussions about philosophy and the larger role of design in social history, but also detailed explanations of single writers or theorists (whose work may be relevant to design practice in some aspects only). The book is therefore intended as a snapshot that, hopefully, will lead students to further reading.

The text is organized in two parts. Part 1 establishes the relationship of visual representation to the contexts for design. My decision to dedicate a significant portion of the book to context is because, historically, so much of graphic design education has been about fitting form to content—as though form, itself, is not content. This traditional, content-driven approach underestimates the importance of people, activities, and settings in choosing and critiquing representational strategies. Similarly, many judgments about design fail to consider broad or long-term consequences, responding only to immediate demands, rather than to the complex systems of which design artifacts are only one part.

I believe it is with respect to these issues of context and complexity that the study of theory is especially relevant.

Part 2 of the book surveys a number of theoretical frameworks, from the beginning of the twentieth century to the present. While it is impossible to catalog all historical positions in a book of this size, or to subject them fully to the rigors of historiography, I have attempted to introduce concepts that have direct implications for the making of design and for the critique of contemporary design practice. The goal of this section of the book is also to prepare students for entry into the reading of more substantive texts by the original authors.

The design of the book is not accidental. The introductions to the chapters in Part 1 offer useful examples and analogies that help clarify some of the key concepts discussed later in the text. It is hoped that these sections present important ideas for new students in far more interesting, accessible, and memorable ways than would be possible via a synopsis of theoretical writing. Key words and concepts that are central to the discussions in the chapters are defined in glossary form in the margins. These words are positioned near their first use in the book to help readers understand the meanings in context. Important theoretical works are named in the text and in the endnotes to help identify seminal literature for further study. Boxes provide deeper examination of issues that are subsections of the main text and that would otherwise divert the reader from the primary discussion. Expanded captions contain discussions of examples, using the theoretical viewpoints for which they were selected.

The book includes a timeline that locates key topics of discussion in relation to each other. Because this is not a book on design history and I have made no attempt at comprehensive coverage of major movements, the visual examples that illustrate various theoretical positions are not always ordered chronologically within the text. But the timeline should enable readers to identify concurrent, overlapping, and successive ideas as a way of making evolutionary sense of design theory. It is assumed that students will study design history at some point in their professional curricula.

It is also important for students to understand the differences between generative and critical theories. Generative theory is used to describe ideas that are helpful in the making of graphic design. For example, the concerns of the designer in terms of his or her audiences; the crafting of messages in material form; the expectations of behavioral outcomes; and the anticipated place of the object in a larger communication system or environment. Discussions of such theory are intended to guide the student designer's view of what is important in defining and developing specific responses to context. Critical theory plays a greater role in the summative evaluation of design as a discipline and practice. It involves worldviews and frameworks for making judgments about the impact of design and its position within larger social, cultural, and historical contexts. While critical theories may shape the generative approaches of designers, they more typically describe shared belief systems about what design is and how it works.

One early decision I had to make in writing this book was what to call the people for and with whom we design. The current terminology in practice favors the word *users*, with a nod toward the interactive aspects of digital media. But this term seemed inappropriate when referring to the print-based culture that comprised much of the twentieth century or to the more recent notion of participants or co-creators when referring to emergent design solutions. *Readers* was a possible term, yet when describing interaction with non-textual material, it held the residue of specific theoretical positions of post-modernism. It also caused confusion when talking of text as being "readerly" as opposed to "writerly." *Viewers* had the opposite problem of not fully describing engagement with verbal language. I use these terms at various places within the text to represent specific relationships between people and designed objects, but none of them serves adequately as a general description of those for and with whom we design.

I therefore finally settled on the term *audiences*, even though I fully recognize its limitations. It is important for readers of this book to understand that my choice does not imply that people are passive recipients of content. Instead, my intention in using this term is to invoke a corollary for design as something that must perform, engage, and elicit a full spectrum of human response within a specific context and through a deliberate design effort to craft the conditions for an experience. This is not a perfect solution, but it is the closest I could come to addressing the range of qualities in the relationships between the designer, the participants in design, the outcomes, and the context.

Finally, it has been claimed for decades that designers do not read. But this has not been my experience in the professional or academic world. Some of the best-read people I know earn their living as makers of visual form. I worry about the future of those students whose coursework permits them to neglect not only the great works of science and philosophy but also important texts on design. This book is in no way a substitute for the deeper reading of original works or more focused discussions about design from a particular theoretical perspective. I am grateful that such writing exists and that the volumes concerning theory continue to grow. Many of these works are positioned outside the discipline, despite their relevance to design, and there is great value in students undertaking their own searches for such material. The purpose of this book is to provide a roadmap that makes the journey just a little bit easier.

The chapters that follow lay the groundwork for a discussion of graphic design theory. The first chapter provides a brief history of communication models as evidence of our increasing awareness of influences on how people produce meaning and on the social life of messages. The second chapter explores the concept of representation and ways in which designers influence the construction of meaning. The third chapter focuses on context and the cognitive, socio-cultural, technological, physical, and economic conditions in and to which designers shape form.

The goal of these chapters is to define key terms and concepts that are essential to the study of design theory. Explanations come from both the humanities and the social sciences and there has been no attempt to privilege one over another. Each, however, is representative of a larger worldview or conceptual framework for visual communication. Gestalt theory, for example, provides a rational explanation of visual perception that is, as we shall see in Part 2, consistent with early twentieth-century modernism's interest in scientific thought, logic, and abstraction. Stuart Hall's description of a constructionist theory of representation is fundamental to the post-modern concept that the meaning of a text can never be fully resolved because every reader brings his or her own cultural position and history to the task of interpretation. Marshall McLuhan's ideas about the influences of media forecast the social effects of the contemporary networked environment.

Each discussion cites seminal works of literature from a variety of disciplines. Readers are encouraged to pursue ideas for further study and to place these works in an historical context of theoretical writing on design. Students of design should also consider these concepts in their own production of studio-based work—they serve as critical frameworks for the evaluation of designed objects and explain potential outcomes with audiences for design.

part 1

laying the groundwork

communication

representing thought and action

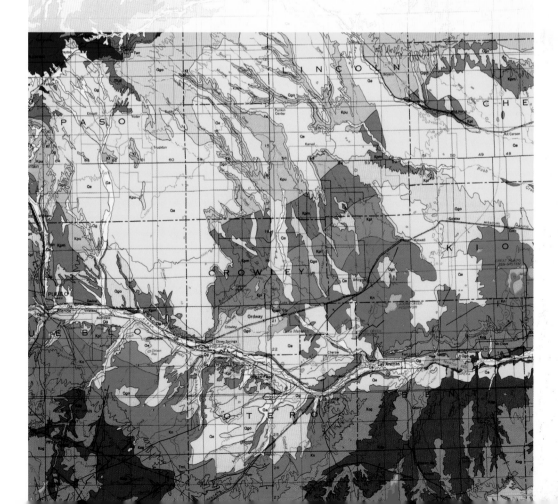

models

1

Models are mental or physical structures that

represent our experience of and knowledge about the world. They shape and organize our perceptions of new experiences and help to make sense of our thought processes. Physical models give our ideas material form, allowing us to visualize, modify, elaborate, and share our thoughts, and to explore complex concepts and relationships that would be impossible to process in our minds alone.

MODEL

A mental or physical structure that represents experience of and knowledge about the world. In conceptual models, meaning resides in the organization or relationships among ideas or concepts. Physical models describe the arrangement of components and the roles they represent within a larger system.

PERCEPTION

The ability to see, hear, or become aware of something through the senses. Perception includes both the observation of phenomena and the understanding that comes from such observation. It therefore involves memory and is influenced by perspective or point of view.

Whether consciously or unconsciously, **MODELS** influence the way we think and act. They also embody theoretical assumptions about things in the world and how they work. For example, the modern concept of the universe includes the idea of the Earth as a sphere that spins on an imaginary axis and revolves around the Sun. Our expectations of periods of dark and light, the shortest routes to certain destinations, and typical climates in different regions of the world arise as much from our mental representations of these spatial relationships as from any knowledge of relevant data. With this in mind, it is easier to understand how people in earlier historical periods created mental models of the universe that helped them to shape their own particular beliefs and customs.

Language gives expression to the mental and physical models upon which we base our **PERCEPTIONS**. Inhabitants of the United States and Europe, for example, often refer to Australia as being "down" and the Arctic as being "up"; they describe Israel as the "Middle East" and China as the "Far East." Such constructions, however, have no basis in concrete reality. They arise from political points of view and socially driven visual conventions related to how we represent the world in maps. The "up/down" references that are used in descriptions of location are a consequence of north-oriented cartography. But this particular orientation of the globe does not reflect a law of nature (we are all clinging to the planet through gravity, regardless of where we live)—it is simply the conventional model through which we learn about and refer to geography. The terms "Far East" and "Middle East" are derived from the perspective of the cartographers who created the maps: not only is it unlikely that the Chinese considered themselves to be "far," but the nautical route from Los Angeles to Beijing is also not east. In these examples, language provides an insight into how our subjective mental models of physical reality shape interpretations and actions.

Physical models allow us to refine and communicate abstract concepts. Architects use models to explore the relationships between built spaces and how people live, work, and move around in them; they also examine the aesthetics of proportion and the technical demands of structural designs on construction. Architectural sketches and scaled-down versions of buildings give physical form to such ideas. In this case, the model physically expresses some optimal arrangement of form that is consistent with the architect's theoretical model of how people use space. A model of a house allows the architect to see whether, for example, the kitchen is too far from the laundry or a room is too vertically proportioned to be cozy. But, crucially, it also ensures that the client and the architect are able to reach a consensus about the final design of the house: the model confirms that both parties hold a similar vision of how to express certain needs, values, and meanings in built form.

Similarly, graphic design objects are models that express mental constructs of how language and communication work. Just as the architect's model of a house is a reflection of his or her ideas about the relationships among form, space, and how people live, the physical objects made by graphic designers are guided by mental models of how communication works. Over and above the subject matter of the communication, our analysis of such objects must therefore address what their physical qualities tell us about the designer's view of audience, representation, and the communication process.

Models can act as powerful tools in shaping or representing perception, behavior, and attitude. The models that are used by graphic designers to understand the communication process and the role of graphic design are highly significant: they define the scope of our work, the types of knowledge and collaborators we think are important to our task, and our understanding of the consequences of our actions. At this fascinating time in the evolution of graphic design, rapid changes in technology and shifting theories challenge us constantly to re-evaluate the models upon which our professional activity is based.

This chapter highlights a few models of communication from recent history. Fairly or unfairly, it critiques what they do and do not include, as well as the attitudes and actions they enable. The aim of the chapter is not to arrive at a definitive conclusion about how communication works, or to prove that one author has more validity than another, but to identify what kinds of theory and knowledge are important to design as a practice and a discipline.

THE SHANNON/WEAVER MODEL OF COMMUNICATION

In 1948 Claude Shannon, a research scientist for the Bell Telephone Company, tried to optimize the process for transmitting an electrical signal with minimum distortion. His "Mathematical Theory of Communication" described message transmission in terms of a signal source, or **SENDER**, which transmitted information along a **CHANNEL** to a **RECEIVER** (SEE FIGURE 1.1)[1]. The signal passed through various types of interference (**NOISE**), resulting in some degree of information loss. Shannon's aim was to reduce noise and thereby improve the telephone's ability to deliver messages with fidelity to the original.

Soon after Shannon published his work, the scientist Warren Weaver recognized that Shannon's model (devised for message transmission between machines) could be used equally effectively in describing interpersonal communication. Warren's interest was in applying models from physical science to the understanding of human behavior. Shannon's original document was republished in 1949, with a preface and additional text by Weaver. The result is what is known today as the Shannon/Weaver model of communication.

SENDER

The origin of a transmitted message.

CHANNEL

A medium for communication or the passage of information. In mechanical terms, the channel is a circuit used as the path for a signal. Under a broader definition, it is the means for delivering messages: print, digital networks, and projection are channels for visual communication.

RECEIVER

The destination of a transmitted message.

NOISE

Anything that interferes with, interrupts, or distorts the successful transmission of a message from its origin to its destination. Noise can be physical, psychological, social, cultural, or technological in origin.

It would be easy to dismiss this model as simply the beginning of a more sophisticated lineage of communication models, if it were not so persistent in shaping contemporary ideas of communication. Many people still refer to the Shannon/Weaver model as an accurate depiction of human communication, despite the fact that Shannon's original intention was to describe the work of machines. Although Weaver deemed Shannon's work a good match for explaining the exchange of information between two people, the model does little to address the interpretive consequences of **CONTEXT** (see chapter 3), the particularly human nature of communicators, and various kinds of communication channels.

1.1   SHANNON MODEL OF COMMUNICATION, 1948
Adapted from Claude Shannon, "A Mathematical Theory of Communication," *Bell System Technical Journal*

In his model of communication, Shannon described the transmission of an electrical signal across a channel to a receiver. Weaver applied the model to an explanation of human communication in 1949, making it possible for others to use it as a theoretical basis for visual communication.

CONTEXT

The circumstances and background that form the setting for the communication and interpretation of messages. Context includes the communicators themselves, as well as the physical, social, cultural, technological, and economic factors that are characteristic of the setting and that place particular interpretive demands on audiences.

CONTENT

The subject matter or topic of a message.

If we accept this model as the basis for visual communication, the Shannon/Weaver sender must represent both the originator of the message (the client) and the designer of its form. The model does not provide a way to account for what the designer brings to the communication process that is more than the literal subject matter of the message, as defined by the client. A description of the channel would have to account for both the physical properties of the designed object (e.g. the poster, the screen-based display, and so on) and its means of distribution across time and space (e.g. online, by mail, on television, and so on). For the purposes of analysis, the material qualities of the designed object could not be separated from the means by which it reaches audiences. Finally, the Shannon/Weaver receiver would have to stand for all the diverse audiences who encounter the message **CONTENT**, now and in the future. Unlike a single telephone transmission that ends when it reaches the intended receiver, visual messages often circulate to many people over time and in many different contexts.

Needless to say, these additional criteria define a difficult representational task for such a simple model, and it is a little unfair to judge Shannon against the characteristics of a system that is far more complex than the one he originally addressed. But when Weaver adapted Shannon's mathematical model to a description of human communication, he opened it up to such criticism. Despite these shortfalls, some graphic design practices reinforce the beliefs that the designer can be a neutral, technical hand of the client; that meaning resides solely in the artifact itself (that is, in its subject matter and form but not influenced by its context or means of distribution); and that reaching a mass audience, in which all participants are seen as roughly equivalent in their behavior and attitudes, is the goal of most communication design. Later models and sections of this book challenge these beliefs.

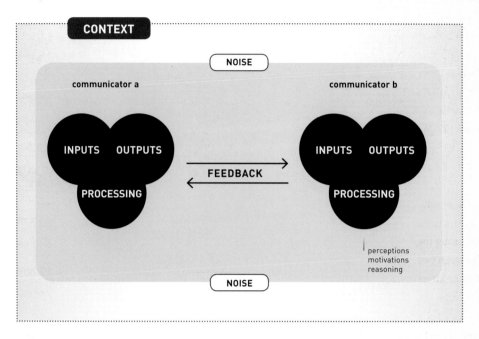

1.2 EMMERT/DONAGHY MODEL
OF COMMUNICATION, 1981
Adapted from Philip Emmert and
William Donaghy, *Human Communication:
Elements and Contexts*

The Emmert/Donaghy model
acknowledges the role of context in
human communication and that meaning
cannot be separated from participants'
communication histories and cognitive
processing behaviors.

THE EMMERT/DONAGHY MODEL OF COMMUNICATION

A deeper understanding of human communication was offered in 1981 by the communication professors Philip Emmert and William Donaghy in their elaboration of the Shannon/Weaver model (SEE FIGURE 1.2).[2] They include important additional factors in their model that describe human communication more appropriately—namely, context, feedback, and the makeup and behavior of communicators.

context

The Emmert/Donaghy model acknowledges that communication always takes place in a context. This context includes the communicators themselves, as well as the physical, socio-cultural, and technological environment through which messages pass. This recognition of context (as present in all communication exchange and as primary in the construction of particular meanings) is especially important for the graphic designer. As designers we seek "goodness of fit" (see p. 57) between the formal aspects of designed objects (the choice of visual elements, their organization in particular artifacts and formats, and their stylistic treatment) and the contexts in which they are to be interpreted. Designed objects and their audiences do not live in an interpretive vacuum— they are *situated* in all the messiness and complexity of real life, and design must account for these conditions whenever possible.

A designer often has to decide how many variables within a given context the design will address, and which aspects of the overall context should be assigned the highest priority when they are in competition. The quality of a design is therefore often judged as much in terms of the designer's contextual definition of the problem as by the formal attributes of the designed object itself. If the designer chooses to ignore critical aspects of the communication context, the design may fail, even though its form may be responsive to other, less important demands of the problem. Imagine, for example, a fundraising pledge card that does not meet mailing regulations; an event poster that can be read only from a short distance away; and a television promotion for a male political candidate in which his wife always walks behind him, never at his side. These examples undervalue the technological, physical, and cultural factors in their respective communication contexts. Regardless of how beautiful or compelling the final form may be, we can judge them as falling short of the obvious communication task.

feedback

FEEDBACK

Information given as a response to a message and that serves as the basis for extending, curtailing, or improving communication. Feedback may take the form of an action, discourse, or observable patterns in behavior or opinion.

Emmert and Donaghy also introduce the concept of **FEEDBACK** and designate *two communicators*, as opposed to the sender and receiver in the Shannon/Weaver model. These concepts acknowledge the two-way nature of most human communication, even in circumstances under which feedback is delayed or communicators are not in the same physical space.

It may appear that print media and television involve one-way communication and lack formal opportunities for feedback. The designer of a poster rarely hears about success or failure from those who have attended an advertised event. And unless we take part in market research or are zealous bloggers, broadcasters have very little information about our responses to particular programming. If people do not show up, watch, or buy, it is not clear how their lack of engagement results from the failure of any specific design attribute or aspect of strategy. Focus-group testing provides some insight into these issues, but it rarely replicates the complexity of the actual context in which the communication takes place. Immediate feedback loops are more integral to the Web and interactive media. In these situations we can observe or record the physical interaction that is required to alter the state of information or review the submission of a formal response.

But if we expand the time frame for considering how an audience responds to visual communication and think of communicators in more subtle ways, we find that the information in designed messages, and evidence of its reception by audiences, often circulate through culture over time. The communication interaction can be viewed not just in terms of its immediate success or failure in achieving a short-term goal, but also as a trajectory of understanding and acceptance for ideas that result from encounters with visual messages. Much of what we define as "cultural literacy" (ideas that are held in common by people who live in the same culture)

CONSENT AND AFFIRMATION

Feedback that responds to existing communication helps designers to shape the problem space for future design activity. It is delivered over time and at scales beyond that of the individual project. In order to have an impact on continuing and future approaches to communication, feedback need not necessarily take the form of letters of complaint or endorsement. It can arise in the form of what "works" in the marketplace—what consumers tolerate and embrace as social and cultural practices.

The twentieth century, for example, witnessed the proliferation and refinement of corporate identities (logos, typefaces, and visual strategies that are associated with particular companies). The journalist Naomi Klein discusses the conventional logo in the 1970s as small and discreet—the Ralph Lauren polo horseman and the Izod Lacoste alligator appeared on the pocket or collar as a subtle reminder of the brand. "These logos," she says, "served the same social function as keeping the clothing's price tag on; everyone knew precisely what premium the wearer was willing to pay for style."[3] Logos eventually became fashion accessories in their own right, "ballooning from a three-quarter-inch emblem to a chest-sized marquee."[4] Klein describes the clothing that followed as less significant than the brand names they carried—we became walking corporate billboards. In recent years companies have expanded their branding to include cultural events, which Klein says became "brand-name outposts." In this case, "Branding was not just a matter of adding value to a product. It was about thirstily soaking up cultural

COMMUNICATION MODELS

can now be attributed to ideas circulated primarily through the media. Such messages constitute a kind of feedback for their originators. Ideas and practices that resonate with audiences enter the zeitgeist or spirit of the times. Those that do not, disappear quickly. (See box: "Consent and Affirmation.")

In terms of the larger cultural response to design, the Emmert/Donaghy description of feedback is not particularly satisfying. It presumes that an understanding of message success or failure is informed only by first-hand responses from the recipient, or exists as some free-floating component of the larger context in which communication takes place. Individual designers, however, are obliged not only to inform their professional activity through observation, research, and various types of discourse that address a wider cultural context (beyond the domain of the individual project), but also to make sense of their work within systems of social and cultural production.

ideas and iconography that their brands could reflect by projecting these ideas and images back on the culture as 'extensions' of their brands."[5]

What Klein describes is the success of a branding strategy, not evident through immediate verbal feedback in response to the formal attributes of its logo design or its short-term ability to sell T-shirts, but demonstrated in our progressive acceptance of its transforming role in culture. We *consent* to these practices and *affirm* the appropriateness of company values by yielding increasing amounts of cultural and public space to such communication strategies. This long-term behavior constitutes feedback for designers and their clients just as much as the response of any focus group or complaining customer.

There has been some resistance to these branding strategies. Kalle Lasn's *Adbusters* magazine and advocacy for a "Do-Not-Buy Day" are evidence of a backlash against the influence of commerce in our culture. Some fashion firms have come under scrutiny for their production practices in developing countries, and fast-food restaurants are under pressure to respond to the growing obesity of their patrons. In other words, designers must pay attention to the evolving inclinations of audiences and consequences of design in society, beyond the parochial needs of specific clients. Whether our intention is to leverage existing strategies for greater effect or to unseat longstanding approaches for cultural or commercial gain, we observe the interactions among people, objects, and contexts over time for clues about how to craft the next message.

two communicators

As previously discussed, the aim of the Shannon/Weaver model was to describe the exchange of information between machines, and its main features included a sender and a receiver. But Emmert and Donaghy's introduction of the idea of two communicators offers a more accurate description of human communication. Their model not only acknowledges that individuals both transmit and receive messages, it also takes into account all the written, visual, auditory, and kinesthetic information present in human encounters and represented in the communication artifacts produced by people. Emmert and Donaghy describe communicators as being comprised of all the communication inputs, outputs, and mental **PROCESSING** of their lifetimes. In other words, our interpretation of a single message is influenced by all our previous experiences.

The authors also describe processing as involving perception, **MOTIVATION**, and **REASONING**. It is important to note that, as designers, we may view the world and messages from perspectives that are different from those of our audiences. Graphic designers cannot assume that their own perceptions and motivations are a good match with those of the people for whom they design, or that they are even typical of the general population. At the same time, the role of the designer is often as an advocate for the audience in the design process. An increasing number of design firms therefore rely on audience- or user-centered research that identifies significant patterns in people's wants and needs, as well as the behavior, values, and attitudes that shape them.

The design researchers Gerhard Fischer and Elizabeth Sanders suggest going a step further and using the intended audience for design as **CO-CREATORS** to

PROCESSING

The human transformation of information (stimuli) into meaning. Processing involves perception, motivation, and reasoning.

MOTIVATION

The reason for doing something or viewing something in a certain way. Motivation activates goal-oriented behavior and can be intrinsic (something essential arising from within the individual) or extrinsic (as a response to something outside the individual).

REASONING

The process of determining a cause, explanation, or justification for something. Reasoning involves forming judgments logically.

CO-CREATOR

A person who engages actively with a designer to determine the best strategies for design solutions. Through structured activities, a co-creator may not only provide information about the useful, usable, and desirable characteristics of products, services, and communication, but may also suggest what to make in the first place.

ensure a "good fit" between the characteristics and features of a designed object and the people who make use of it in specific contexts. Rejecting the term CONSUMER as contributing to "the degeneration of humans into 'couch potatoes,' for whom a remote control is the most important instrument of their cognitive activities," Fischer suggests that the role of design lies in creating opportunities for informed participation.[6] He laments situations in which "1) someone wants to be a designer in personally meaningful activities but is forced to be a consumer; and 2) someone wants to be a consumer in personally irrelevant activities and is forced to be a designer."[7] The goal of well-designed communication objects is therefore to engage audiences or users in reasoning and actions that are appropriate to their motivations and perceptions of relevance.

As the complexity of communication problems increases, so do the demands on reasoning. The designer is often a mediator between a system (physical, technological, cultural, social, or economic) and the audience's or user's idea of that system, how it works, and its role in supporting the activities people really care about. The goal of design is to represent the system appropriately in ways that aid reasoning. Whether this involves intuiting the use of a software operation, reflecting on a work of literature, accepting a political position, or making an informed purchase, designed objects stand between the audience and an external system or framework. The physical or virtual object may therefore enhance or diminish the audience's understanding by the degree to which it effectively represents that system. Further, the system's meaning and usefulness are often understood in terms of people wanting to accomplish something, so the configuration of the system must appear to be consistent with that intended goal.

For example, as a long-time user of Microsoft Word, I understand it to be word-processing software. I expect it to provide features and functions that allow me to check grammar and spelling, add emphasis to certain words through type weight and italics, and format a document using margins, line spacing, and tabs. This is my idea of a word-processing or authoring system. Microsoft, however, has decided to take some formatting control out of my hands. When I type a number at the beginning of a sentence, the program automatically assumes I am making a list and places numbers at the start of each subsequent line. To turn off this function, I must go back and enter commands that counter the programmed system. When I bullet a list of items, the program assumes I also want to indent that list. These are design, not authoring issues, even though my idea of Microsoft Word is not that of a design program. In other words, there is a mismatch between my understanding of the system and motivation for using it and those of Microsoft. This mismatch engages me in more reasoning than may be necessary for the task.

The Emmert/Donaghy view of communicators acknowledges that meaning is constructed in the mind of the interpreter and is not controlled solely by the originator of the message (as implied by the designation of sender and receiver in the Shannon/Weaver model). The best we can hope for, as designers, is to put in place the appropriate elements and conditions that help an audience arrive at a similar interpretation to the one we intend. Later chapters of this book discuss CONSTRUCTIONIST or writerly theories of design, which suggest

---

CONSUMER

A person who buys and uses goods and services. In design, consumers are those for whom products, services, and messages are created. Human-factors studies and marketing research are used to determine which characteristics and behaviors the members of the target audience have in common.

CONSTRUCTIONISM

The theory that knowledge and meaning are derived from life experiences in a social world. This is in contrast to the idea that meaning is either inherent in objects or that an individual can assign meaning that will be understood automatically by others without explanation. See also constructionist approach (p. 36).

COMMUNICATION MODELS

that the reader actually creates or writes the meaning of the work through his or her own interpretive experiences (see pp. 36–37).

According to Emmert and Donaghy, noise is not only a by-product of the context but is also internal to the communicators themselves: perception, motivation, and reasoning (i.e. aspects of an individual's mental processing of stimuli) can result in interpretations of meaning that differ between the originator of the message and the recipients. This principle argues for a deeper understanding of cognitive processes as fundamental to design practice. It indicates that the audiences for design are more complex and diverse than implied by the demographic definitions favored by most marketing studies, and that patterns in how we think influence both what and how things mean.

This expanded definition of the communication process tells us that the work of the designer involves more than simply subjective decisions about what looks good or is novel; confirms that design arises from and influences general values and attitudes in the culture; involves the detection of pattern in determining which characteristics of designed objects compete successfully for people's attention in an environment of information overload; and suggests that decisions about form must be linked to how people process information as well as to the nature of the subject matter.

SENDER	MESSAGE	CHANNEL	RECEIVER
Communication skills	**Content**	Seeing	Communication skills
Knowledge	**Elements**	Hearing	Knowledge
Social system	**Structure**	Touching	Social system
Culture	**Code**	Smelling	Culture
Attitudes	**Treatment**	Tasting	Attitudes

1.3   BERLO MESSAGE MODEL, 1960. Excerpted from David Berlo, *The Process of Communication: An Introduction to Theory and Practice*

Berlo's model of communication identifies the components of messages. While some of these components are physical, others are cultural conventions that account for what things mean beyond the literal inventory of subject matter.

BERLO'S MESSAGE COMPONENTS

The communication theorist David Berlo provided another useful model for designers in his identification in 1960 of message components (SEE FIGURE 1.3).[8] Admitting that these components are often difficult to separate, he describes the role each one plays in the construction of meaning.

content, elements, and structure

Berlo explains that the message has **CONTENT**—subject matter that is the topic of communication. The message takes physical form through **ELEMENTS**: text, headlines, illustrations, photographs, graphic marks, and symbols. These are the tangible forms from which the message is composed and about which the designer makes choices.

CONTENT
The subject matter or topic of a message.

ELEMENT
Any text, image, or graphic component of a visual composition. In design, white space is considered an element because its physical qualities are designed and contribute to meaning, in the same way as text, images, or graphics.

STRUCTURE

The arrangement of and relationships among the parts of something complex. In visual terms, structure is composition and involves not only the organization of elements but also their relationship to the field of vision (i.e. on a page, on a screen, or in the environment).

STRUCTURE is the visual/spatial/temporal arrangement of elements. This arrangement is often referred to as composition in graphic design and as sequencing and pacing in time-based media (motion graphics, film and video, and so on). Meaning can be embedded in or implied by these structures. It is possible, for example, to talk about the visual composition of type on a page as being "stable" or "playful." Such descriptions refer to the degree to which visual elements are organized according to the laws of physics (balanced or tipsy) or some other parallel experience in the physical world. Time-based media often use such devices as flashbacks or multiple views of the same event as a **NARRATIVE** reordering of the linear structure of time. We learn to read such structures through our experiences of watching movies.

NARRATIVE

Storytelling. An unfolding of connected events or actions.

Structure indicates which elements are related or most important and should be seen or read before others in the same space. In writing, an author influences the perception of importance through the linear ordering of ideas. The start of a paragraph tells us something about the primary thesis, and later sentences expand the content through greater detail. A story has a beginning, a middle, and an end. But in visual space all elements are often present at the same time, and the order of reading may or may not be defined by conventional linear arrangements of top to bottom or left to right. Variables other than position (typographic weight, color, size, complexity, and so on) may be necessary to create contrast or similarity among elements in order to signify the importance of certain information components over others. In establishing the hierarchy among elements (and the content they represent), choices about structure bear considerable responsibility for conveying meaning. The conventions of visual structure and their disruption have played an important role in the history of twentieth-century design. (See box: "Reading Structure in Design.")

code

CODE

A set of conventions or principles governing how the audience interacts with the elements of a message in various media or formats. The left-to-right, top-to-bottom pattern of reading English, for example, demands a certain pattern of engagement with printed text that is different from the ways in which a photograph is read or a film is watched.

In Berlo's model, **CODE** refers to the rules governing the reading of elements. In the strictest sense, code is grammar. "The dog bites the man" means something very different from "the man bites the dog," even though the same words appear in both sentences. Speakers of English understand the difference in meaning because a particular linguistic code establishes the relationship between subject and object in English.

Similar codes operate in visual communication. Our interpretation is influenced by where different elements are positioned in relation to one another and to the perimeter of the page. For example, a financial bar chart that shows the declining revenues of a company over a five-year period is interpreted less easily

READING STRUCTURE IN DESIGN

The history of graphic design reveals that the manipulation of visual structure has always been fundamental to our thinking about how communication works. In the early twentieth century, for example, writers, poets, and designers worked closely together, using typographic structure to awaken audiences to ideas of political and social change (see chapter 5). It is fair to say that they succeeded less by their words than by their *arrangement* of words.

Structures with less political motive are found in the grids and typographic systems of contemporary magazines. These underlying divisions of space and palettes of typographic variables organize reading behavior and our understanding of what kind of content appears on the page. Column width and style, typeface, and point size define the functional differences among information components. We know a sidebar from a feature article and a headline from a quote because the choices about form are applied systematically. The author's designated hierarchy among information elements is represented visually and through the recurring placement of different kinds of content in particular areas of the layout. If the structure of these layouts is not clear, we are unable to make quick decisions about which of the many articles to read or where one article begins and another ends.

1.4   FINANCIAL CHARTS *(opposite)*

The vertical orientation of the bars showing succeeding years of profit is read easily as *gain* and *loss*. Because we have a weaker association of these concepts with left and right orientation, we are less likely to understand financial decline in the horizontal chart.

Deliberate attempts to subvert this structural distinction can be found in the *advertorial*, a hybrid in which advertisements assume the structural identity of editorial content, presumably to gain credibility with the reader.

These structures also define the *identities* of magazines. Without seeing a masthead or reading text, we can easily differentiate the somewhat cluttered *Family Circle* magazine from the more ordered *Martha Stewart Living*. The wide columns of text, limited palette of typefaces, and liberal use of white space in *Martha Stewart Living* contribute to a clear editorial hierarchy and separate it from other publications in the supermarket checkout line. By contrast, the four-column grid, random use of multiple typefaces, and frequent boxing of text by colored shapes and lines create a frantic structure for *Family Circle* that is virtually interchangeable with competing women's periodicals. Although the two magazines address similar content, their structures communicate very different messages that extend their attitudes toward home interiors and fashion. They also provide not-so-subtle clues about social class, taste, and whom they see as their intended audience.

Structure, in this sense, is integral to the meaning of the message. It is not simply an arbitrary or neutral ordering of more content-infused elements, but rather an extension of particular ideologies about how form contributes to meaning.

when the bars are oriented horizontally than when they are oriented vertically (SEE FIGURE 1.4). Our interpretive code typically associates "gain" and "loss" with top and bottom rather than left and right. The health of the company will therefore be clearer if the designer orients the chart in a manner consistent with this code.

A grammar of visual form that describes the physical world has evolved gradually. For example, the code of linear perspective, evident in the work of sixteenth-century Renaissance artists, dates back to the mathematical experiments of the architect Filippo Brunelleschi (1377–1446) (SEE FIGURES 1.5–1.6). The depiction of three-dimensional space in work executed prior to Brunelleschi's system of horizon lines and vanishing points is not "convincing" to modern eyes (SEE FIGURE 1.7). As a result of these efforts, we now take for granted such cues as the relative size of objects, their relationship to the horizon, the convergence of parallel lines in the distance, foreshortening, and shadows and shading as the grammar of spatial representations.

The French semiotician Jean Baudrillard (1929–2007) discusses code from a cultural perspective. In his analysis of interior design in *The System of Objects* (1968), he suggests that, historically, the interiors of our homes were constructed from objects that were handed down through families. They consisted of a diverse assemblage of furniture and bric-a-brac amassed across generations. These objects were rich narratives of family history.[9] They held meaning through their associations with people, places, and experiences, often expressed through their idiosyncratic appearance. Twentieth-century modernism

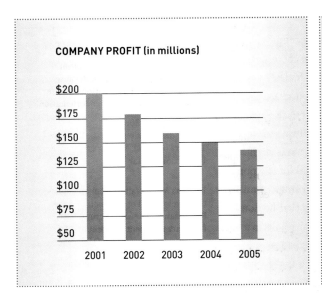

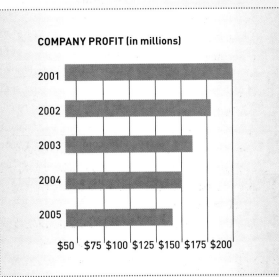

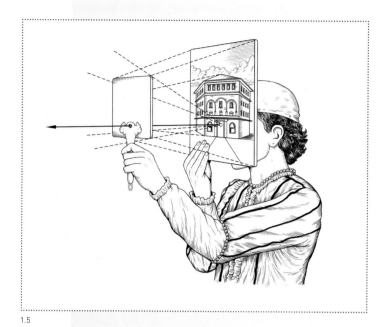

1.5

1.6

1.7

(see chapter 5) reduced the form and meaning of furniture and housewares
solely to that of function. Stripped of all historical detail by industrial manufacturing processes and the new materials of the twentieth century, the design
of such objects expressed a unity of purpose. Like the industrial machines that
served as the metaphor of the modern world, these objects were void of any
details that did not contribute to their primary function. Their value was as
components within a larger system for living.

Today's interiors strive for the same sense of unity among components. We
are told by advertising images what does and does not fit the code, and which
parts are necessary in order to achieve the desired look and feel (SEE FIGURE 1.8).
It is not enough simply to purchase the sofa—we must also purchase the right
pillows and the appropriate armchair if we want to complete the ensemble.
The behavior encouraged by such advertising is to consume, always to want the
next object that is necessary to the completion of a system that is slightly out
of our economic reach. For example, a television commercial for the popular
furniture store Rooms to Go presents a testimonial from a single man who
purchased an entire, pre-coordinated living-room. He brags that he does not
know "what these little round things are" (referring to decorative balls in a bowl
on the coffee table), but he is glad the Rooms to Go designer had the savvy to
know they "belonged." In this sense, code is a visual template for "good taste,"
a system that guides the selection and organization of parts.

1.8   IKEA CATALOG

According to the cultural theorist Jean Baudrillard, furniture catalogs encourage us to consume by presenting interior environments that are complete only when we purchase all the matching components of the system. Baudrillard describes the value we assign to any individual item as arising less from its singular qualities than from its membership of the larger system.

The antique, according to Baudrillard, is now "exotic," someone else's story acquired on weekend jaunts through cluttered shops, flea markets, and back-road estates. Its meaning to the antique hunter resides not in the character of its life with the original owner but in its role as a member of a larger collection, as part of a more general set of grammatical rules about how things go together in eclectic interiors.[10] In this way, interior design and advertising write the code according to guiding principles that are present in the culture.

treatment (style, aesthetics)

Berlo defines **TREATMENT** as the subjective contribution of the creator/author to the meaning of the message. In design, this is often referred to as *style*, or, incorrectly, as **AESTHETICS**. Style defines a particular kind of relationship between the function of something and how it looks. The material, sensory qualities of the artifact produce emotional responses and meanings that might not otherwise be evoked by the literal subject matter itself. Style is often an expression of **IDEOLOGY**, form that arises from beliefs and theories, as much as from the subject matter of the work.

Thomas Starr, a design professor at Northeastern University, illustrates the role of treatment or style in his account of events surrounding the publishing of the American *Declaration of Independence* in 1776. (The text that follows is a summary of an interview with Starr.)

TREATMENT

The subjective contribution to the meaning of a message by its maker or author. In design, these aspects of a representation are often referred to as *style*.

AESTHETICS

A branch of philosophy concerned with the fundamental nature of beauty or taste, not with a specific style or arrangement of form.

IDEOLOGY

A set of ideas and beliefs characteristic of a social group. Ideology frequently forms the basis of social, economic, or political theory and, in the case of design, may be expressed through particular aesthetic principles.

Following the final editing of the Declaration of Independence on July 4, 1776, the authors turned over the manuscript to the typographer and official congressional printer John Dunlop. Dunlop set the text in metal type and, on July 5, delivered printed copies to Congress, which distributed them to the colonies. They were eventually reprinted in twenty-four colonial newspapers to inform the colonists. On July 19, however, Congress also ordered calligraphic versions of the document, one of which is now in the National Archives in Washington, D.C., and represents what most of us mistakenly consider to be the original form of the Declaration of Independence. Calligraphy was the style of the most important documents of the time and a remnant of the monarchy. The colonists could not leave behind, even after winning their independence, this stylistic convention.

Starr makes the point that typesetting is the style of democracy and mass communication; it was the typeset version that actually did the "declaring" to citizens. On the other hand, the handwritten calligraphy is elitist and implies a single author and a single reader.[11]

Style, more than any other aspect of a visual message, is subject to shifting cultural attitudes. The history of design is replete with examples in which ideological differences of opinion gain expression through breaks with styles of the past. For this reason, stylistic references in design are charged with meaning and serve as primary vehicles for communication.

THE MESSAGE CYCLE

The previous models discussed in this chapter illustrate an increasing awareness of context and of the specific attributes of the communicators themselves as fundamental to the construction of meaning. Such models have been used to describe written, spoken, and visual communication, yet there is little elaboration of how the message influences its surrounding context or how the media culture is responsible for shared interpretations of its meanings. And there is no description of the afterlife of messages beyond the initial encounters of audiences. These previous models are therefore more effective in describing individual interactions between two people than communication on the scale of mass audiences.

Even in Berlo's description of message components, little is said about the particular contribution of certain kinds of elements, structures, and treatments to the interpretation of meaning. While Berlo acknowledges different channels of communication, he provides little discussion about how the meaning of various elements is linked to technologies for their creation or how messages gain or lose meaning through processes of distribution.

If we shift our focus to the visual message and its interpretive life cycle in society at large, we can describe communication as consisting of message *creation, reproduction, distribution,* **RECEPTION** *by individuals,* and *consumption by culture* (SEE FIGURE 1.9). In this cycle, the message is first made concrete through a creative process of **REPRESENTATION**, an encoding of the message in material form that has the intention of bringing to mind the appropriate concepts. This encoding process is the traditional domain of the graphic designer, who draws upon the language and understanding of the culture to craft visual, spatial, and temporal messages that stand for something to the intended audience. If the

RECEPTION THEORY

The theory that the meaning of something is created not by the inherent qualities of the communication (or literary text) but by the relationship between the object and the reader.

REPRESENTATION

A depiction of something (an idea, concept, quality, person, place, thing, or event) in a form other than the one in which it originated; or, a process through which such forms are created that is motivated by context and intention.

COMMUNICATION MODELS

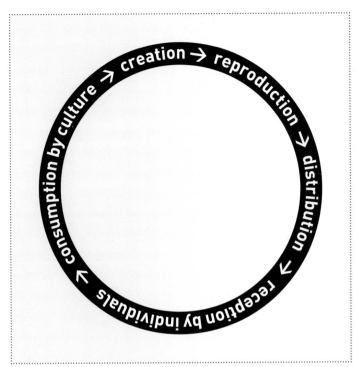

Historically, message *creation* and
reproduction have been the primary
focus of the graphic designer. More
recently, a broader understanding of how
communication works has emphasized
the importance of message *distribution*,
reception, and *consumption by culture* in
determining what designers make.

message is to be interpreted by a mass audience,
it must be reproduced in a way that enables its
circulation through the culture, frequently
across time and physical space. The form of the
message must be compatible with its means of
distribution, placing technological as well as
creative demands on the maker. The scale of
reproduction influences the choice of medium.

distribution

More importantly, the message alters the
interpretation of meaning through its means of
distribution, and as a result it may or may not
be read exactly as intended. For example, messages that are circulated through an interactive
environment, such as the Web, are assembled
in sequences that are often determined by the
user: the choice to explore a link, to roll over,
or to change the ordering of content affects the
user's overall interpretation of meaning. In this
way, the author of the message is not entirely in control of its meaning because
the sequencing of message components will vary with each user and may even
include content created by another author. In some cases, the user may actually
leave the site through a link to read material by a completely different author.
To the user, this hypermedia assemblage is one communication experience,
the nature of which is defined, in part, by the very means of its distribution.

Similarly, messages that circulate across significant intervals of time are
understood within the context of other intervening or subsequent messages,
all of which influence the interpretation of the first message. We all experience
those moments when primetime television programming and advertisements
feel as through they are part of the same discourse: the pharmaceutical ad
following a drama about addiction; the vacuously flirtatious girl in the sham-
poo advertisement adjacent to a documentary on the success of women in
the workplace; the promotion for the supermarket tabloid, *National Enquirer*,
on CBS Morning News. These compound messages result entirely from the
programming structures and economics of broadcast television. It is almost
impossible for the originators of feature programs and the sponsors of advertising to anticipate this collision of specific content, although there are attempts
to increase product credibility or reach certain audiences by advertising during
particular shows. Through the choice of the medium for distribution, therefore,
the designer determines the extent to which he or she can control how messages
acquire new significance.

The means of distribution also carry meaning of another sort. The media
theorist Marshall McLuhan (1911–1980) wrote that the introduction of a technology changes the world around it forever (see pp. 87–88, 209–12).[12] The
experience of reading and owning a book is very different today than it would
have been before Johannes Gutenberg's invention of printing with movable

type in the fifteenth century. The time and expense of producing hand-lettered texts determined who could and could not read, reinforcing class distinctions that were already established by wealth and privilege. The role of pictorial representations in communicating to a largely illiterate population, and the type of content deemed worthy of the tedious labor dedicated to bookmaking were other consequences of the limited technology for the distribution of ideas. As books became easier and cheaper to produce, these meanings changed.

Similarly, the introduction of the computer changed forever what it means to "author," now that anyone can copy or change original text. It also redefined what it means to "publish," when the endorsement and financial backing of a company or organization are no longer required for the mass dissemination of ideas. And it changed our perception of the value of documents, now that "saving" something is no longer a matter of physical space and materials. In other words, the values and meanings we attach to certain means of message distribution are interpreted as part of our response to the message itself, and these meanings change over time.

reception by individuals

The models discussed so far describe the mechanics of *message reception by individuals*; later chapters address how we perceive and process information cognitively. But in considering reception with respect to the message cycle we must acknowledge the true nature of the contemporary communication environment. We live in a time of unprecedented information access, of message overload and increasingly temporary relationships among people, places, and things. It is impossible to process on a conscious level all the information to which we are exposed in a single day. The information designer Richard Saul Wurman describes this as the "ever-widening gap between information and understanding," as too many messages reach us in incomprehensible form.[13]

If visual messages are to compete in this environment of information overload, they must first communicate their relevance through content and forms that are well matched to the audience, and then deliver meaning that is appropriate to the context of use. In recent years, the means for accomplishing this match has been to tailor messages for highly specific target audiences (see pp. 61–77). Design strategist Larry Keeley describes such **TAILORING** as the current trajectory of communication strategy.

Keeley suggests that in the 1930s, the approach to strategy was *selling*. Like the snake-oil salesman, communication touted the attributes of the product or service, delivering the same message to anyone who would listen. By the 1950s, advertisers had discovered *marketing*—selling products differently to broadly defined segments of the population. For example, because women made most choices about home appliances, the communication appeal in refrigerator advertising was to women. The "homemaker" was shown in high heels and a party dress standing next to her new Amana freezer, which identified her as an efficient woman who had time for parties because her life was made easier by modern kitchen conveniences. In the 1970s the dominant communication strategy was *positioning*—instead of buying the product, people bought the lifestyle afforded by the product. Notions of value were wrapped up in the

TAILORING

The design of goods and services to respond to the needs and wants of specific audiences and to adapt over time as circumstances change.

COMMUNICATION MODELS

CHANGES IN CIRCULATION, 1992

READER'S DIGEST	- 3%	INSIDE HOLLYWOOD	+ 326%
TIME MAGAZINE	- 20%	NORTH AMERICAN FISHERMAN	+ 67%
NEWSWEEK MAGAZINE	- 19%	DISNEY ADVENTURES	+ 124%
WOMAN'S DAY	- 4.9%	MEN'S HEALTH	+ 54%

1.10   CIRCULATION FIGURES FOR
POPULAR MAGAZINES, 1992
Source: Audit Bureau of Circulations

The market today favors publications that direct content and advertising to ever-narrowing definitions of audience. Even within broad market segments—women, for example—there is increasing attention paid to preferences and behaviors that distinguish one group from another. Since the early 1990s, companies have promoted tailored products and communications as a business strategy. The design characteristics of these objects reinforce perceptions of audience identity.

intangible aura of a company and the social status that buying its products or services signified, not in the tangible attributes or performance of the product or service itself. Nike's athletic spokespeople told us to "Just Do It," without even showing shoes in their television and magazine advertising. The popular Niketown showrooms, which immersed customers in wall-sized media displays of active lifestyles, were experiences in their own right and bore little resemblance to buying shoes at other stores. According to Keeley, the 1990s heralded the age of *tailoring*. Smart companies promoted adaptable products that acknowledged the diverse and evolving needs of consumers.[14]

1.11   MAGAZINES FOR WOMEN

Newsstands today carry a staggering array of special-interest magazines that enable advertisers to reach their exact target readership. The circulation figures for magazines in 1992 (SEE FIGURE 1.10), around the time tailoring emerged, showed declining numbers of readers for general-interest magazines but a skyrocketing readership of special-interest publications.

The design of these publications reflected their specifically defined audience groups (SEE FIGURE 1.11). For example, recognizing that the readership of most teen magazines was ten- to thirteen-year-old girls, the visually edgier *Sassy* entered the market for the attention of older teens. The publishers followed this magazine with *Dirt*, a publication tailored for boys in the same age group. *Lear's* focused on the forty-something working woman, consistent with the publisher's status as a sophisticated but worldly-wise divorcée with expendable income. *Town & Country* magazine still addresses the interests of conservative middle-aged women who stay at home and have money to spend on the advertisers' luxury products. Many such publications had short but highly visible lifespans, fading away as their demographically defined readership advanced in age or changed its socio-economic status.

This continuing *demassification* of audiences raises questions about the viability of conventional design strategies. If success depends on communicating to highly targeted groups of people, what are the characteristics that define meaningful differences among audience groups? Are the socio-economic definitions of audiences, as addressed by marketing studies, the only significant ways in which we are different or alike? And can we so fragment the population through tailored products, services, and communication that we lose all sense of a common cultural experience? These are questions that face the next generation of graphic designers.

consumption by culture

The message originator's aim is usually to influence individual understanding, opinion, or action. But the concepts embedded in a message also affect the culture at large by their individual presence or in combination with other messages that accumulate over time. The culture assimilates or *consumes* ideas from such communication as an ongoing process.

For example, a television advertisement for the tax preparer H&R Block, launched during the Super Bowl broadcast in 2003, was set to the Beatles' song *Taxman*. Three men, dressed identically in conservative, blue business suits, were shown walking in unison through an anonymous, Federal-style building. The song lyrics proclaimed, "one for you, nineteen for me," followed by a pitch from H&R Block to assist citizens in navigating the complexities of Federal tax preparation. The company's message depended entirely on the widely held American belief that the Internal Revenue Service (IRS) is a big, unfriendly government agency, out to make as much money as possible from the average citizen. The three men appeared in almost military formation, confirming the impression that the average taxpayer does not stand a chance against an army of bureaucrats without the aid of a professional tax preparer. The ad then cut to a warm and fuzzy conversation between a client and an H&R Block employee.

The designers of this ad did not have to build the impression of a greedy, adversarial government agency from scratch. The television images functioned as shorthand reminders of long-held ideas in our culture. This shorthand allowed H&R Block to devote the majority of its minute-long broadcast to explaining how the company protects citizens from the villain. If the public challenged this perception of government or required greater detail in the explanation of IRS behavior, the ad would not have worked. The offering up of a prevailing assumption about reality is so fundamental to how advertising works that we rarely see it as being a cultural response to the accumulated cultural messages that precede the ad itself. The ideas have been assimilated or consumed so effectively by the culture that we no longer identify them as message content delivered or perpetuated by the sponsor. Designers study such phenomena for clues about commonly held perceptions and values that may be reinforced or subverted in future communications—and so the message cycle begins again. Later chapters of this book will address the cultural context for design and how it shaped twentieth-century design history.

The message-cycle model illustrates that our concept of what constitutes the message is both *relational* and *dynamic*: that messages have multiple meanings within various contexts; and that our perception of their meanings changes over time. Some relationships and changes are predictable and are the domain of the graphic designer; others are not, but define the future context in which the designer must work.

This model represents an argument for educating graphic designers in more than the formal and technical aspects of design and communication. By expanding the domain of graphic design to include the distribution, reception, and consumption of messages, we see the value of studying the social sciences and the need for design research.

SUMMARY

In the middle of the twentieth century, the scientist Claude Shannon and the researcher Warren Weaver attempted to describe human communication as the transmission of a message from a sender to a receiver. Despite the popularity of their model, it did not meet the challenge of capturing those aspects of the communication process that are truly human. Professors Philip Emmert and William Donaghy expanded this model to include the important addition of context, feedback, and the makeup of two communicators. Their suggestion that interpretation results from the communicators' lifetime experiences and their mental processing behaviors is well matched to constructionist theories of meaning-making that underpin post-modern design.

David Berlo focused attention on the message itself by identifying as its fundamental components content, elements, structure, code, and treatment (style). In doing so, he supported the concept that messages have organizational and material differences that are culturally determined. The message-cycle model extends this understanding in graphic design terms by identifying reproduction and distribution as discrete processes through which the intended meaning of a message may be enhanced, diminished, or altered. It further identifies differences in the reception of messages by individuals and assimilation of message ideas by culture, which forms the context in which the meanings of subsequent messages are interpreted.

What is apparent in these models is that, for better or worse, they arise from theories about the relationships between messages, audiences, and contexts. They are speculative, not grounded in empirical data, and are expressions of belief (hypotheses in the scientific sense, intuition in the design sense) about the basis on which design action should proceed. In this way, how we believe meaning is made and exchanged tells us how to define design problems, what we need to inform our task, and how form must perform in response to communication needs. Whether mental or expressed through physical form, complete or incomplete, conscious or unconscious, these models drive design.

the nature of

what and how things mean

representation 2

You are in a restaurant with a friend and are planning to go to a movie together after dinner. You will be driving in separate cars but your friend does not know how to get to the theater. So you draw the route between the restaurant and the theater on a napkin. This map is a representation: it describes, depicts, or stands in some way for the experience of driving from the restaurant to the specified location.

Your map, however, differs significantly from the one provided by the auto club. Both maps include roads and landmarks, but your map excludes any features or aspects that are not essential to the task of getting to the movie theater. It focuses only on the sequence of decision-making points along a specific route, and these are likely to have been depicted slightly inaccurately by the scale of your drawing. In contrast, the auto-club map has the far larger task of providing accurate navigation routes to and from anywhere in the city.

Your map includes specific roads and landmarks that you know your friend will recognize. Knowledge of your friend and of the route allow you to shape the map references in very particular ways: the intersection where there used to be a gas station, the school where you both went to kindergarten, the store where your friend's mother works. In other words, the representation is motivated by the histories of you, your friend, and the location, as well as by the specific task of getting to the theater.

If a stranger were to find your map on the ground in the parking lot of the theater, information about its origin would be encoded in its form. Even without knowing who made the map, someone could tell that it had been created under particular circumstances (over a meal or a drink, for example) and had probably been accompanied by a verbal explanation, which presumes some degree of familiarity between the maker and the user. The forms used in the map tell the stranger something about how comfortable the maker was in his or her mapmaking role and to what degree personal observation informed the task.

WHAT DO WE MEAN BY REPRESENTATION?

As this example shows, *representation* (see p. 26) is a process through which people make something that expresses an interest in some particular aspect of something else and that is motivated by both context and intent.[1] Representations are substitutions for something else, surrogates in some alternative form that provide information about things, as well as about the makers and, possibly, the audiences for those things. The map to the movie theater is a substitute for both the physical route (a configuration of landscape features and roads) and the mental concept of driving the route (a conceptual

THE NATURE OF REPRESENTATION

plan that gives a sequence of physical actions to enable someone to reach a goal and that shows the order of particular stimuli along a path on the way to the goal). It also expresses a relationship between the maker and the audience.

Representations may be expressions of intangible ideas, concepts, or feelings in some physical form (for example, a gesture, a drawing, or a poem). They may also communicate information about tangible objects, people, or places in the real world in a different physical form (for example, diagrams, photographs, or maps). And in other instances, one representational form may be substituted for another, such as a film for an oral history or a picture of five apples for the Arabic numeral 5.

The most basic unit of representation is the **SIGN**, which is something that stands for something else to someone in some respect. For example, C-O-W is a linguistic sign. There is consensus among speakers of English that this combination of letters and the sounds associated with them stand for a large farm animal that gives milk. A soldier who salutes with his or her right hand is also a sign: there is a common understanding in many cultures that this gesture signifies respect for those of higher rank among members of the military. And a red cross composed of two intersecting lines of equal length and width is a sign. In non-Arab countries, this symbol stands for a politically neutral organization dedicated to emergency relief in times of war or disaster.

In these examples, the relationship between the physical attributes of the sign and what it stands for is **ARBITRARY**. Nothing about C-O-W looks or sounds like a real cow. The same letters may be used in other words and have no meaning associated with animals, farms, or milk (for example, MosCOW, COWard, or CO-Worker; see also p. 106).

The arbitrary nature of the Red Cross symbol is evident in its history (SEE FIGURE 2.1). Standing for an organization founded in 1863 by five men from Geneva, Switzerland, to aid wounded soldiers, the symbol is the inverse of the Swiss flag (a red cross on a white background, rather than the Swiss white cross on a red background). As such, it borrows the country's signification of neutrality in times of war. In other words, the meaning of one sign was assigned arbitrarily to the meaning of another.

Because any cross also has cultural associations with Christianity, the organization operates as the "Red Crescent" in Arab countries—what one group of people associates with neutrality is charged with less-than-neutral religious significance for another. In 2005, an international committee addressed the dilemma of a two-symbol system for the same relief effort. A new symbol adopted by the two organizations, the "Red Crystal," is described as "free from any religious, political, or other connotation."[2] But many Arab countries saw the adoption of a third symbol as an unnecessary accommodation to Israel, which refused to use either the cross or the crescent. A frustrated Swiss diplomat said, "We're actually trying to get a solution for the Red Cross, but some seem to want us to try to solve the entire Middle East conflict."[3]

2.1   RED CROSS, RED CRESCENT, AND RED CRYSTAL, 2007
International Federation of Red Cross and Red Crescent Societies

All three symbols stand for a neutral organization that provides relief in times of war or disaster. The relationship between this meaning and each of the three forms is *arbitrary*. There is no meaning inherent in the cross, crescent, or diamond; significance is established solely through their use in cultural practice. Three different identities are necessary because various countries associate the symbols with ideas unrelated to the organization's work.

SIGN

The most basic unit of representation. According to Ferdinand de Saussure's linguistic model, a sign consists of a signifier and a signified. According to Charles Sanders Peirce, a sign is something that means something to someone in some respect.

ARBITRARINESS

Ferdinand de Saussure suggested that the relationship between a sign and what it stands for is arbitrary. In visual and verbal language, the correspondence between the sign and its meaning is a matter of cultural agreement, not an inherent property of the sign itself.

This ability to read abstract symbols in many ways, and to assign new meaning to a form that previously had no meaning, demonstrates the arbitrariness of signs.

THE CONTEXT OF CULTURE

The intention in all three previous examples (the cow, the soldier, and the red cross) is to exchange meaning with other members of our culture. Such a meeting of minds is usually achieved through language, which is, according to the cognitive psychologist Donald Norman, a representational system in which the *represented* world (those things about which we communicate) is expressed in terms of a *representing* world (the signs, sounds, and symbols we use in that communication).[4] Were there not some cultural consensus about the meaning of signs and symbols among members of a linguistic community, communication would not be possible.

The sociologist Stuart Hall dissects this notion of the signifying practices of culture in his book *Representation* (1997). He cites three different theoretical approaches to explaining the concept. The **REFLECTIVE APPROACH** suggests that meaning resides in the object, person, or event in the real world and that the language system simply reflects or mimics what is already there.[5] But he says that if this were the case we would not be able to communicate about things never seen or through metaphor or analogy: the atomic structure of a chemical element would be incomprehensible as a diagram and a rose would simply be a flower with thorns, never a poetic expression of affection or beauty.

The **INTENTIONAL APPROACH** takes the opposite stance, whereby meaning is imposed on the object, person, or event by the author or maker of the representation.[6] But if this were true, says Hall, we would be able to communicate through entirely private languages. We could simply decide that a sign stands for something (a circle for childhood, for example) and that everyone, without explanation or education, would instantly understand the association of the sign with this idea.

The **CONSTRUCTIONIST APPROACH** acknowledges the public, social character of language. This third theory posits that we construct meaning through the use of representational systems that link concepts to signs.[7] The conceptual system is made up of our mental representations of things in the world and we correlate it with a language system made up of sounds, images, gestures, or words in order to exchange their meanings with others.[8] The material world of people, things, and places is therefore linked to the symbolic social practices through which meaning is made. A church is not a church simply because it has certain physical components (steeple, altar, pews, and so on), but because it is a place of cultural rites and rituals, spiritual associations, and community, and because we have come to associate its form with these activities through our social and cultural experiences.

The graphic example of the swastika illustrates the *constructedness* of representational meaning through cultural practices. Used for thousands of years, the abstract form held meaning for cultures as diverse as the ancient Trojans and Egyptians, Europeans in the Middle Ages, and Native Americans. The word swastika comes originally from the Sanskrit *svastika*, meaning "good,"

REFLECTIVE APPROACH

Stuart Hall used this term to refer to a view of representation in which the meaning of something is inherent in the person, object, place, or event itself and the representation simply mirrors what is already there.

INTENTIONAL APPROACH

Stuart Hall used this term to refer to a view of representation in which the meaning of something is imposed on the representation by its author or maker.

CONSTRUCTIONIST APPROACH

Stuart Hall used this term to refer to a view of representation in which the meaning of something is shaped partially by the social practices that surround it. See also constructionism (p. 20).

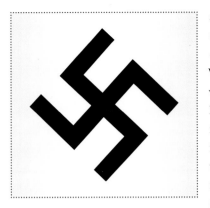

2.2   SWASTIKA

The swastika is used by various religions and dates back to prehistory. For most of its history, the swastika had positive associations; its use by Nazi Germany, however, recast its meaning irreversibly for modern times.

and throughout history the symbol has been used to connote life, sun, power, strength, and good fortune.[9] The Germans appropriated it in the nineteenth century as a symbol for German nationalism and used it as their battle sign. When Hitler resurrected the form in 1920 all former positive associations gave way under the brutal practices of the Third Reich (SEE FIGURE 2.2). As much as the Nazis viewed it as a symbol of the Aryan struggle, others saw hate and genocide in its form. In this instance, the aesthetic qualities of the abstract graphic form itself, its long history of positive associations, and the significance assigned to it by those in charge of its application were insufficient in overcoming the negativity of social practices surrounding its use in Germany in World War II. So strong are these social meanings that, even decades later, it is inconceivable that the symbol can be recast in modern times.

Stuart Hall describes these associations as **SEMANTIC NETWORKS**, as fields of related meanings, with each network having its own characteristic language or discourse. In *Doing Cultural Studies* (1997) Hall analyzes the Sony Walkman as an object that could be "read culturally," through its semantic network (as a cultural representation as well as a functional object for playing recorded music). Not long after its invention in 1979, the Walkman came to stand for Japanese high technology, youth-oriented active lifestyles, and the world of recorded music and sound.[10] The object itself was not especially novel in appearance and used the same materials and power source as its predecessor, the transistor radio. But a consensus was very quickly achieved regarding the Walkman's position in culture and its wider range of meanings, much in the same way as today's iPod has cultural connotations and social practices—personal music mixes, the digital connectedness of today's youth culture, challenges to the traditional practices of the recording industry, media convergence, and so on—that extend its meaning beyond the mere function of listening to music. In fact, the cultural role of the iPod is so well understood that manufacturers of other products now respond to it in their own designs—the Toyota Yaris, for example, was first advertised as being "iPod-compatible"—and new practices incorporate the iPod into their lexicon ("podcasting"). An industry has been built around designing "apps" for the iPod Touch and its sister products, the iPhone and iPad.

This expanded field of associations and affiliations is referred to as the **CONNOTATIVE** function of a sign. For example, the saluting soldier, mentioned earlier, could connote respect, authority, allegiance, blind obedience, or camaraderie. Depending on his or her uniform and the past experiences of the viewer, he or she may be interpreted as an enemy, hero, oppressor, peacekeeper, or liberator. Within different contexts he or she may constitute a threat, provide a sense of security, or encourage someone to join the service. All are possible connotations of the gesture by a person in uniform, and the variability of such meanings allows the graphic designer to craft richer messages for specific audiences than if such meanings were not available.

By contrast, the **DENOTATIVE** or literal meaning of a sign is less open to variable interpretation. Our soldier is simply a gesturing person in a uniform and the Walkman is merely a small, portable stereo in the denotative sense. We often deploy denotative representations when seeking objectivity or

SEMANTIC NETWORK

Stuart Hall's term for the field of related meanings or connotations that are affiliated with a person, thing, place, or event. It is through such affiliations that objects can be "read culturally."

CONNOTATION

An idea or feeling that a representation invokes in addition to its literal meaning. Because such meanings are not explicit, objective descriptions of fact, they generally arise from cultural and social experiences in which people, things, places, and events become associated with particular abstract ideas, emotions, or behaviors. Sometimes referred to as second-level meaning.

DENOTATION

The literal or surface meaning of a sign. Denotative meaning is explicit and direct and usually avoids metaphor. Sometimes referred to as first-level meaning.

rationality. The auto-club map, for example, tells us nothing about the subjective experience of a particular journey, the perceived duration for which we might travel on various roads, or our frustration with the characteristic traffic on one route versus another. In contrast to the more connotative map on the napkin, it simply denotes that the roads exist and the geographic relationships among them.

CHOOSING AN APPROPRIATE SIGN

Choosing an appropriate sign is therefore a complicated task, especially when communicating to mass audiences that belong to diverse interpretive cultures. The designer must search for signs that are generally understood to represent the appropriate concepts and also present them in a way that competes successfully among other demands for people's attention. Signs must be familiar but used in an inventive way to be successful in today's climate of information overload.

categorization

The work of Eleanor Rosch, a psychologist at the University of California, Berkeley, provides insight into the possible choices among signs for a particular concept. Rosch's experimental work focuses on a mental process called **CATEGORIZATION.** This term refers to how we identify stimuli in our environment and group them in memory as members of a category, similar to others in that category and different from members of other categories.[11] A category could be "things that are soft," "people not to be trusted," or "redness." Our cultural experiences determine many of the categories into which we sort stimuli and the members within each group. For example, the list of members in the category of "success" or "authority" may differ among people from various social groups or of different ages or gender. This *categorization* of concepts is thought to be fundamental to perception, thought, language, and action.[12]

Categorization allows us to think and communicate metaphorically. We need not see the actual thing being represented, in a literal sense, as long as, to the people who are viewing the sign, it shares some important quality with the thing it stands for. Metaphor is a powerful tool in design (see p. 189). It allows us to make the strange familiar by comparing something new or unknown to something known. The desktop metaphor, for example, enables us to communicate intuitively with the operating system of our computers. We understand how to perform certain functions, or the role of particular objects in the real world, and we bring those behaviors and objects into the virtual world as substitutions for lines of computer code. For example, our knowledge of the behavior associated with a file allows us to execute certain computer operations without reflection. We intuit from past experience the difference between a file and a folder, recognizing that the former is information and the latter is a container. Such metaphors create a user-friendly environment through which a system that would be indecipherable to many is made accessible to people without technological expertise.

CATEGORIZATION

The act of identifying stimuli in the environment and grouping them in memory as members of a category, similar to others in that category but different from members of other categories. Categorization allows us to think and communicate metaphorically. Eleanor Rosch and George Lakoff use the concept of categorization in their work.

THE NATURE OF REPRESENTATION

Metaphors also allow us to make the familiar strange by revealing over-looked aspects or perspectives of a known thing through its comparison with something else. The designer John Rheinfrank (1944–2004), for example, challenged the design professions to drop the language of war and adopt the language of biology as a metaphor for the role of design in business (instead of speaking of "strategies," "campaigns," and "target" audiences, to frame our thinking in terms of "growth," "sustainability," and "evolution"). By using the metaphorical basis of representations to shift the categories to which we think a concept belongs, we reconfigure the string of associations and expectations. We see something in a new way.

In his book *Women, Fire, and Dangerous Things* (1987), the linguistics professor George Lakoff cautions us that categorization is not just the collection of properties shared by the things in a category. He cites research suggesting that our categorical reasoning is embodied (in other words, has a basis in our physical experience of the world), and is in some cases as much a matter of culture as of biology.[13] If categories are only about the properties inherent in the thing itself, how could thinking about them be independent of the object itself and how could we have categories about abstract concepts (for example, "power" or "innocence")?[14] And if categories are defined only by the qualities of objects, then no examples in the category should be more representative than others in that category.[15]

To explain this last point, Eleanor Rosch describes categories as having a graded structure of better-to-worse examples, with many categories having unclear boundaries.[16] There are prototypical "best examples," members that are clearly central to the category and that we may be able to identify as arising from some common experiences. These **PROTOTYPES** tend to be processed in the mind as concrete, information-rich images from which we generalize (transfer expectations) to other examples.[17] Rosch tells us, for example, that we may agree that a particular red object is "red" but debate in our minds the "redness" of a second object. The reference for the redness of the second object is likely to be the red of the first object that we assessed as a best example of the category "red." We may describe the second red as being "too pink" when what we really mean is that it is "pinker than the best example of red."[18]

If we think of the graphic design task as triggering the appropriate concept category in the minds of viewers, it makes sense when possible to construct representations that use best examples or prototypes shaped by the audience's physical, social, or cultural experiences. An analysis of the images in FIGURE 2.3 employs Rosch's perspective of categorization in thinking about visual representation.

FIGURE 2.3A is likely to be described by many people as "erotic": the woman's manner of dress (fishnet hose), posture (reclining with legs crossed), the setting (satin-sheeted bed), and point of view (concealing the face, focusing on the lower half of the body) recall multiple aspects of images that many in Western cultures would associate with erotica. Some people may even refer to this image as a cliché, a *prototype* that suffers from overuse by the culture in representing the category.

PROTOTYPE

Eleanor Rosch's term for the "best example" of a category. A prototype is a member so central to the category that it contains most or all of the characteristics that define the category, unlike other members that might be more peripheral and likely to invoke other categories.

choosing an appropriate sign

FIGURE 2.3B is a photograph of a nude woman. While some people may also describe this image as "erotic," others may label it as "fine art." As a member of the latter category, the human figure is viewed by the photographer as an object with qualities not unlike those of items in a still life. We are less able to deliver a narrative about the woman or her circumstances in this image than in FIGURE 2.3A because she is photographed less as a person associated with certain social behaviors than as an object with particular formal characteristics. This approach has a stronger affiliation with fine art than with erotica, although the boundaries between the two categories are blurred.

FIGURE 2.3C is a Georgia O'Keeffe painting from 1926 of an iris. For many this is simply a flower. For others who know O'Keeffe's work and have a larger frame of reference in the history of art, the image is "erotic" through its resemblance to the female anatomy, even though a human figure does not appear in the work. From this perspective, the image has status as an example of "erotica," while for others it is a best example of "flowers" (a denotative rather than connotative meaning).

FIGURE 2.3D is a painting by Edouard Manet from 1863 entitled *Le Déjeuner sur l'Herbe*. In Manet's time, the erotic nature of a nude woman in the presence of clothed gentlemen would have been scandalous. Today, however, this meaning is likely to be secondary to the overall impression of "a famous painting from the past." Its best-example status for the concept of "erotic" is therefore time- and culture-specific.

FIGURE 2.3E shows a teapot in a tea cozy. If this image was viewed on its own, few people would consider it to be "erotic." But if it was surrounded by images that clearly belong to the category of "erotic," its image content might be re-evaluated, even though a human form does not appear in the representation and the general category of the object is more likely to be associated with a prim and proper grandmother than with sexual behavior. By referencing the category "erotic" through surrounding images, we call forth the relevant physical features of the object that might otherwise have stronger associations with other categories. What initially appears to be out of place among the other objects in the group gains new meaning as we search for the feature or attribute of the teapot that is consistent with the category.[19]

This collection of images demonstrates that the literal, denotative meaning of subject matter in a representation is insufficient, in itself, to trigger the concept category. In the case of the Gibson photograph and the Manet painting, nudity alone lacks the power to call up the highly emotional concept of "erotic." O'Keeffe's iris and the teapot demonstrate that inanimate objects can take on abstract meanings (in this case, human sexuality), despite their denotative content. They are, however, more ambiguous and culturally peripheral as "erotic" than FIGURE 2.3A—they risk being misinterpreted because they have

2.3 (A–E)

Each of the images in this collection can be interpreted as "erotic," yet some are "better examples" of the concept than others. Some depend on the cultural experience of the viewer, while others rely on their position within the collection.

2.3A WOMAN WEARING FISHNET STOCKINGS

2.3B *NUDE, CHICAGO*, 2009
Ralph Gibson (b. 1939)

2.3C *BLACK IRIS*, 1926
Georgia O'Keeffe (1887–1986)
Oil on canvas
Metropolitan Museum of Art, New York, Alfred Stieglitz Collection

2.3D *LE DÉJEUNER SUR L'HERBE (THE LUNCHEON ON THE GRASS)*, 1863
Edouard Manet (1832–1883)
Oil on canvas
Musée d'Orsay, Paris, France

2.3E TEAPOT AND TEA COZY

2.3A

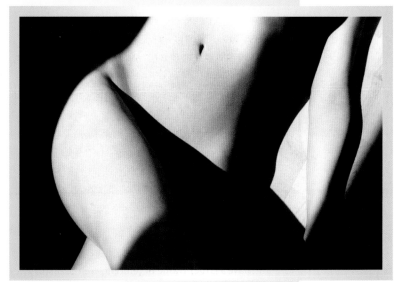

2.3B

2.3C

2.3D

2.3E

stronger membership in other categories (fine art, flowers, tea, housewares, and so on) for some viewers.

It is critical to graphic design to understand how such images reinforce concepts through metaphor or deflect interpretations of meaning to other categories. If the image fails to exhibit the appropriate features or qualities of the metaphor that establish the sign's association with the desired concept, the representation may confuse the audience. Or if the image is outside the audience's experience as a member of the desired category targeted by the design, it also may fail as a representation.

representational style

In addition to the denotative and connotative content of the subject matter, meaning can be communicated by the representational style through which it is rendered. FIGURES 2.4A–C show a variety of ways of representing a simple object.

2.4A

FIGURE 2.4A is what semiotician Roland Barthes (1915–1980) calls **ANALOGOUS** or *natural*—the photograph replicates or is congruent with our experience of the object in the real world (see pp. 128–31). The camera, as a machine, makes no choices about what to record and what to leave out. Everything within the frame is captured on film or as digital information. Barthes tells us, however, that the photograph is also paradoxical. While the photographic image may be denotative in its accurate recording of the objects, people, or places that are its literal subject matter, there is a second, connotative meaning that results from special effects, pose, lighting, the inclusion of other objects, and its position within a series or sequence of other images.[20] We learn the meanings of such representational codes largely through our exposure to images in our culture: soft focus = romance or a dream state; framed portraits of a wife and children = family values; lighting from below = sinister qualities; and so forth. Despite this understanding that photographic meaning can be manipulated, we generally trust photography to be more "objective" or denotative than other types of image.

On the other hand, we easily accept the drawing in FIGURE 2.4B as someone's subjective interpretation of reality. Through the rendering style, we recognize that the maker of the drawing revealed some aspects of the object and omitted others. We make judgments about its meaning on that basis; the decision to include and omit certain details connotes what the maker of the sign thought was important, relevant, or interesting. Further, we can usually place the choice of a drawing style within an historical or cultural context. A loose gestural drawing of the object is quite different from a technical or classical rendering of the form. A cartoon of Bugs Bunny and

ANALOGOUS

Roland Barthes's term for a representation that is natural or that physically resembles what it stands for. A photographic representation is analogous to the subject being photographed, whereas a gesture drawing may be less so.

2.4 (A–C)

These three images represent different interpretations of the same object, a can opener. The first image is analogous to reality in its photographic reproduction. Interpretation of the other two images, however, is based on our understanding that the designer included some of the available information about the object in the rendering, but left out other details. Drawing, therefore, is generally seen as a subjective representation of reality, while photography is often considered to be objective.

THE NATURE OF REPRESENTATION

2.4B

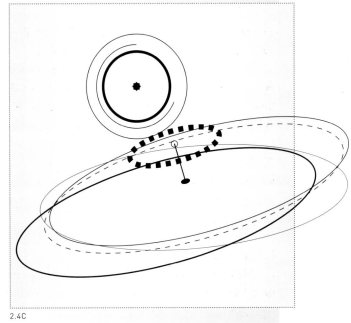

2.4C

2.5 COVER FOR *BEGINNING POSTMODERNISM*, TIM WOODS, 1999
River Design Company

SECOND EDITION

BEGINNING
POSTMODERNISM

irony
simulacrum
pastiche
heteroglossi

quotation
transgression>>
random>>

intertextuality

pluralit

Tim Woods

a realistically rendered rabbit by the sixteenth-century artist Albrecht Dürer are both representations of the same animal species, but they mean very different things based on their respective representational styles. The same basic elements may be present in all types of drawing, but the representational style connotes a different expressive intent or status of the image within a culture.

The representation in FIGURE 2.4C barely resembles the object in its natural form, focusing instead on its action. Here, the meaning is very specific but communicated through an abstraction that we have learned through other similar representations to mean "action" or "rotation." We are free to ignore all other attributes and possible meanings of the object because the representation directs our attention exclusively to the gadget's behavior.

In this way, form *is* content. The gadget is the literal subject matter in each image, but the meaning of each sign is different precisely because of its representational style. In the case of the photograph, we make assumptions about truth and accuracy, even knowing there is a human being behind the machine that made it. In the other two examples, we clearly recognize subjective viewpoints.

Representations sometimes communicate not only their subject matter but also meanings implied by the technology through which they are made. Such meanings are subject-matter-independent and arise from the semantic network of connotations associated with the technology itself. In the cover design for a book on post-modernism

**2.6   POSTER FOR AMERICAN
CENTER FOR DESIGN SIXTH *LIVING
SURFACES* CONFERENCE, 1998**
Geoff Kaplan (b. 1963)

Kaplan represents the history of
communication technologies in his
approach to imagery. The subject matter
of the images is less important than
references to the technologies through
which they are produced or distributed.

by River Design Company (SEE FIGURE 2.5), for example, the printed typography behaves in the same way as motion typography behaves on a digital screen. The book title need not include the word "media" for this message to come across. The cover design is not merely an illustration of type on a computer screen, but type that appears to behave as though it is actually changing its state of being, which is in fact possible only through dynamic media.

Geoff Kaplan's poster for the *Living Surfaces* conference on new media (SEE FIGURE 2.6) recalls various technologies from the history of design. The range of typographic choices (spanning centuries in their historical references) and images, which juxtapose a classical print-based layout with bitmapped form, call forth the historical lineage of narratives and venues for their dissemination, the topic of the conference. The poster communicates its meaning largely through these representations of technology, not through the literal subject matter of the text or images.

FIGURE 2.7 is Scott Clum's design for a rock-and-roll issue of *Stick*, a magazine for snowboarders. The gritty typography (poorly copied, badly spaced, with ink blots) reminds us of band posters stapled to telephone poles in college towns and on urban street corners. The form of the typography is intentionally "low tech," recalling associations with alternative music, free from the control of slick record producers, and the counter-culture of snowboarding. Again, the meaning is less about what is shown or said than about how it was made.

In all these examples, the primary message carriers are representations of the technologies that shape the quality, not the literal content, of form. Such qualities are not inconsequential by-products of the means of image or type production—although those aspects have representational value as well—but technological references used specifically for their associative meanings.

2.7 COVER FOR "THE NEW ROCK AND ROLL," ISSUE OF *STICK* MAGAZINE, 1996
Scott Clum (b. 1964)
Photograph by Trevor Graves

ORDERING THE ELEMENTS WITHIN THE REPRESENTATION

The visual arrangement or ordering of elements within the representation, called syntax, also influences how we interpret meaning. We assign significance to the placement, orientation, and perceived hierarchy among elements within the visual field.

narrative

In *Reading Images* (2005), Gunther Kress and Theo van Leeuwen offer a strategy for analyzing the influence of visual structure on the construction of meaning. They call the elements of the composition **PARTICIPANTS**—any object, person, or shape within a photograph, for example, is a participant—and the dynamic forces or tensions among them **VECTORS**.[21] The vector may be an actual line or a line implied by other directional cues within the composition, such

PARTICIPANT

Gunther Kress and Theo van Leeuwen's term for any person, object, or element within a visual composition or a photograph. A participant is an "actor" in the narrative.

VECTOR

The dynamic forces or tensions among participants in a visual composition or photograph. A vector may be visible (as in a line) or implied (as in the direction of a person's gaze or the perceived trajectory of a shape in space).

2.8   *TIME CATCHER*
Saul Selwyn Flores (b. 1989)

This image can be read narratively, using Kress and van Leeuwen's idea of a vector connecting the man to the object beneath the water. The story is grounded in the perceived relationship between the two established by the visual composition.

as the direction of a person's gaze toward an object, the pointing quality of a geometric shape, or the gesture of a diagrammatic element.

Kress and van Leeuwen suggest that when participants are connected by a vector, they are represented as doing something to or for each other; and that the role of vectors in visual compositions is akin to action verbs in language.[22] In this way, visual compositions are narratives—they present unfolding actions and events, processes of change, or transitory spatial arrangements in a sequence of possible arrangements or states of being.[23]

Applying Kress and van Leeuwen's analytical framework to FIGURE 2.8, for example, the vector is established by the fisherman's arm and fishing line and reinforced by his gaze. The man is an actor and the object of his attention, which is under the water, is a goal. The vector connects the two, even though the goal is hidden. If the vector did not direct our attention to a particular kind of transactional relationship between the fisherman and his goal, it would be more difficult to construct a story about the image. The narrative meaning of the representation arises, not merely from the attributes of the man (from his age, assumptions about his nationality or social class based on his dress, and so on) or of the imagined fish beneath the water, but also from the relationship between the two that is apparent only through the visual arrangement of the composition. Without this visual relationship we might think he is simply out for a boat ride.

In some images, the person in the photograph is connected by the vector to something outside the picture frame. Kress and van Leeuwen tell us that we interpret this kind of gaze differently for each gender—we see women as

2.9   URBAN OUTFITTERS CATALOG, 2005
Jim Datz, art director;
Annie Wolf, photographer

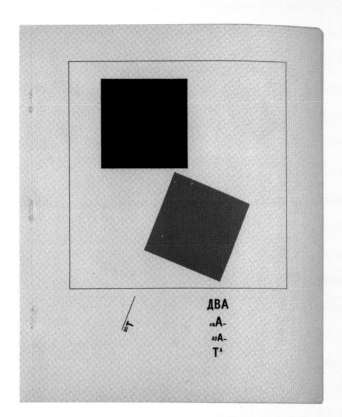

2.10 PAGE FROM *OF TWO SQUARES: A SUPREMATIST TALE IN SIX CONSTRUCTIONS*, 1922
El Lissitzky (1890–1941)

withdrawing mentally, as lost in contemplation, while we typically describe men as focusing on a distant horizon.[24] In either case the vector extends the interpretive space and therefore the possible story of the image. In this way, the cropping of images changes their meanings.

The historian Stuart Ewen discusses fashion photography in his book *All-Consuming Images* (1988). He describes the tendency to crop such photography as an attempt to depict the "dream of wholeness" through fragmentation. Because no single model can be perfect in all ways, the "ideal" woman is created through multiple photographs of many women, each with one perfect attribute—an "inventory of disembodied parts, in order to construct the semblance of wholeness."[25] In this case, the cropping robs us of rich narratives because the elements in the photographs lack individuality, moving them from what Ewen calls "self as subject" to "self as object."[26] In Kress and van Leeuwen's terms, they become non-transactional—static, detached taxonomies of human form.

In FIGURE 2.9 the vector moves from the man to the woman to the photographer. The goal of the man in the photograph is the woman, but we also detect her awareness that she is being watched from outside the frame of the picture as well; that she holds the power to attract attention from two participants. The man in the photograph continues to watch her, even though there is another participant outside the frame who could conceivably distract him were she less compelling. The fact that he does not look away is meaningful. By establishing herself as the goal of two participants, as the point where two vectors converge, she represents the sexual attraction through which she commands attention. As consumers, we are led to believe that such attraction arises from her clothing, the advertised product.

In FIGURE 2.10 the black square teeters on the corner of an unstable red square, suggesting a possible collapse. The narrative, in this case, is the implied future trajectory of the two dependent squares. This toppling of shapes is as much an unfolding of events as are the previous examples in which we have literal subject matter. In this example, we lack the specific semantic meanings of the more naturalistic content of photographs. We are, however, no less capable of describing the directional qualities of the dominant shape, as well as its past or future trajectory within the picture space. The narrative in this case is a stripped-down representation of action, but it is as much an unfolding of events in time as are the previous examples.

the relationship between text and image

Multiple images or images and text in juxtaposition hold the same potential for establishing meaning on the basis of their visual syntax. In such configurations the relationships among signs are as important as the signs themselves. In the layout in FIGURE 2.11A, the arrangement of typography responds to the perimeter of the photograph. Nothing about the composition of elements *within* the photographic frame exerts any influence on the placement or shape of the block of text. In Kress and van Leeuwen's terms, there is no vector established from image to type that represents any connotative or narrative meaning, no transaction among participants; the two forms simply coexist in the same space and their relationship is only one of physical alignment and proportion. In contrast, the composition in FIGURE 2.11B aligns the text with the horizon line in the image—the type emphasizes the relationship of the house to the land by extending the topography as typography. The addition of the second image (the close-up of a door latch) in FIGURE 2.11C takes the viewer conceptually from the street to the front door of the house, a goal. This shifts the narrative, raising questions about why we are there, and what lies inside the door. The original image of the house has not changed from one layout to the next, but the possible narratives it represents are expanded through typography and the presence of the additional image.

In his analysis of photographic representation, Barthes discusses a historic reversal in the relationship between text and image. The image—once simply an illustration of the text that was designed to elucidate the ideas expressed in words—now reigns as the primary carrier of meaning in most visual communication. He describes contemporary text as "parasitic to the image," as

2.11A

2.11B

2.11C

2.11   (A–C)

The content and cropping of the primary photograph is identical in these three layouts, yet the meaning of each composition is different. In **2.11A** the text simply conforms to the perimeter of the image, reinforcing an abstract formal relationship. The typography in **2.11B** extends the horizon line in the photograph, focusing our attention on the relationship of the house to the land. In **2.11C**, the addition of the second image takes the viewer to the front door, establishing a narrative relationship between the viewer and the house.

THE NATURE OF REPRESENTATION

an accessory rationalizing the image, a "secondary vibration, almost without consequence."[27] "Formerly there was a reduction from text to image; today, there is amplification from one to another."[28] The image introduces the cultural connotations previously reserved for the text. By this Barthes means that in the past the image served as an objective, denotative version of the text, as apparent in textbook illustrations or in journalistic photography (SEE FIGURE 2.12). Today's images, through their deployment of culturally charged signs and compositions designed to foreground certain aspects of the representation, introduce connotations that were previously the responsibility of the text. Barthes is not saying that the design of typography is irrelevant, only that text is no longer the only information that functions connotatively and culturally.

Consider, for example, the photograph of President George W. Bush in FIGURE 2.13. Staged for a press release by the White House staff, the image cleverly places the President's head in line with those of former presidents George Washington, Thomas Jefferson, Theodore Roosevelt, and Abraham Lincoln in the monument at Mount Rushmore. The speech delivered that day, to be covered by newspaper reporters, had no particular content relationship to the monument—it could have been delivered anywhere. The connotation of the representation (that President George W. Bush has something in common with the country's most revered leaders and will be remembered as one of the great presidents) overshadows the accompanying text. In this way, the image is culturally charged in a manner that the text of the speech or news report of the event was not.

2.12 PAGES FROM *GATEWAYS TO ART*
Designed by Geoff Penna
First published 2012 by Thames & Hudson Inc.

In an art history textbook, we expect images to serve as more detailed visual examples of the theme or movement discussed in the adjacent text. These images rarely introduce new content that undermines the narrative.

2.13 PRESIDENT BUSH DELIVERING A SPEECH AT MT. RUSHMORE, August 15, 2005
Photograph by an employee of the Executive Office of the President of the United States

This image, cleverly staged by the White House staff and made available to newspaper journalists, places the President's head among the grouping of former presidents on Mt. Rushmore. The implied meaning is that Bush's leadership ranks in significance with that of Washington, Jefferson, Roosevelt, and Lincoln, something not discussed in the article. What upset many readers was the subjectivity of the myth-building introduced solely by the image in a medium that professes to uphold standards of objectivity (i.e. journalism).

MATCHING THE REPRESENTATION TO ITS CONTEXT OF USE

More than two thousand years ago, the Roman architect Marcus Vitruvius Pollio (fl. 1st century BCE) described the essences of design as firmness, commodity, and delight.[29] Today's designers translate these qualities of design as usability, usefulness, and desirability. While the goal is to achieve all three, the contexts that define design problems frequently place a greater burden on representations for achieving one outcome more than the others.

In some cases, the primary goal of the representation is efficient use. The audiences for income-tax forms and signage in airports, for example, do not expect to contemplate the patriotism of paying taxes, or how the signage system complements the architecture of the terminal. This is not to say that form is irrelevant, aesthetics do not matter, or that there are not emotional consequences in making one visual choice over another. Usability is *not* the opposite of appealing form; it is *not* a rationale for a detached, default solution that ignores the full spectrum of audience needs and wants. The priorities in such contexts as taxpaying and airport navigation, however, are clarity, accuracy, completeness, efficiency, and objectivity; such representations must be usable over and above all other possible considerations.

Donald Norman discusses the appropriate use of representational form in his book *Things That Make Us Smart* (1993). In one example, he shows the typical inconsistency in the representation of dosage instructions for prescription medicines [SEE FIGURE 2.14].[30] The patient who takes multiple medications each day often confronts conflicting narrative descriptions that must be reconciled to ensure he or she receives the correct dosage. The form of the information requires more reflection than patients want to expend in reading such instructions. In a reconfigured representation, Norman shows that ordering medications in a matrix by the time of day places all instructions in a consistent format and allows the patient to ignore medications that are not required at the current time; the visual pattern is more usable in this task than is the narrative form.

In other contexts, the goal of the representation is to engage the audience more deeply in reflection about concepts and to inform judgments about significance and possible courses of action. Under these circumstances, we value attributes of representations that invite the analysis of importance or consequence, provide insight through enlightening stories, and connect meaning to future action. The priorities in such projects are about managing complexity, revealing patterns and relationships, and establishing hierarchies. Good solutions are not merely efficient, they are also effective. They extend our ability to think about things, demonstrating that they are useful and worthy of time spent in contemplation.

The chart in FIGURE 2.15, comparing company revenue across several years, is similar to one that appeared in an annual report for consumers who make stock purchases and was recognized in a prestigious design publication. The colored bars (which create the illusion of a receding plane) carry no meaning other than to hold the typeset numbers represented by the sizes of the vertical gray bars. Attention is drawn to this feature by the most vibrant colors in the chart, yet the reader must debate whether the diminishing sizes of the colored bars represent varying amounts of something or are simply the illusion of perspective among elements of the same size. In actuality, the sizes of the colored bars are meaningless and have nothing to

ZANTAC	Take twice a day at meals
LISINOPRIL	One tablet daily
SINGULAIR	Once a day in the morning
LIPITOR	One at bedtime
AMOXICILLIN	Twice a day with meals

	BREAKFAST	LUNCH	DINNER	BEDTIME
ZANTAC	X		X	
LISINOPRIL	X			
SINGULAIR	X			
LIPITOR				X
AMOXICILLIN	X		X	

2.14   TRANSLATION OF MEDICAL INSTRUCTIONS
Based on a chart by Donald Norman, published in *Things that Make us Smart* (Cambridge, MA, 1993)

Norman makes the point that prescription information arranged by time, rather than in the narratives that appear on the labels of medicine bottles, is less confusing to patients about what medications to take at any particular time.

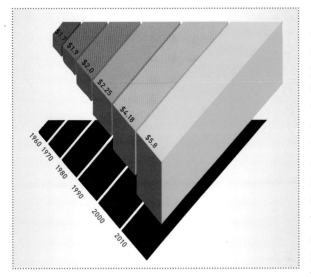

2.15 FINANCIAL CHART
Based on an award-winning diagram

This chart shows successive years of revenue for a company. The relevant financial comparison resides in the vertical gray bars. The colorful bars confuse the viewer by an ambiguous spatial representation and the changing sizes of black bars represent no statistical information.

Food Guide Pyramid
A Guide to Daily Food Choices

Fats, Oils, & Sweets
USE SPARINGLY

KEY
▢ Fat (naturally occurring ▢ Sugars
and added)   (added)
These symbols show fat and
added sugars in foods.

Milk, Yogurt,
& Cheese
Group
2-3 SERVINGS

Meat, Poultry, Fish,
Dry Beans, Eggs,
& Nuts Group
2-3 SERVINGS

Vegetable
Group
3-5 SERVINGS

Fruit
Group
2-4 SERVINGS

Bread, Cereal,
Rice, & Pasta
Group
6-11
SERVINGS

Source: U.S. Department of Agriculture/U.S. Department of Health and Human Services

2.16 USDA FOOD PYRAMID, 1992
United States Department of Agriculture

This version of the food pyramid encouraged consumers to make nutritional choices based on comparisons among differently sized wedges of a polyhedron, a tough perceptual task that is unrelated to how we plan meals (by servings). The most useful information appears in the text surrounding the image.

do with the data. The black drop-shadows—which merely contain the typeset years for which financial data is provided—reinforce the perspective illusion and distract readers from the more important data comparisons among the vertical gray bars. Because the comparative data is at an angle, it is difficult to determine how much actual difference there is between any two gray bars. So if consumers depend on this chart to make crucial judgments about the health of the company and stock purchases, they might reasonably question why the form of the chart confuses the very information necessary for reaching such conclusions and why there is no payoff for the additional time spent in reflection. The chart is ultimately usable (with work, we can identify what the form represents), but many of its elements are not very useful.

Many people are familiar with the original Food Guide Pyramid designed by the United States Department of Agriculture (USDA) to explain what constitutes a healthy diet. The USDA represented various food groups as pictorial illustrations located within wedges of a five-sided pyramid (SEE FIGURE 2.16). The number of objects illustrated in each wedge of this diagram (fruits, vegetables, dairy products, and so on) has nothing to do with the recommended consumption of any food group. Instead, readers are asked to equate food intake with differently proportioned sections of a polyhedron representing the various food groups, a difficult perceptual comparison. While the more obvious differences in the sizes among the polyhedron sections and their vertical locations in the pyramid are moderately useful in determining that we should eat less meat than fruits and vegetables, people rarely plan meals or make food choices on the basis of surface area or volume. The truly useful information appears in the text in the margins of the diagram, indicating the number of recommended daily servings from each food group (although there are still questions about what constitutes a "serving"). In this case, numbers are better matched to the way in which we plan meals than are spatial representations. The usefulness of the chart is compromised by a perceptual mismatch between the form of the information and the means through which people are to adopt the recommended behavior.

In some cases, the purpose of the representation is to aid us in forming a perspective about something. In this type of communication, representations may be evaluated as insightful, revealing, credible, compelling, or convincing. They are valuable to us in making judgments and in forming or confirming opinions. Other representations appeal to our emotions in an attempt to persuade us to some opinion or action, frequently addressing a want rather than a need. In these types of representation we usually expect subjectivity, a point of view, and consider the motivation of the message source in our interpretation of meaning.

The photograph of President Bush at Mount Rushmore, discussed earlier (see p. 49), demonstrates a point of view, both literally and figuratively. The camera angle from which Bush was photographed inserts the President physically into the sequence of other presidential heads in the monument. This placement is intentional. The position of the photographer is not a natural one were Mount Rushmore simply a backdrop for the President as an important speaker, but it is necessary to reinforce the political point of view that Bush's record is consistent with those of his great predecessors. For readers who agree, the photograph is confirmation of that belief. But for those who take a different political stance, the photograph represents media manipulation.

What is disturbing for the latter group is the relationship between the loaded connotations of the photograph and the objectivity we expect from journalistic photography. Our interpretation of meaning depends not only on the attributes of the representation itself, but also on the extended meanings of the category of imagery to which the representation belongs. We trust newspaper reporting—as opposed to editorial commentary—to be accurate and free from bias. For those who consider the Bush photograph biased, outrage results both from its content and from what is perceived as a violation of journalistic integrity, maneuvered by White House media moguls.

We generally consider maps and diagrams as "objective" representations, yet many are used to promote particular points of view, values, or social outcomes. The view of the world that many of us hold in our minds, for example, is represented in the Mercator projection, a sixteenth-century attempt to depict landmasses on the surface of a sphere in flat form. The result is an east–west distortion of geographical shapes that diminishes the relative sizes of South America and Africa and enlarges Europe and North America (SEE FIGURE 2.17A). The Peters projection from 1973, on the other hand, represents land of equal area equally, but distorts the shape of the Earth (SEE FIGURE 2.17B). The publication of the Peters projection spawned controversy over whether one map was more "fair" than another, especially in policy decisions that affect developing nations. While the Mercator projection is still the dominant representation, the debate makes apparent that the choice to use one representational form over another, however mathematical its origin, can be seen as a value-driven decision.[31]

In contrast, we fully expect some representations to be subjective. **PROPAGANDA**, an attempt to sway opinion, is understood to have a point of view and has employed a variety of techniques across history. *Testimonials* by people we respect lead many of us to adopt political positions without independent judgment: "If my hero believes this, it must be right for me because I aspire to be like this person." Given today's equivalency between "hero" and "celebrity," this technique need not employ testimony from anyone knowledgeable on the issue or of exceptional character. *Bandwagoning* encourages acceptance because "everyone believes or does" something, playing on our desire to be

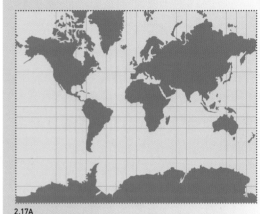

2.17A

2.17B

2.17 (A–B)

The Mercator Projection (top) distorts the sizes of landmasses in order to depict them on a flat plane, while the Peters Projection (bottom) shows landmasses of equal dimensions equally. Both are accurate representations when considered under the limitations of their mathematical models, but they create very different perceptions of geography. Such perceptions guide policy making, as well as assumptions about distance and time.

PROPAGANDA

A form of communication aimed at influencing opinion or inciting action, based on a particular, usually political or cause-related, point of view.

2.18 *THE ETERNAL JEW*, 1937
Hans Stalüter

The propaganda technique of scapegoating, blaming a common enemy for negative circumstances, often depicts the "villain" in the most unflattering light. Physical and behavioral characteristics are exaggerated to distance audiences from feelings of empathy.

part of a dominant social group. To disagree with the commonly held opinion is to declare our own inability or unwillingness to see what is obvious to everyone else. *Scapegoating* blames a detractor, uniting those with otherwise dissimilar beliefs in their opposition to a common enemy and relieving them from responsibility for the negative consequences of making a decision on the issue alone. The scapegoat is usually depicted in an unflattering or exaggerated way (SEE FIGURE 2.18). Other approaches use *reward or punishment*, warning of the negative consequences of holding a particular opinion or associating the "rightness" of a position with some personal benefit. In all cases, these appeals are visceral or emotional and do not depend on deep reflection or judgment about the subject matter. Their power lies outside the content of the issue itself and resides, instead, in the relationship between the context of use and the psychology of the viewer.

SUMMARY

While graphic designers are professionals whose job it is to build meaningful representations, all people use signs and symbols to exchange meaning with others in their culture. The construction of meaning involves a complex interplay of factors relating to the creator of the representation, who encodes the message in some culturally negotiated form, and the interpreter, who brings past experiences and context to a determination of its significance.

We sort stimuli into categories in our minds in ways that allow us to recall them when confronted with new stimuli. These categories include members that share something in common, with some being more central or prototypical to the category than others and with fuzzy boundaries between the categories.

The style of the representation and its composition carry meaning over and above the literal content. Today, cultural meanings reside in images that were once thought simply to illustrate more culturally charged text. We read significance in the choice of style and means of production, attributing subject-matter-independent meaning to both. We also view the arrangement of signs within the representation as meaningful, with the visual relationships among elements serving a narrative function. The relationship between text and image has shifted over time.

We expect communication artifacts to be usable, useful, and desirable, but recognize that different contexts often demand more of one quality than another. Representations succeed in achieving these outcomes when there is a good fit among the choice of signs, the ordering among signs in the same physical space, and the context of use.

the dimensions

of context

3

Think about the problem of designing a cup. It may seem to be a fairly simple task because the vocabulary of the form is well known (a handle, a bowl, a rim, and a base). But as the examples on these pages show, cups can vary greatly in shape and materials.

The cup in FIGURE 3.1A is well suited to drinking coffee while driving. It has a wide base and a narrow rim, making it fairly stable. The small opening and thick stoneware allow it to retain heat on a car journey and the rubber bottom prevents it from sliding on slick surfaces.

The cup in FIGURE 3.1B is my grandmother's china teacup. It has a very small base and a wide mouth, making it tipsy and sacrificing heat retention for a graceful shape. The handle accommodates only the forefinger and thumb in a gesture that causes the pinkie to rise. Its "fussiness" (painted roses and gold trim) speaks to old-world notions of formality and elegance. Although very fragile, it has the qualities of something that a family passes from generation to generation.

The cup in FIGURE 3.1C is a Heller mug designed by Massimo Vignelli. It is made of plastic with a beveled bottom, which allows several cups to be stacked easily in the cupboard. The handle accommodates all five fingers and is convex where the human hand is concave and concave where the hand is convex. It is available in black, white, and primary colors and is suitable for casual dining and a modern aesthetic.

The cup in FIGURE 3.1D is a Solo cup. It is made of thin plastic and is unstable when empty. The ridges on the side improve traction when cold liquids cause it to sweat. It nests with others of its kind, consuming little space on supermarket shelves or in picnic coolers. And it is cheap and disposable.

These four cups respond to different problem contexts: driving, expressions of high culture and heritage, casual dining, and temporary utility. In meeting and reflecting the particular demands of these contexts, the cup designers had to ignore others. It is a difficult task to design a cup that is both stackable *and* retains heat or that is both disposable *and* elegant.

Now think about the design problem of containing liquid for drinking. Instantly the scope of the problem context expands beyond the more narrow range of conditions that influence the design of a cup. What kinds of liquid, for whom, and under what conditions? Drink boxes, canteens, squeeze bottles, and freezer pops are just a few contemporary responses to a context only slightly broader than that of a cup. Had the designers of these objects viewed their

3.1A

3.1C

3.1   (A–D)

Despite the differences in shape and materials, these four cups serve the same general purpose: to contain liquid for drinking. Their distinct characteristics, however, privilege some aspects of the problem context over others (for example, heat retention, stability, social use, stackability, and disposability).

THE DIMENSIONS OF CONTEXT

respective problems as yet another cup, rather than as another way of drinking, these objects would not be part of our product world.

THE FIT BETWEEN FORM AND CONTEXT

In his *Notes on the Synthesis of Form* (1964), the architect Christopher Alexander described the real objective of design, not as form alone, but as "the goodness of fit between form and context."[1] Form is that which we can shape, and context is the complement of factors that determines the nature of appropriate form. Alexander is referring here to the fact that design problems are *situated*, that solutions must respond to specific human motives and activities, conditions, and settings that may be viewed at a variety of scales or perspectives and across time. While the nature of the context is beyond the designer's immediate control, a primary design responsibility is to determine which factors, and how many factors, within that context the design will address. When it is not possible for a design to reconcile the inevitable array of competing priorities, we must decide to value some things as more important than others. Alexander suggests that although the ultimate objective of design is form, "when a designer does not understand a problem clearly enough to find the order it really calls for, he falls back on some arbitrarily chosen formal order. The problem, because of its complexity, remains unsolved."[2]

3.1B

3.1D

Herbert Simon (1916–2001), Nobel Prize-winner in economics, described design as "action aimed at changing existing situations into preferred ones."[3] Simon's view focuses on the goal of design not just as the appropriateness of the object itself, but as the influence the designed object has on its surrounding context. For example, the design of the automobile made living in the suburbs easier, extended opportunities for the communication of personal status, and encouraged the development of commerce and leisure activities by providing on-demand transportation.

These ideas of *good fit* and *preferred situations* place the criteria for the evaluation of design as much in the designer's definition of the problem as in the quality of the solution. We can judge design, then, not only on the basis of the object and the qualities of its form, but also on how the designer framed the problem-context to which the form responds. The designer may be criticized for having ignored certain possible outcomes that others deem critical to the preferred conditions, as suggested by Simon, or for his or her ranking of competing priorities in the ensemble of relevant factors, as acknowledged by Alexander. For example, our dependency on automobiles also increased pollution and our reliance on foreign oil; suppressed the development of energy-saving mass transit; and crisscrossed traditional neighborhoods with interstates and off-ramps. Had we understood initially, or indeed over time, that these would be the negative consequences of private transportation and adopting the technology of the internal combustion engine, we may well have taken a different design path.

Although these examples come from the product world, the formal attributes of graphic design objects are equally accountable to audiences and the contexts in which they must perform. Contrary to many perceptions, the task of the graphic designer involves more than the fit between form and content. While subject matter plays a significant role in determining how graphic design objects look, defining problems solely in terms of content is unlikely to produce effective communication. Consider the following descriptions of four communication assignments:

> Persuading teenagers to practice HIV prevention.
> Persuading teenage girls, between fifteen and seventeen years of age, to practice HIV prevention.
> Persuading teenage girls, between fifteen and seventeen years of age and who have dropped out of school, to practice HIV prevention.
> Persuading teenage girls, between fifteen and seventeen years of age who have dropped out of school and live on the streets, to practice HIV prevention.

The aim of all four assignments is to convince the targeted audience to abstain from sex or to practice safe sex and not to share needles in intravenous drug use. The basic intent and content for preventing HIV is consistent across the four descriptions of audience, but the contexts are not. The first problem-statement, for example, defines the audience as teenagers in general, directing the designer's attention to the conditions surrounding young men and women between thirteen and nineteen years of age. The resulting contexts in which the proposed communication must function under such a broad audience definition (composed of people with extreme differences in maturity and access to privileges, as well as gender) involves an enormous range of physical settings, social experiences, media influences, and intellectual and emotional capacities. Consider, for example, the very different worlds inhabited by a sixth-grade boy and a woman in her first or second year of college.

By narrowing the audience definition in the second problem-statement to include only fifteen- to seventeen-year-old girls, the designer is better able to imagine—or, more importantly, to conduct research about—a tighter range of attitudes and behaviors associated with the specific social situations and places in which teenage girls hang out. This more limiting problem description narrows the conditions under which girls, in particular, would be receptive to information on abstinence or safe sex and intravenous drug use. It also surfaces the conflicting messages that foster unsafe activities, such as storylines in movies and magazines that encourage premature adult behavior. The designer can identify role models and relevant influences for this audience and explore visual styles and approaches to language that are consistent with other successful communication for teens.

THE DIMENSIONS OF CONTEXT

The third problem-statement introduces the further complication that the girls have dropped out of school and, once again, the context shifts. With the elimination of school as a setting, there are fewer predictable environments through which visual communication about HIV prevention can be distributed. Teachers, and possibly parents, are less likely to exert significant influence on the choices made by these young women—peers therefore rise exponentially in importance as shapers of values and sources of information about sex and drug use. The reasons for students leaving school may also be relevant: messages that feel like a science lecture, or that preach from a more conservative value system, or fail to acknowledge the high-risk behavior frequently exhibited by dropouts, are unlikely to succeed.

In terms of the final problem context, it is reasonable to ask whether visual communication is likely to persuade these girls to practice preventive behavior. With the almost total loss of predictability in the physical settings inhabited by the audience and the escalation of high-risk factors, personal intervention and counseling (i.e. social solutions) may be more effective than any graphic design strategy.

In each of these cases, the underlying facts of the message are the same. Technically, how someone becomes HIV positive does not change with the audience. But how the designer crafts that message (the choices about persuasive strategy, visual and verbal language, and the means by which the message is distributed) depends largely on how we define the context. In other words, a successful design must respond to a situated problem, and the more specific the description of that situation, the clearer the path to an appropriate design.

THE SCALE OF CONTEXT

In *Design Methods* (1970), the design methodologist J. Christopher Jones challenged the design professions to think about context at differing scales.[4] He devised a hierarchy of design problems that moves from components, to products, to **SYSTEMS**, to **COMMUNITIES** (SEE FIGURE 3.2). Examples of graphic design problems at the lower two levels (components and products) would be typefaces and brochures. Designing at these scales requires limited research and simple methods; trial and error solves most component problems, and such strategies as focus groups often address the needs of users with respect to individual communication products.

Jones observed, however, that most contemporary problems do not exist at the levels of components and products.[5] Single actions at the product level today could have a ripple effect on systems and communities (interrelated systems) well into the future. Jones's use of the word "system," in this case, does not refer to the typical graphic identity system consisting of logos, typefaces, color palettes, and related graphic applications. In Jones's sense, an identity system is a "product." His term implies the more comprehensive scale of a communication system, consisting of all the ways in which messages are constructed and

COMMUNITIES   (interrelated systems)

↑ **SYSTEMS**   (interrelated products)

↑ **PRODUCTS**   (interrelated components)

↑ **COMPONENTS**

3.2   HIERARCHY OF DESIGN PROBLEMS. Adapted from J. Christopher Jones, *Design Methods: Seeds of Human Futures* (New York, 1970)

Design problems may be viewed at different levels of complexity. Jones argues that the problems of post-industrial society reside mostly at the levels of systems and communities, while our methods are stalled at the levels of components and products.

SYSTEM
J. Christopher Jones's term for a set of interacting or interdependent products that make up an integrated whole. Donella Meadows defines a system as a set of things interconnected in such a way that they produce their own pattern of behavior over time, as interconnected elements with a purpose.

COMMUNITY
J. Christopher Jones's term for a set of interacting or interdependent systems that define the scale of design problems in post-industrial society.

circulated inside and outside an organization. It includes all the conflicting or competing information in the culture against which a message may be judged. His notion of "communities"—interrelated systems—tells us that the concern of the graphic designer is not only for the consequences of design action on the communication system, but also for its effects on other systems.

For example, how the online bookseller Amazon.com markets books through the design of its website affects practices in independent and chain bookstores as well as book reviews and bestseller lists. It also alters the book-buying behavior of college students and literature searches by researchers. In addition to understanding the formal and technical aspects of web design, designers of the digital system need to know about the social and cultural experiences of users—from their browsing patterns in libraries and real book-stores to their use of catalogs and search engines. Although the designer's specific task may be confined to the visual aspects of screen displays or the information architecture of the site, decisions about form are driven equally by what the designer understands about user knowledge, behaviors, and attitudes, before and after any individual interaction with the site itself. The site also has a relationship with how Amazon.com functions as a business, including its research, marketing, financial, and distribution operations. In other words, the designer must be concerned with the full lifespan of user interactions with Amazon.com as a company, related components of the reading and book-buying context, and the business model of which the website is only one part.

In another example, the immediate task of a magazine designer may be to sell the latest fashion to young women in the much-valued fifteen- to twenty-five-year-old age bracket. When viewed as a product, a successful magazine design appeals to the aspirations of young women with expendable income for beauty and social status; it converts desire into purchases for the advertisers in the magazine. When viewed from a community perspective, however, we must consider the social and cultural consequences of equating beauty with unattainable images of perfection; self-worth with possessions; and accomplishment with physical attractiveness.

In *All-Consuming Images* (1988), the historian Stuart Ewen (see p. 159) laments the social consequences of the images that are promoted by advertising:

Economic wealth is derived, more than ever, in the circulation of detached and imponderable representations of value . . . . Advertising, public relations, and other industries of image and hype are consolidating into global megacorporations; their prime role is to envelop a jerry-built material world with provocative, tenuous meanings, suggesting fathomable value, but occupying no clear time and space.[6]

Ewen's critique attributes this dissociation from the material world of real goods to "the ever-increasing prominence of abstract conceptions of value, conceptions that celebrate representation divorced from matter."[7] Advertising and design are of course complicit in promoting this world in which having a big credit line is more important than having real money, in which celebrity is more important than achievement, and in which the status associated with owning something is more important than how that object actually performs. Whether we agree with Ewen's less-than-rosy view of advertising or not, there is little doubt that consumption is fueled by design. And while many clients' descriptions of professional design assignments are at the product level, our ultimate social responsibility is to systems and communities. The lessons from these examples are that the designers of such communication have obligations to more than the short-term profits of business and clients, and that meanings accumulate, have a very long half-life, and define the society in which we live.

So, if our first and primary task as designers is to determine what aspects of context should drive our decision-making about communication strategy and form, where do we look for things that are important in defining the problem space in which we work? What aspects of design shape consequences in larger contexts? And on the basis of what knowledge and which theories can we make choices among competing concerns? If we are standing in for the audience and society in the design process, as well as representing the client and business, how do we make sure that our choices are in everyone's best interests?

The relevant aspects of context vary with the audience and communication goal. There is, however, a fairly short checklist of domains about which we should ask questions. As advocates for the individual interpreter or user, we must be concerned with all the cognitive and physical behaviors that are enhanced or diminished by the performance of the designed artifact. As citizens, we must care not only about the ways in which the designed object both shapes and reflects the culture of which it is a part, but also about how it supports positive social practices among members of that culture. As makers, we must pay attention to the means by which artifacts are created, reproduced, and circulated, as well as to the meanings of objects within broader technological contexts. And we must recognize that most designed objects have economic consequences for the clients of design, and therefore for society at large.

To illustrate these dimensions of context better, the discussions that follow provide a brief inventory of relevant theories. Many of these theories originate in disciplines other than design. Designing at the system and community levels responds to the complexity of today's information environment and argues for the role of interdisciplinary teams. The expertise of a designer alone is frequently insufficient in addressing the full range of concerns and the complicated nature of today's problems. To collaborate with other disciplinary experts, however, designers must be well informed on issues beyond form and technology. If design is to be considered in the initial stages of developing a communication strategy, not at the cosmetic end of a process aimed at short-term profit, designers must address the contributing roles of human cognition, social behavior, culture, technology, economics, and the physical aspects of audiences and settings in the definition of design problems.

THE COGNITIVE CONTEXT FOR DESIGN: HOW WE ARE ALIKE AND DIFFERENT

It is important for graphic designers to know how people perceive and process information. Human perception, motivation, and reasoning comprise one dimension of the overall context for design and define how audiences are both alike and different.

Much of our cognitive perception and processing of visual stimuli has its origins in the biological world and survival responses. Other interpretive behaviors are learned and shared among people with the same general cultural experience. Such common responses to visual phenomena ground design decisions in a set of basic perceptual assumptions.

On the other hand, contemporary graphic design and communication strategies frequently favor tailored approaches. Rather than create general messages for a broad set of audience characteristics, strategists often target communication to particular audience groups with very specific interests and backgrounds (see pp. 28–30). We can observe this trend in the number of highly focused magazines, the popularity of cable television, weblogs, personal playlists, and cell-phone plans that sort user groups through specific features and functions. Communicators look for ways to craft messages that attract specific audiences in an environment in which too much information competes for our limited amount of attention. The first goal of tailoring is to communicate quickly the "goodness of fit" between the message and an audience that is forced to edit a complex information landscape (see pp. 28–29). The task for the designer, therefore, is to determine meaningful ways in which audiences are different, as well as alike, at scales that can be addressed by design.

While marketing provides one model for identifying audience differences—usually based on socio-economic factors and issues of gender, race, and age—psychology provides another, based on perception and reasoning. In some cases, designers use psychological research to construct persuasive strategies that motivate or change the opinions of consumers. They also depend on human-factors studies of users' interactions with products and technology. In these instances, the application of psychology is often quite specific to the project or setting and may not be transferable to other design challenges. In other cases, the relationship between psychology and design addresses fundamental theories of perception and processing that are not project-specific. The aim in these studies is to understand how thinking and feeling relate to any design problem and to integrate such research as part of an overall approach to design.

how we are alike:
the contribution of gestalt psychology

Among the visual studies most frequently referred to by designers are those conducted by a group of German psychologists in the early twentieth century, which sought general principles in the perceptual organization of stimuli. Their goal, consistent with the modernist ideas of the times, was to establish an objective science for making sense of the relationships between human perception and the physical world. GESTALT in German means "configuration" and favors the perception of pattern over individual elements.[8] Such patterns are not part of the stimulus itself (are not physically present) but are created by the perceiver in his or her own mind. Gestalt scientists were interested in how people perceive grouped stimuli (i.e. discrete elements in a visual composition) as larger wholes and as segregated from other organized wholes. These visual phenomena underpin many foundation studies in basic two-dimensional design classes, but they also govern our perception of sound

GESTALT THEORY PRINCIPLES

Principles developed by German psychologists in the early 1900s in an attempt to establish a scientific understanding of the relationship between human perception and the physical world. These principles focus on the ability of the human mind to recognize whole figures within a collection of individual elements, based on the self-organizing nature of the human brain. From the German word for "configuration" or "essence or shape of an entity's complete form."

and motion. The following examples illustrate some of the best-known Gestalt principles.

Principle of proximity: According to this principle, we tend to perceive individual elements as a whole or complete form when they share common spacing among them that is different from the spacing of other elements on the page. In FIGURE 3.3A we see a small square inside a field of dots because the proximity among some dots is closer than elsewhere in the composition.

Principle of similarity: This principle states that we tend to perceive a whole form or pattern when similar characteristics are shared by individual elements. In the case of FIGURE 3.3B, we see distinct horizontal rows because of the change in shape among the elements, despite the even distribution of same-sized elements in the overall pattern. In the typographic example in FIGURE 3.3C, the same principle is at work. Type color and weight connect the three words "the right opinion" by their common attributes, overriding the normal syntax of the larger sentence through the principle of similarity. The full message implies one thing, while the second message, formed only by the gray type, means another. The second message raises questions about the first by implying that some opinions may be more "right" than others. Were the principle of similarity not in play, we would not see the second message.

Principle of good continuation: This principle explains how elements can be organized as continuous wholes, despite some interruptions and changes in form. FIGURE 3.3D shows a series of individual dots that read as straight and wavy lines. Even though these dots are identical elements surrounded by white space, we perceive them as two distinct, continuous lines. In the typographic example in FIGURE 3.3F, we have no problem reading the larger display type as a single thought, even though it is interrupted by the paragraph of smaller text type. The illusion of the larger line of type as piercing the paragraph occurs because of our perception of continuation. If the two parts of the headline were not perceived as a single line, the content of the individual segments would make no sense.

Principle of closure: This principle states that we tend to perceive some groupings of elements as simple, closed shapes, even when outlines are broken and independent of other properties of similarity, proximity, and continuation. A circle drawn with small gaps in the line, for example, is still perceived as a circle even though the containing line is broken. In the typographic composition in FIGURE 3.3E, the four letters in color are perceived as a square, not as four independent letterforms. Our perception of the shape as a square reinforces the verbal message, even though the letters in the word "cube" do not appear in a straight line. In FIGURE 3.3G, the two paragraphs of text

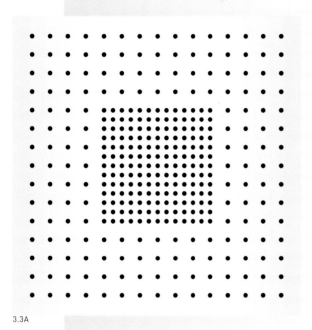

3.3A

3.3B

Everyone has the right **to freedom of** opinion **and expression**

3.3C

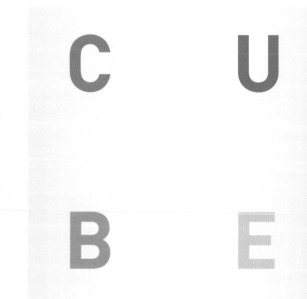

3.3D

3.3E

imagination and reasoning

In our attempts to interact forcefully with objects and persons in our environment, we often encounter obstacles that block or resist our force. When a baby learns to crawl, for instance, it encounters a wall that blocks its further progress in some direction. The baby must either stop, ceasing its exertion of force in the initial direction, or it must redirect its force. It can try to go over the obstacle, around it, or even through it, where there is sufficient power to do so. In such a case the child is learning part of the meaning of force and of forceful resistance in the most immediate way. The experience of blockage involves a pattern that is repeated over and over again *throughout* our lives.

The bodily basis of meaning,

3.3F

You construct visual worlds from ambiguous images in conformance to visual rules. No one teaches you these rules. Instead, you acquire them early in life in a genetically predetermined sequence that requires, to its unfolding, visual experience. Just as a child acquires the grammar of its language without being taught, so also a child acquires the rules for constructing visual worlds without being taught, but simply by being exposed to visuals.

And just as an adult, using rules of grammar, can understand countless sentences (in principle if not in practice), so also an adult, using rules of vision, can understand countless images (again, in principle if not in practice). Indeed, it is this infinite capacity to understand that provides a strong argument for rules in language and in vision.

3.3G

the cognitive context for design: how we are alike and different 65

appear as complete but overlapping rectangles, because of closure and continuation. Even though all words in the red paragraph are visible and make an L-shaped form, we read it as a complete rectangle sitting underneath the black text.

Many logo designs depend on the principle of closure (SEE FIGURE 3.4). Because logos appear on a variety of surfaces, the open contours and reversal of positive and negative space within their designs help to integrate them with their diverse backgrounds. Yet the principle of closure guarantees that they are also viewed as distinct, whole forms, recognizable and memorable within complex visual landscapes.

Recent studies show that sound and visual sequences in film are also subject to some of the same Gestalt principles. The durations of silence between sounds determine whether sequential sounds are perceived as part of the same whole or as isolated stimuli (for example, as a song rather than random notes). In another experiment, Gestalt psychologists studied the perception of motion in the absence of actual movement by the stimulus. In what is known as the *phi phenomenon*, two adjacent lights flashing on and off in succession are perceived as the same light changing its location.[9] We find applications of this phenomenon in lighting displays at holiday times (during Christmas, for example) and it is the means by which computer-generated motion typography works: a single letter appears to be moving across the screen when, in fact, multiple versions of the letter are simply generated in different locations at different times. Too much delay between the letter iterations breaks the perception of a single form in motion.

These Gestalt principles describe perceptions that human beings are likely to have in common. They acknowledge the importance of the total visual field, not just the design of discrete elements, and inform visual compositions and our assumptions about how people read form.

3.4   WORLD WILDLIFE FUND LOGO, 1986
Sir Peter Scott (1909–1989)

our common approaches to picture processing and memory

Psychologists also study the relationship between picture processing and memory: how we scan images, what we look at in order to construct meaning, and what conditions influence how much and how long we remember things.

Many of these studies are based on eye movement and on how much attention we pay to the specific features of an image. The assumption is that the longer we spend looking at something, the greater our investment in processing meaning and therefore the more likely we are to remember it.[10] Scientists identify two distinct types of eye movement: **FIXATIONS** and **SACCADES**. Fixations are the brief rests during which the eye is stationary and focused on an individual element or part of the image. Saccades are the rapid eye movements between fixations, so quick and automatic that they are undetectable by the perceiver.

Psychologists find that most of our fixations occur on the areas of an image that we think are most informative. When scanning images of people or animals, for example, we are most likely to fixate on the face because we expect this feature to contain more information about emotions and intent than other parts of the body.[11] Informative areas are also those with the least probability of being in the image, based on the viewer's past experience.[12] For example, in a composition of farm animals and buildings, a tiger would be an unexpected item and likely to command the most fixations among all picture elements. We appear, as a species, to be attracted to novelty and to things that are not predictable— probably as a survival strategy.

Picture scanning is also influenced by the viewer's reason for looking at the image. When asked to determine the ages of people in a photograph, for example, viewers scanned their faces. But when asked to remember the positions of the people in the same image, the viewers' eye movements zigzagged among the figures in order to gauge distance.[13]

This finding is important to the graphic designer when determining the relationship between text and image. Magazine readers, for example, generally scan spreads before reading any specific article in detail. They make decisions to return to an article on the basis of this scanning and memory of content that appears relevant to them. A headline can tell the viewer how to process the image. The two layouts in FIGURE 3.5 guide the reader to two interpretations of the same image, solely on the basis of their respective headlines. They create very different top-of-the-mind perceptions of what the article is about. Both are accurate and will stand up to further scrutiny by readers, but they may differ in attracting particular readers. If we think of headlines as telling the audience how to process the image, we make a compelling argument for designers and copywriters to work together in shaping messages.

Studies also show that the longer we look at an image, the more likely we are to remember its content—the greater the amount of processing activity, the greater the retention and reporting of detail.[14] This is a significant finding for creating messages for certain contexts. For example, a study of museum exhibitions in Washington, D.C. found that the average time spent by viewers with a single exhibition component (a discrete explanation of an object or

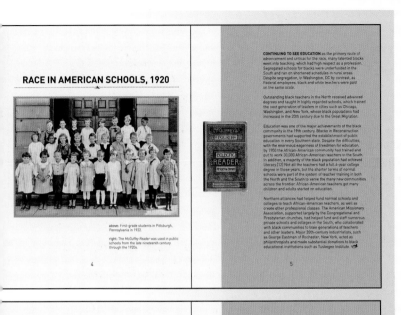

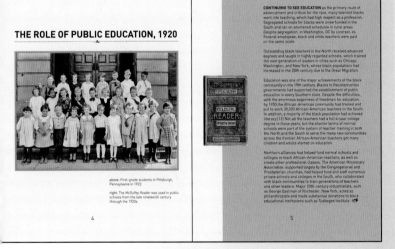

3.5

Although the two layouts are nearly identical, the different titles influence how we process the image. In the top layout, the reference to race in the title guides our viewing pattern; we fixate on the children's faces to determine racial differences. In the bottom layout, the title makes no reference to race or any other distinguishing characteristics of individual children. The image is simply a class picture in which children are arranged in rows by height.

concept) was about three seconds. This typical viewing pattern was almost identical to that of window shopping in a mall.[15] In addition, many museum-goers report entertainment, not learning, as their primary reason for visiting museums.[16] Such short exposure to content, not motivated by an explicit inten-tion to learn, raises questions about many curatorial and exhibition-design strategies. Long textual discussions on labels and sequential presentations of content that require a specific viewing order may be at odds with the visual processing behavior and somewhat random movement of viewers through exhibition spaces. Just as in window-shopping, something visually compelling must interrupt the general scanning behavior for the viewer to invest time in processing content.

3.6A

Another study concludes that there are at least three types of picture memory: one in which we retain an inventory of the objects in the picture; another in which we remember the appearance of those items; and a third that captures the location of the items within the picture frame and with respect to each other.[17] Two images, similar to those in FIGURE 3.6, were shown separately to viewers for very short periods of time. The viewers' memories of the size and the orientation of the items in the two compositions were roughly the same. What differed was their retention of spatial information. They were more likely to remember items and where they were located in response to the ordered composi-tion, and they read the image vertically; if they were unable to remember something, it was usually an item at the bottom of the page. In response to the tumbled composition,

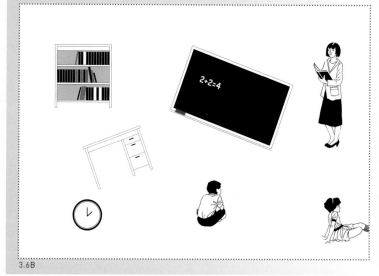

3.6B

viewers were less likely to remember the object placement and read the images horizontally, defaulting to the left-to-right reading pattern for text in the absence of a recognizable schema (i.e. a classroom) that explains the presence of these items in the same composition.[18]

This research demonstrates that there are no hard-and-fast rules about how viewers process images that designers can apply in every design setting. Viewers deploy the cognitive behavior that is appropriate to a particular interpretive task or context. Such research also emphasizes the importance of defining a communication task not only by the inventory of subject matter, but also by the perspective for viewing it.

3.6
PICTURE PROCESSING
Based on studies by Potter and Levy (1969) and Potter (1976) described in Kathryn T. Spoehr and Stephen T. Lehmkuhle, *Visual Information Processing* (San Francisco, 1982)

Two similar configurations of images, when shown to viewers for short periods of time, produced very different results in viewers' speed of recognition and memory of elements.

sensing and feeling:
the affective response to design

If design decisions were only about initiating physical responses to stimuli, there would be less debate about how things should look. Yet design also seeks to bring about some kind of **AFFECT**, **EMOTION**, behavior, or reflection. In his book *Emotional Design* (2004) the cognitive psychologist Donald Norman (see pp. 36, 50) defines these terms:

The affective system makes judgments and quickly helps you to determine which things in the environment are dangerous or safe, good or bad . . . . The cognitive system interprets and makes sense of the world . . . . Emotion is the conscious experience of affect, complete with attribution of cause and identification of its object.[19]

Norman describes three levels of emotion that can be represented through the physical characteristics of products, and by extension, in communication artifacts.

The **VISCERAL** level of emotion relies on appearance. Norman suggests that this type of emotion is "pre-wired" in our brains and is not the result of reasoning—exposure to the object or image actually changes the chemistry of the brain and our processing mechanisms.[20] Through pattern matching we respond to some things positively (smiling faces, sensuous shapes, rhythmic beats) and other things negatively (crowds of people, looming objects, discordant sounds).[21] The claustrophobic, jostled view photographed from within a crowd is visceral; we usually react to the visual and kinesthetic experience of crowding with anxiety. This is not the case with a diagram of population density or an attendance number for an event, which require far more reflection about abstractions.

The material qualities of design objects often elicit visceral responses: the woody texture of paper; the hefty weight of a book; the mesmerizing fluidity with which one shape morphs into another on a computer screen. Apart from the content they represent, these appealing physical qualities of things frequently account for our attraction to one object over another. Our interest in such qualities has little to do with culture—we all respond to touch, sound, and sight as physical beings. In this way, then, aesthetics really matter. Norman reminds us that we actually believe that attractive things work better.[22]

Television advertising makes frequent use of the visceral response: the frosty glass of beer with foam spilling over its rim in slow motion; the extreme close-up of pouty, hot-pink lips glistening with a new coat of lipstick; the tires of a shiny SUV leaving the ground, then landing with a dramatic splash in a mountain stream. So basic is our response to these types of representation that advertisers need not worry that they are too complicated for a thirty-second experience or are likely to become dated. Because we do not reflect on them, we can watch them repeatedly during prime time, without diminished reaction—that beer looks just as frosty and enticing the third and fourth time around. The goal is to make us want something; it is about an immediate emotional response, not about the rationality of that desire.

The **BEHAVIORAL** level of emotion arises from the effectiveness and pleasure derived from use; it is not conscious and, when successful, is the facility of experts.[23] Norman gives the example of being able to drive while thinking about something other than the car and the road. The psychologist Mihaly Csikszentmihalyi goes a

AFFECT

Donald Norman used this term to refer to the experience of feeling or emotion, as distinct from other kinds of thought.

EMOTION

Donald Norman used this term to refer to the conscious experience of affect, in which it is possible to identify the cause or object of the emotion.

VISCERAL EMOTION

Donald Norman used this term to refer to an instinctive or unreasoned emotional response to something.

BEHAVIORAL EMOTION

Donald Norman's term for the satisfaction or pleasure that comes from the use of something or from doing something well.

step further and refers to *flow*—a state of mind in which the act of doing something is so pleasurable that we lose all track of time.[24] Computer gamers, for example, often reach behavioral flow. They are so engaged in the characters, environment, action, and storyline of the game that the physical interactions necessary to sustain them become automatic and all but disappear from consciousness.

The goal of many design solutions is to eliminate the need for reflection on the actions necessary to make use of a tool—to make intuitive and natural (often by mimicking behaviors from another context we already understand) those things that are not the ultimate goal of the design. The computer desktop metaphor serves this function. Unlike the intense reflection required to read and write code—or even the more moderate demands of pull-down menus— "dragging something to the trash" is an action we do not have to think about. It resembles a behavior in the real world about which we are already experts. Appropriately, our reflection is about what we are throwing away, not about how to do it. So unconscious is this gesture that the system often asks us if we really want to discard the item.

Many design objects are primarily about function and performance, about usability and usefulness. For example, the last thing the harried driver in an unfamiliar city wants is to contemplate the cultural significance of highway signs or to struggle with their legibility. The performance we expect of a signage system is to direct us to the appropriate destination and confirm when we have arrived, as efficiently as possible. Because the Federal Highway Administration has adopted general standards (white sans-serif type on green backgrounds and a numbering system that tells us whether we are on ring roads or direct routes through cities, running north–south or east–west), we develop some behavioral expertise for making sense of new situations. We spend our time thinking about the content of the signs, not about their design or who is directing us by placing them along the roadways. The graphic system frees us from such reflection.

A challenge for designers of behavior-oriented objects, where the mastery of doing something well is at stake, is to discern what and whose needs are most important or typical in a given context. Should filling out a tax form require a degree in accounting? Is a software interface designed for the novice or the expert? Can it adapt to changes in skills over time? Should hitting the right sequence of buttons on equipment in a medical emergency require a lot of practice? Must we reinvent our patterns of use with a travel website under every new change in style?

A major focus of contemporary design practice (see chapter 7), and the aim of a growing number of design research firms and work in universities, is to develop a better understanding of the needs and wants of audiences or users. These enterprises do more than ask people what they do or what they need or want. Instead, they develop user-centered research methods—such as ethnographic studies—in which they observe and collect data from people about their everyday lives. A user's diary, for example, may offer a far richer and more accurate account of actual behavior than the user is able to recall in an interview. Similarly, observations of how children interact with various types of media throughout the day may not be something a busy mother can provide.

THE DIMENSIONS OF CONTEXT

Such studies are important in bridging the potential gap between the designer's and the audience's notions of need and use. In *The Design of Everyday Things* (1990) Norman discusses the possible distinctions between the designer's and the user's conceptual models of the object and how it is used.[25] Problems arise when the object fails to mediate between these two conceptual models. In this textbook, for example, definitions of terms appear in the margins of the book next to the paragraphs in which they are first used. As an author, my value-driven conceptual model is that definitions need to be handy when readers first encounter a new word, and that clusters of definitions tell readers something about a field of related ideas in ways that alphabetical listings do not. The book in your hands articulates that model. If the reader cannot decipher my conceptual framework and how to use it through the design of the object, the page-by-page definitions may appear to be random. Were the glossary not repeated as an alphabetical listing at the back of the book, the resulting behavior would be lots of flipping back and forth among pages, causing reflection about the tool, rather than about the content it is supposed to communicate.

The **REFLECTIVE** level of emotion, says Norman, involves contemplation, memory, and learning; we develop an understanding of new concepts and generalizations about the world through reflective thought.[26] This level is most susceptible to the influences of culture and individual experience and lasts longer than the visceral.[27] How we feel about successfully using an especially demanding software program or what we think about the design of certain books that makes us display them on the coffee table are not momentary thoughts. We can trace how we felt about such things in the past and project what they might mean to us in the future. They inhabit our memories and inform future actions and beliefs.

In *Complicity and Conviction* (1980) the architect William Hubbard discusses typography as a model for architecture. He argues that even if we were able to determine the perfect typeface, point size, leading, and page proportions for the maximum legibility of text, it is still unlikely that we would repeat such typographic specifications for every layout we produce, despite its behavioral efficiency.[28] Instead, we are willing to sacrifice some ease of use to gain the emotional benefits of contemplation that result from variations in typographic form.

For example, Jonathan Barnbrook's spread (SEE FIGURE 3.7) in an issue of the anti-consumerist magazine *Adbusters* that was devoted to design anarchy does more than imitate the style of rebellion against traditional displays of text. It is a literal collision of ideas, expressed in typefaces that have strong historical associations, and in a form that demands re-evaluation of each sentence in juxtaposition with another. Barnbrook reveals his intentions in the smallest paragraph of text in the layout:

Making texts visually ambiguous and difficult to fathom is a way of respecting our readers. Let's lay obstacles, diversions, and false leads. Let's halt and disrupt the discourse in devious ways.[29]

In this case, the aim of the designer is to place the reader in a highly reflective mode, to slow him or her down in the difficult task of deliberating about ideas expressed in the work. This is an appropriate mission for visual text in a

REFLECTIVE EMOTION

Donald Norman's term for the type of emotion that involves contemplation, memory, and learning.

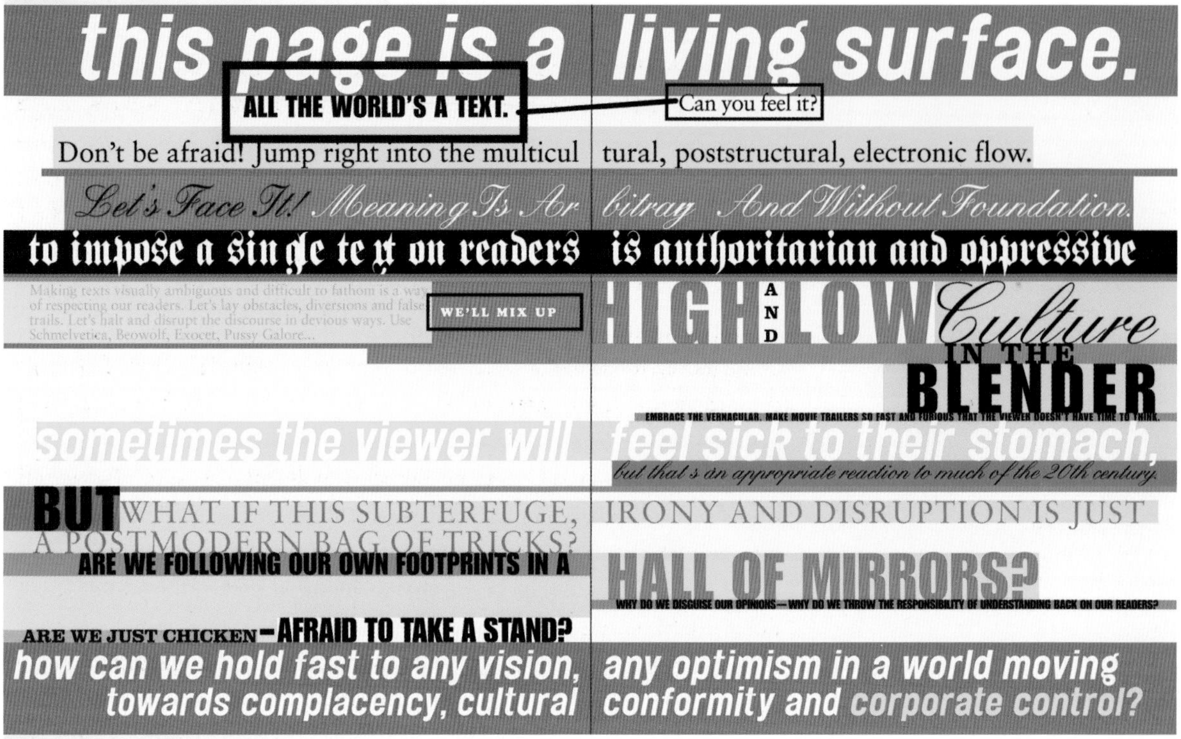

this page is a living surface.

ALL THE WORLD'S A TEXT. · Can you feel it?

Don't be afraid! Jump right into the multicul | tural, poststructural, electronic flow.

Let's Face It! Meaning Is Ar | *bitray And Without Foundation.*

to impose a single text on readers | **is authoritarian and oppressive**

Making texts visually ambiguous and difficult to fathom is a way of respecting our readers. Let's lay obstacles, diversions and false trails. Let's halt and disrupt the discourse in devious ways. Use Schmelvetica, Beowolf, Exocet, Pussy Galore...

WE'LL MIX UP **HIGH** **AND** **LOW** *Culture* **IN THE BLENDER**

EMBRACE THE VERNACULAR. MAKE MOVIE TRAILERS SO FAST AND FURIOUS THAT THE VIEWER DOESN'T HAVE TIME TO THINK.

sometimes the viewer will | feel sick to their stomach,

but that's an appropriate reaction to much of the 20th century.

BUT WHAT IF THIS SUBTERFUGE, A POSTMODERN BAG OF TRICKS? | IRONY AND DISRUPTION IS JUST

ARE WE FOLLOWING OUR OWN FOOTPRINTS IN A | **HALL OF MIRRORS?**

WHY DO WE DISGUISE OUR OPINIONS — WHY DO WE THROW THE RESPONSIBILITY OF UNDERSTANDING BACK ON OUR READERS?

ARE WE JUST CHICKEN —AFRAID TO TAKE A STAND?

how can we hold fast to any vision, | any optimism in a world moving
towards complacency, cultural | conformity and corporate control?

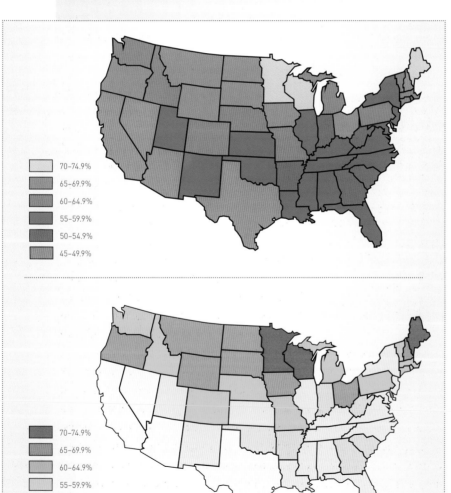

3.7   SPREAD FROM *ADBUSTERS* 37, ISSUE ON DESIGN ANARCHY, 2001 Jonathan Barnbrook (b. 1966)

3.8
VOTER TURNOUT PERCENTAGES IN THE UNITED STATES, BY STATE, 2004 Data from StateMaster.com

The two maps represent the same data, but it is easier to determine whether Missouri or Kansas has a higher percentage of voter turnout in the map on the bottom than in the map on the top. The graduated changes in color have a more natural relationship to increasing percentages than do the random colors of the map on the top.

Legend (top map):
70–74.9%
65–69.9%
60–64.9%
55–59.9%
50–54.9%
45–49.9%

Legend (bottom map):
70–74.9%
65–69.9%
60–64.9%
55–59.9%
50–54.9%
45–49.9%

critical magazine. The time spent with a magazine is self-paced—the reader can devote the time necessary to process the ideas and opinions in the work, to place it in context with the rest of the issue, and to consider the perspective and history of the maker.

In other situations, medium or timing may not be well suited to reflection. Norman cautions us that tools can be designed in ways that cause us to reflect when we should be behaving less consciously. For example, the dialog box that intrudes with an annoying question during our otherwise fluent use of software, or diagrams that make comparisons of magnitude using a perceptual strategy that is at odds with the nature of the data (SEE FIGURE 3.8)—we often spend more time thinking about these items than they deserve.[30]

Norman expresses even greater concern over design that causes us to experience viscerally or behaviorally when we should be reflecting.[31] Television often presents such circumstances: too much violence not processed on a reflective level; advertising appeals to the visceral that should be judged with more conscious discrimination; and acceptance of cultural stereotypes without self-reflection about our own biases. We have become experts at viewing and are often awash in the pattern of broadcast media without conscious thought about its content.

On the other hand, Norman makes the point that these three levels interact with one another, that communication does not always fall entirely into one category or another. Our cognitive activity can be bottom-up (initiated from the visceral level) or top-down (coming from the reflective level).[32]

3.9   TRUTH ANTI-SMOKING TELEVISION AD, JULY 2000
Arnold Communications for the American Legacy Foundation

This scene from a television public-service announcement depicts body bags piling up at the foot of a building occupied by a tobacco company. It leads viewers to reflect on the consequences of smoking through an image that produces a visceral emotional response.

Public service announcements (PSAs), for example, often use the visceral as a bottom-up alternative to more reflective sermons or lectures on social causes. A thirty-second smoking prevention television spot by the truth® youth-smoking-prevention campaign in 2000 showed a crew of young people piling up 1,200 empty body bags at the foot of a tobacco company's high-rise building. The ad sought to illustrate in a visceral fashion how 1,200 people die each day in the United States from tobacco-related diseases (SEE FIGURE 3.9). After the initial shock, viewers were encouraged to reflect on the consequences of smoking. An industry that itself relied on selling its product through visceral messages feared a counter-message that used highly emotional content as well. In another PSA, the Committee for a Drug-Free America showed a teenager drowning in her water-filled bedroom as a way of describing the feeling of an overdose. In both cases, the goal was to encourage the viewer to reflect on the self-destructive behavior, but the entry to that reflection was through an emotionally charged, visceral image. Equally important, the intentionally negative quality of these images is in stark contrast to the upbeat, frenetic nature of most television advertising. They grab our attention by breaking the expected pattern, and we sense a change in the emotional content of the broadcast.

Even abstraction can be visceral. In a response in 1985 to the proliferation of nuclear-weapons testing, Joan Kroc, the wife of the McDonald's founder Ray Kroc, purchased full-page ads in major newspapers around the country. The only content on these pages was an edge-to-edge pattern of small bomb icons and, by implication, a representation of the commitment to nuclear weapons. The newspapers report the same statistics in their front-page news, but Kroc achieved greater reflection about the extent of the country's commitment to war through a visceral representation of numbers. It mattered very little what the actual number was—we knew instantly that it was a lot. In this case, a visceral response was elicited, not by images of destruction to which we had become numb through the nightly news, but through an abstract representation of magnitude or frequency.

The emotional content of design is increasingly important to the success of products and communication. Now, more than ever before in history, the purely functional or qualitative differences among many competing products and messages are negligible. Advertisers must make us want something because the real differences among the products we need are increasingly irrelevant, or because they are selling us something we do not need at all.

responding to differences in cognitive style

There are important ways in which we are different from one another in our cognitive behavior. A segment of research in psychology focuses on learning, on how we acquire understanding and skills, and on our preferences for certain ways of structuring experiences with unfamiliar information. Although not all communication interactions focus on traditional classroom learning, a case can be made that preferences for ways to learn relate closely to preferences for ways to access and process new information in a variety of contexts.

As mentioned previously, the contemporary communication environment presents enormous competition for our attention. No one can perceive or process the totality of information available at any given moment. We therefore make choices about what we attend to. Such choices are guided, in part, by the relationship between the perceived structure of the information and the demands that structure places on our interpretative behavior. We edit according to both need and preference.

The learning theorist Bernice McCarthy, building on original studies by the psychologist David Kolb, describes people's preferences for ways to learn. Through evaluations of learning style, she measures and classifies learners as **ABSTRACT** or **CONCRETE** perceivers and as active or reflective processors. Abstract perceivers reason experience; the

ABSTRACT

Theoretical, conceptual, apart from the physical world. Denoting an idea, quality, or state.

CONCRETE

Physical, tangible, real. Existing in a material form that can be understood through sensory experience.

REPRESENTING THE CONCRETE

Visual communication, by definition, often represents or simulates concrete experience. The material properties of a printed publication (paper choices, color, or size, for example) or the gestures used to interact with some computers (such as finger movements on an iPad or iPhone), enhance the concreteness of experiences with certain representations. But the majority of sensory cues in graphic design are visual facsimiles of a physical, concrete world: a blurred photograph represents motion; letterspaced typography simulates rhythmic or spoken sound; and overlapping red and yellow shapes appear to make orange.

On the other hand, there is a tendency for graphic designers to rely on abstraction in communicating certain kinds of content. Imagine describing the height of a skyscraper. Were we to approach the explanation of its height as an abstract concept, we might place an image of the building next to other known tall buildings, illustrating a juxtaposition that we are unlikely to see in the real world. Such comparisons encourage understanding of a mathematical concept of height. The building is "twice the size" of another building, or "ten stories higher" than the Empire State Building, or equal to multiples of some unrelated object the size of which we already know. For example, to understand the height of the Empire State Building, we could compare it to a two-story house. In contrast, an image of the street taken from the top of the building, looking down, with our toes at the edge of its cornice, is more likely to help us "sense and feel" building height than an abstract, mathematical comparison. It would recall the concrete, bodily experience and resulting anxiety of being in high places. While such concrete representation is not useful in making some kinds of comparisons or

intellect makes the first appraisal in an attempt to be objective and free from bias, to stand apart.[33] Theories, concepts, models, and strategies are comfortable points of entry to new content for these individuals. Concrete perceivers, on the other hand, sense and feel. These individuals prefer to access new ideas through immersion in actual experience or through the recall of actual experience. They enter content through the physical information of the senses; they are intuitive and connect information to deeper meaning and personal points of view.[34] (See box: "Representing the Concrete.")

calculations, it can be helpful when trying to communicate on a more emotional level.

Some information lends itself naturally to concrete representation. Several decades ago, the United States attempted to align itself with the rest of the world by broadening its use of the metric system of measurement. Unfortunately, the method promoted for US adoption was conversion, which asked citizens to think in abstract numerical equivalencies (between yards and meters, for example). The problem with this strategy was that distances, weights, and volumes are things we first understand through concrete experience in the execution of physical tasks. We hold, see, or estimate an amount of some real thing that represents the abstraction of a "cup" or a "foot." We sense how long it takes us to walk or drive a mile. In fact, our system of measurement was once based entirely on physical experience. A yard was said to equal the stride of King Henry I of England. The cubit was the distance from the elbow to the fingertips in ancient Egypt, and an inch in fourteenth-century England was the span of three grains of barley placed end to end. In the case of Americans and the metric system, the abstract, reflective task of conversion was not well matched to learning the concepts of measurement. Practice in measuring real things with metric instruments or thinking of metric units in our travel of distances would probably build a better understanding of the system.

Interactive media present an opportunity to address both abstract and concrete perceivers in the same presentation. For example, the typical periodic table of the elements as it appears in science books is a static chart that groups like elements in specific zones of the table (the noble gases are clustered in an area that is distinct from metals

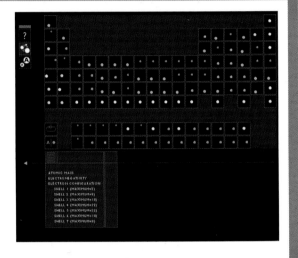

and non-metals). Elements are also ordered by ascending atomic number (shown in the corner of each element's rectangle. In this alphanumeric chart, one element looks essentially like another. In contrast, the interactive version of the periodic table by Stacie Rohrbach, shown in this illustration, explains reactivity through a small white ball that bounces within each element's rectangle at a specific speed. Movement is reinforced by a pinging sound as the ball hits the edges of the rectangle. When all elements are activated, sections of the table pulse at different rates, depending on how reactive the elements in that section are. We sense the differences in reactivity through sound and motion and, in doing so, understand patterns across the 118 elements. Again, we cannot perform calculations through this form, but the sensory variables allow us to recognize and reflect upon pattern and difference in ways that are not possible through the more abstract alphanumeric display.

**LEARNING
PREFERENCE**

A preferred way
of interacting
with, taking in, and
processing stimuli
or information.

The second dimension of **LEARNING PREFERENCE** measured by McCarthy is processing. Some people prefer to process information by thinking (reflectively), others by doing (actively). This difference in processing behavior may be described by two approaches to assembling a toy or piece of furniture: one person reads the instructions to build a mental concept of the components and rules for their assembly before acting, while another person dumps the contents onto the floor and discovers the rules by physically testing combinations in response to the physical features of the parts. (See box: "Understanding by Doing.")

Although individuals may show preferences at various locations along McCarthy's perceiving and processing continuums (abstract to concrete perception and active to reflective processing), the system classifies learners into four basic types and provides a "favorite question" as a shorthand description of each:[35]

→ Concrete perceiving/reflective processing—the "why" people

→ Abstract perceiving/reflective processing—the "what" people

→ Abstract perceiving/active processing—the "how does this work" people

→ Concrete perceiving/active processing—the "[what] if" people

These favorite questions offer interesting opportunities for structuring content in visual communication. Design strategies frequently focus on the "what" issues in content explanations; choices about text and image "identify" content related to the concept. For example, a poster advertising a jazz festival may use a saxophone and piano keys to tell viewers that the poster relates to music. The rendering of the instruments and choices of typeface may go a step further to signify jazz through some stylistic tradition, but the intention is still to recall objects we associate with jazz. On the other hand, if we view the design task as describing how jazz works, or why we might want to spend an evening listening to a live jazz performance, we open up communication about jazz to a wider range of interpretive perspectives.

In thinking about how the verbal and visual forms of information address these various cognitive preferences, individually or simultaneously, we expand the conventional repertoire of design strategies. Further, we layer meaning, providing a richer representation of content—text does not merely "label" an image, and images do not simply "illustrate" text. Instead, text and image can present two complementary but different aspects of the same concept, providing the audience with choices about how to engage with the subject matter.

Graphic design has a limited history of concern for the cognitive behavior of audiences in terms of research and theoretical perspectives. Most designers assume that audiences see what the designer sees and operate intuitively about how visual information is perceived and processed in the mind. Because we are usually not present when audiences confront print-based design objects, and because it is impossible to observe someone's thought processes, we have little information about the cognitive consequences of design decisions. In recent years, however, the move from print- to screen-based interactive communication has presented unprecedented opportunities to study and record

UNDERSTANDING BY DOING

The active processing of information is, in many cases, neither efficient nor economically feasible. It makes little sense to judge the healthful attributes of a breakfast cereal by sorting ingredients into cups when a pie chart serves the same function. And if we assemble a bicycle incorrectly, based on intuition about how the parts go together, the results could be costly. Yet there are communication challenges in which the physical engagement of the audience can be a powerful means for understanding something. Digital technology expands the possibilities of "virtual" activity, making such strategies more practical. The Sodaconstructor website (http://www.sodaplay.com/constructor/), for example, allows users to build virtual robots and other models with muscles and springs that respond within an environment of user-determined variables (gravity or rates of movement). Interaction with the site teaches about physics through something other than traditional presentations of static illustrations, text, and numbers.

In another example, the much-published thesaurus by Plumb Design (http://www.visualthesaurus.com/) offers a visual semantic web of synonyms and definitions in response to 145,000 user-entered words. The semantic web is dynamic: clicking on a synonym reveals yet another web of meaning as an extension of the first word. Click-and-drag behaviors physically reconfigure the point from which the web is viewed. The reader actively

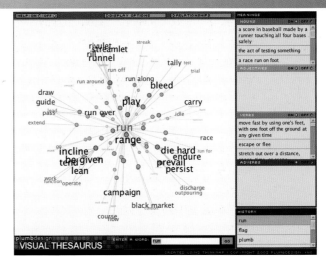

Visual Thesaurus, 1998. Mark Tinkler, Plumb Design and Thinkmap, Inc.

constructs the field of definitions, unlike a traditional thesaurus in which the arrangement of information is fixed and the individual's path through definitions is never recorded in physical form.

In both examples, the physical interaction of the user with the site involves more than deploying standard software functions (scrolling, pulling down menus, clicking from a fixed number of options, and so on). Instead, the actions required to change the state of the information are equivalent to actions in the real world, with consequences that are quite particular in a visual and spatial sense. Users "build" information in a virtual environment, much as they would in actual experience with material objects.

how users process information. The cognitive implications of design represent a growing area of research. Chapter 7 addresses the rise in importance of cognitive theory, brought about by the recent shift in practice from designing objects to designing experiences.

THE SOCIO-CULTURAL CONTEXT FOR DESIGN: THE SEARCH FOR PATTERN

Even when tailoring communication to the cognitive needs of individuals, it is important for designers to understand patterns in the social and cultural values and practices of groups. Much of our thought and how we process meaning is conditioned by living in a social world.

Stuart Hall (see p. 36) cites the cultural theorist Raymond Williams (1921–1988), who examined varying definitions of **CULTURE** across history. Originally referring to the cultivation of crops and animals (agri-culture), the term came to mean the process of human development during the Enlightenment (see p. 136). Europe was viewed as "more cultured" than other

CULTURE

A particular way of life that expresses certain meanings and values in ordinary behavior. According to Raymond Williams, culture is "a network of relationships with congruent ways of seeing the world."

societies as the definition asserted a hierarchy among peoples on the basis of social progress.[36]

The term acquired a more specific meaning in the late nineteenth century and became associated with intellectual achievement, learning, and the arts. Today we hold a distinction between *high culture* and *popular* or *mass culture* that has much to do with this perspective.[37] This dichotomy presents a dilemma for the identity of design. On one hand the field is rooted in the fine arts, with many contemporary designers having been trained through an aesthetic education, and most clients thinking that the only purpose of design is to make things look beautiful. The earliest documentation of graphic design history was conceived largely within the canon of art history, which emphasizes exceptional individuals and the exemplary objects they made in a chronology of important visual or ideological movements, which may or may not be as emblematic of their times as were the anonymous items of everyday life. In many art history texts, design and typography are still treated as footnotes to major artistic movements in painting, sculpture, and photography, thus confirming the demarcation between high and mass culture. With a few recent exceptions, museums have affirmed this distinction by typically collecting one-of-a-kind and high-culture artifacts as "objects of art," and mass-produced products and printed communication as "objects of history." The first major exhibition of graphic design in an art museum in the United States did not take place until 1989, when the Walker Art Center in Minneapolis mounted *Graphic Design in America*; and the Cooper-Hewitt National Design Museum in New York is the only major museum in the nation devoted exclusively to historical and contemporary design.

On the other hand, design involves the creation of messages for mass consumption and concerns itself with an enormous variety of audiences, settings, and communication problems. More recent design histories address the anonymous, unsigned objects of popular culture and the broader social contexts that gave rise to them. Technological changes in how we produce design further distance the field from its associations with high culture. In democratizing the

3.10 *THE NIGHT GALLERY*, 1991
Art Chantry (b. 1954)
Poster for performance at the Center on Contemporary Art

3.11 DESIGN FOR THE UNIVERSITY OF VIRGINIA, CHARLOTTESVILLE, 1825
Thomas Jefferson (1743–1826)

Jefferson understood the *illustrative* and *formative* power of design. His design for the university quotes ten styles from architectural history; none of the examples is British. Earlier, Jefferson had designed the Virginia State Capitol building based on a building from the Roman Republic, his model for American government.

means of production through computer software and networked communication, technology moved design beyond the hands of highly trained professionals and the privileges of corporate wealth to untrained users and do-it-yourself strategies for publishing and communication. And following a characteristic post-modern strategy, designers frequently make reference to mass culture in their choices about form. The vernacular inspiration for Art Chantry's poster for the Center on Contemporary Art (SEE FIGURE 3.10), for example, does little to reinforce the upper-class connotations we typically associate with the high culture of art museums. Design has therefore had a varied life under definitions of culture that focus only on its artistic qualities.

During the twentieth century, and consistent with the rise of the social sciences, we came to view culture as a particular way of life that expresses certain meanings and values in ordinary behavior.[38] Williams stressed the strong links between culture, meaning, and communication in this definition. He viewed cultural experience as a "network of relationships," in which the meaning of communication artifacts cannot be separated from the social environments and practices in which they reside.[39] More recent theories question the notion of "one way of life" and focus on the process of meaning production and circulation, rather than on a unified vision—on *how* things mean rather than *what* things mean.

formative and illustrative roles for design

In *An Introduction to Design and Culture* (2004), the design historian Penny Sparke describes design as having both **ILLUSTRATIVE** and **FORMATIVE** roles to play within culture.[40] From one perspective, design reflects the culture and society in which it is produced. Through their subject matter and form, designed objects express the values and preoccupations of the social environment. From another perspective, Sparke says, "Design is part of a dynamic process through which culture is actually constructed."[41]

The history of architecture is replete with examples of the illustrative role of design in culture. The design for the University of Virginia by the architect and president of the United States Thomas Jefferson (1743–1826) distributed ten architectural pavilions, each housing a different academic discipline, around a rectangular lawn (SEE FIGURE 3.11). A small version of the Roman Pantheon stands at the head, a bricks-and-mortar representation of the ideals of the Roman Republic, upon which Jefferson modeled American government. Each of the ten pavilions uses a different building style, making an encyclopedia of architecture to be

ILLUSTRATIVE ROLE

Penny Sparke's term for the concept that design expresses the culture in which it is produced and illustrates the ideas and values that are already present in the social environment.

FORMATIVE ROLE

Penny Sparke's term for the concept that design shapes the culture in which it is produced and is actually a means for constructing the values and ideas that eventually become part of the social environment.

studied by students of that discipline enrolled in the university. There are, however, no British examples in Jefferson's plan—an expressive "thumbing of his nose" to the monarchy from which he sought to distance the young country.

Likewise, the history of graphic design illustrates our shifting cultural values. FIGURE 3.12 shows a collection of magazine advertisements, produced for Listerine mouthwash, spanning a period of roughly forty years, much of it under the same advertising agency. These ads are not likely to make anyone's "100 Best" list for their design, but they are typical of the thousands of messages that define the zeitgeist of particular times. In the earliest image (SEE FIGURE 3.12A), the ad reflects the prevailing perception of black people in the 1930s and 1940s—a servant class in support of the dominant white culture. The image seems shocking to us today, through the lens of several decades of social transformation. By the 1950s (SEE FIGURE 3.12B–C), political and social change had recast the role of black people in images that were "separate but equal." Not only were there two versions of the ad for different racial audiences, but the black woman is also modeled entirely in the image of the white woman. Finally, the ad produced after the civil rights movement (SEE FIGURE 3.12D) shows a confident African-American woman sporting a hairstyle and attitude all her own. We can trace similar changes in representations in fashion magazines, which reinforce public attitudes about female "beauty," or sports magazines and television advertising, which illustrate the dominant social schemas of what it is to be "male."

In contrast to these illustrative examples, there are situations in which design is formative and actually shapes the nature of the surrounding culture. This is most evident in the application of new technologies. For example, networking sites have transformed social behavior for certain audiences. Google Maps and mobile GPS systems have changed the way many of us understand our cities and navigate the physical environment. Online versions of the news and newspapers create certain expectations of what is "current" about current events and actually contribute to changes in traditional reading habits.

Older media have also had a lasting impact on cultural behavior. Propaganda posters during the two world wars shifted our views about women working in industry, people with ethnic and national origins that matched those of our enemies, and what we thought was absolutely essential for living a comfortable life. Our preference for SUVs in the 1990s responded to the auto industry repositioning attitudes toward the station wagon and military vehicles through its advertising. Contemporary magazines tell us how to dress, what a fashionable home should look like, and who we should look to as role models. Information graphics shape our views of public policy or influence our decisions as we exercise the privileges of democracy. This role for design is powerful. It assigns to design considerable responsibility for the transmission and production of culture.

social schemas

Schema theory focuses on how we assign meaning to things through social experience. **SCHEMAS** are mental structures that contain general expectations and knowledge about people, social roles, events, and places. These structures tell us how to behave and what to think in certain situations and are formed through our social encounters, in real life or as represented by the media.

SCHEMA

The psychologists Martha Augoustinos and Iain Walker used this term to refer to a mental structure that contains general expectations and knowledge about people, social roles, events, and places. These structures tell us what to think and how to behave in certain situations and are formed by experiences in a social world.

3.12 (A–D)
LISTERINE MOUTHWASH ADVERTISEMENTS

A chronology of advertising images for this product reflects the social history of race in America during the same period. In this sense, designed artifacts reflect the prevailing social values of the culture.

A Listerine advertisement, *Cosmopolitan*, 1941

B Listerine advertisement, *Life*, 1962. J. Walter Thompson Company

C Listerine advertisement, *Ebony*, 1962. J. Walter Thompson Company

D Listerine advertisement, *Ebony*, 1971. J. Walter Thompson Company

THE DIMENSIONS OF CONTEXT

3.12A

3.12B

3.12D

3.12C

Schema research aims to explain how people represent information in memory and how new information is assimilated with existing knowledge—that is, how people are able to process, interpret, and understand complex social stimuli.[42] When we confront a new stimulus, we quickly identify or categorize the general domain to which it belongs and respond accordingly with attitudes and behaviors that we have assigned to that domain through our prior experience.

Many of these schemas are shaped or amplified by media representations. For example, what teenagers think is "cool" or what someone with average income thinks is "wealth" is established through television, magazines, and movies as much as by any real experiences with cool or wealthy people. Because schemas act as templates against which we compare future stimuli, they are very important to perception and interpretation. This is the power of visual communication, and designers must consider every image-making act carefully for its consequences in creating larger social expectations and attitudes.

ROLE SCHEMAS contain the norms and expected behaviors of specific positions in society and can refer to *achieved* or *ascribed roles*. "Achieved roles" refers to roles that are acquired through effort and training (such as "doctor," "dancer," or "student"); ascribed roles relate to gender, race, age, or any other human attribute over which we have little control.[43] Such schemas are cognitively efficient—they allow us to deal with the inherent complexity of the social world through a kind of shorthand. When meeting a new person, or viewing an image of someone, we use our history of interactions with people who share the same attributes, until we discover other information that tells us that our behavior may be inappropriate or misguided. Schemas do not require deep cognitive processing—they are efficient, first-level responses to stimuli.

A **STEREOTYPE** is a particular type of role schema that contains social expectations and behaviors. Research indicates that the social content of these schemas is richer in structure and able to elicit more concrete attributes than schemas based on traits alone.[44] Stereotypes are especially difficult to dislodge because a number of traits are grouped in the mind, any one of which may call forth the others. (See box: "The Power of Stereotypes.")

Schemas may also contain information about places and objects. In *A Pattern Language* (1977), Christopher Alexander defines recurring **PLACE SCHEMAS** that support particular kinds of human activity in the built environment. For example, the pattern of intimacy gradient describes a schema for the arrangement of rooms in a typical American home. Public spaces are generally placed toward the outside of the home while more intimate spaces tend to occur deeper in the home's interior.[45] Think how

ROLE SCHEMA

Martha Augoustinos and Iain Walker used this term to refer to a type of schema that contains the norms and expected behaviors related to people's achieved roles (those acquired through effort or training) and ascribed roles (those assigned by society to age, gender, race, and so on).

STEREOTYPE

A type of role schema in which a number of traits are grouped in the mind and may be called forth by a single visual cue, such as skin color or dress.

PLACE SCHEMA

Martha Augoustinos and Iain Walker used this term to refer to a schema in which the content and spatial organization of elements arise from experience with place.

THE POWER OF STEREOTYPES

The design writer Steven Heller addresses the problem of stereotypes in his article "Exploiting Stereotypes: When Bad Is Not Good" for *Voice*, the online journal of the American Institute of Graphic Arts (AIGA). He focuses on the 2005 Art Directors Club (ADC) Call for Entries, which uses the images of a black Ronald McDonald and a bling necklace with the copy line "Pimp My Brand" to comment on what designers do for a living (http://creativity-online.com/work/art-directors-club-pimp-my-brand/7947). Heller suggests that the image may be a "critical poke at how white mass media exploit contemporary black stereotypes to sell products." But his critique finds the image distasteful in its "playing to a stereotype of hip-hop as nasty, tastelessly extravagant, and ultimately foolish."[46] He cites the importance of context, affirming that had the image been used "on the cover of a hip-hop CD that critiqued rap language or gangsta style, then perhaps the message would be more palatable" and within the genre of Blacksploitation films.[47] Later in the article, Heller raises questions about what the work is actually saying: whether it suggests that advertising styles are changing; or gratuitously ridicules a streetwise style that could not succeed in a design competition; or simply references popular culture.[48]

Readers' postings on the AIGA site on which Heller's article appeared were mixed—evidence of the degree to which the stereotype does or does not resonate with the social experience of the various authors of the postings. Self-identified African-American respondents were as diverse in their comments as others, with some framing the image critique within the larger media context, including MTV's "Pimp My Ride" and other advertising campaigns. The point

odd it would be to enter the home as a first-time guest through the kitchen or bedroom instead of the foyer.

Such conventions are culturally driven. In some Arab countries, for example, public space ends and private space begins at a high wall that surrounds the property. People who are not members of the family would not think of penetrating the wall without an invitation. But in the United States we sunbathe and barbecue in open yards, well within view of the neighborhood—privacy begins at the front door of the house itself.

There are graphic counterparts to some of these cultural patterns in the built environment. A book design, for example, generally moves through an

in this diversity of feedback is that the image means different things to different people on the basis of their experiences. The designer's assumption of a common reading is erroneous. At the same time, the image is highly charged for most people. It is not simply a clever advertisement for the ADC but a social stereotype, which calls up complex and strongly held social values and attitudes.

What this example demonstrates is that stereotypes are powerful because they direct attention, guide the encoding and retrieval of information, and save cognitive effort.[49] The ADC image grabs attention because it is in many ways familiar, but unexpected in this particular setting (a design competition). In fact, on the *Voice* site, some of the Internet postings address the shocking nature of the depiction specifically because it is used to advertise a previously non-controversial competition. In other words, "shock" is one result of a stereotype appearing outside its normal context, hence Heller's comment that we would find a CD cover more palatable. Also, how well we remember an image depends to some degree on how consistent it is with our memory of the stereotype. The ADC image would not have caused as much discourse had it not seemed familiar, had it not been congruent with already formed stereotypes promoted through the media.

What makes negative stereotypes so difficult to dislodge is that an array of social and behavioral expectations is grouped within a mental category that is recalled simply by the presence of any single visual trait. If the ADC call for entries had used a white Ronald McDonald the resulting message would have been very different. All that was necessary to incite the emotional content of the advertisement and concern over the ambiguous intention

of its designer was the presence of a black face. The typographic reference to bling was far less emotionally charged because the field of associations with flashy jewelry is much smaller. The inanimate object signals fewer associations with motive, behavior, and cultural history than does race. But when coupled with a black face the reference becomes more emotional.

Attitudes toward gender and race are particularly difficult as they have strong social reinforcement. A study with five- and six-year-old children (Cordua, McGraw, and Drabman, 1979) exposed them to a schema-inconsistent image of a female doctor and a male nurse. In response to a later question about what they had seen, the children recalled a male doctor and a female nurse, switching the roles to make them more consistent with the gender stereotypes they had been taught through social experience. Such impressions develop over time and through the continuing reinforcement of schema-consistent messages.

This issue of schema consistency raises questions about the use of stock photography by designers. Stock photography is based on the premise that we have enough role and place schemas in common that producing stock images will be profitable. The most valuable stock image is one that is either so consistent with the prevailing schema (for example, mother or businessman) that it transcends the range of audiences' individual experiences with these concepts, or so general (for example, sunsets or flowers) that it can elicit an array of abstract emotions depending on its application. In this case, the stock image falls short by being neither inventive nor specific. It either adds nothing new to the timeworn cliché or opens up such broad interpretation that it is ineffective in delivering the message with conviction.

information gradient of typographic scale and content specificity from cover to title page, table of contents, chapter heading, body copy, and notes. We exit to marginalia from the primary text and expect smaller, less aggressive typography in these elements. Because of these visual conventions, it would seem strange to go directly from the book's cover to a chapter heading without any transitional pages.

The masthead of a newspaper, like Alexander's main entrance of a building, is separated from the other content of the front page by placement, shape, symmetry, and scale. It is usually positioned higher than other content and is surrounded by white space in the same way that attention is drawn to the front door of a building.

Design can reinforce these conventional schemas or subvert them to change our relationship to the content and reading experience. The Dutch designer Irma Boom and the Canadian designer Bruce Mau both designed large books in the 1990s (SEE FIGURES 3.13–3.14). The number of pages in these books far exceeds typical editions of the same height and width. By their very sizes, these books defy linear reading. Instead, they comprise compendia of images and texts that may be entered at any point, with covers that simply contain the pages, rather than signify the beginning and end of a story. The altered proportions of these books also make them formidable objects with their own material presence, not just neutral containers for more expressive two-dimensional narratives.

3.13   *S, M, L, XL*, 1998
Rem Koolhaas (b. 1944) and
Bruce Mau (b. 1959)
Office for Metropolitan Architecture

THE DIMENSIONS OF CONTEXT

3.14   *(above, below, and right)*
BOOK FOR SHV, 1996
Irma Boom (b. 1960)

These oversized objects push the limits of the conventional book format, thus reconfiguring the traditional reading experience. Readers are not directed by structure to move in sequence from page to page, cover to cover, as in traditional books; rather, they enter the books at any place with no expectation of continuous stories.

Boom goes so far as to print on the foredges of pages, treating the book more as architecture than as publication. These design solutions sit materially between the traditional book and some other kind of object, expressly to challenge the typical interaction of the reader with content.

EVENT SCHEMAS are cognitive scripts that describe the sequential organization of episodes in everyday activities, such as our morning routine of getting ready for work or the sequence of decisions and actions necessary to make an online purchase. They allow us to make plans and to imagine the steps through which we may achieve a goal or bring about another set of conditions. We bring these sequential patterns of cognitive, physical, and social behavior to our interactions with objects and assign significance to the ordering of events. Software designers make use of event schemas as metaphors for the operation of computers. We understand, for example, that placing a digital file in the trash does not mean it is gone forever, unless we follow that action with emptying the trash. Web and software designers construct scenarios—narratives of use by real or fictional users—in order to anticipate the paths or series of actions people might take through information or in the execution of tasks. And signage designers predict the need and readiness of viewers for certain information at various points along a route, hoping to deliver just the right message at just the right time. In designing for events or experiences, we must imagine the steps or key frames necessary to complete the task and study social behavior for clues about how people do things.

Historically, the interest of graphic designers in theory has focused primarily on the social and cultural implications of design. Modernist movements in the early part of the twentieth century shared the aim both to illustrate and shape a social world that was vastly different from preceding centuries (see chapter 5). Formal experimentation in the 1980s and 1990s frequently drew its inspiration from writing in literary and social criticism. Post-modernist discourse of the same period elevated the importance of cultural pluralism and the vernacular (see chapter 6). And the tailoring of products for members of various subcultures within society shaped design strategy in the 1990s. Later chapters of this book provide further discussion of approaches to theory, linking the history of design to cultural production.

THE TECHNOLOGICAL CONTEXT FOR DESIGN: MATERIAL MATTERS

The signs produced by graphic designers hold meaning for audiences, not only through their subject matter and style, but also through the tangible attributes of their physical form. **MATERIALITY**, or the physical qualities of a representation that give it individuality and allow it to be categorized, is an important aspect of what signs mean. The specific visual, spatial, auditory, kinesthetic, and temporal characteristics of form *are* content. The materiality of designed objects arises from choices about media, surfaces, formats, or structures, and the technology and tools used to produce them.

THE DIMENSIONS OF CONTEXT

A **MEDIUM** is a mode or system of communication that extends our ability to exchange meaning. It is the locus of representation. Drawing, typography, film, and networked digital communication are media and have characteristic material attributes that result from how they are produced, reproduced, and distributed.

TOOLS are the means by which we make form or accomplish some other kind of task in a particular medium. Tools leave traces of their use in material form. For example, lines drawn with charcoal, ink, and pixels differ in their expressive qualities and references to how they were made. In hand-drawn forms, we can tell something about the gesture, speed, and pressure of the hand that made the lines; we can detect if technical instruments were involved and the confidence with which the forms were hand-rendered. We can also assign meaning and intention to these tool-based processes and their particular use in certain contexts—a line that emphasizes, that softens, that hesitates. The choice to remove the mark of the hand through machine-generated form may also reveal intent—a desire for precision, for anonymity, for objectivity.

Even digital representations have material properties in a virtual sense, in that they mimic behaviors and simulate the qualities of objects in the physical world. We recognize these properties from our life as physical beings, and impose our understanding of experiences in the real world on our interpretations and judgments of simulations. Ask any gamer about the compelling nature of movement through the imaginary environments of first-person-shooter computer games. There is also a material language that is unique to digital media, such as the mutability of objects that transforms them seamlessly across time, that allows them to disappear and re-emerge, to exist simultaneously in more than one state of being.

media and tools

Choices about media and tools not only influence the meaning of a single representation in a specific context, but they also establish a field of associations that shapes our perception of meaning beyond the individual sign itself. Media refer to the character of our culture at particular times in history, as well as to our general expectations of information, how it behaves, and what it means.

Before Adobe Photoshop, for example, we made assumptions about the "truth" of photographic images. The technical means for altering a photograph usually left some visible residue and required highly trained specialists. We could all see the cut lines on the cover of the tabloid with the two-headed baby. Today, the average consumer has access to high-powered digital tools for assembling and retouching images; he or she understands that photographs can be altered, and also has the means to accomplish the task at home. Because it is now almost impossible to determine the veracity of images and because audiences understand that images can be manipulated, the objective role of the photographic medium in our culture has been forever compromised.

The media theorist Marshall McLuhan (see pp. 27–28, 209–12) compared the meaning of things in a print-based culture (since Johannes Gutenberg's invention of printing with movable type in the fifteenth century) with those of an electronic age, describing both as altering their respective cultures. The mass dissemination of ideas in the medium of print fostered nationalism, widespread literacy, and the spread of commercial markets. It emphasized

MEDIUM

A mode or system of communication that extends our ability to exchange meaning. Photography and drawing are media.

TOOL

The means by which someone accomplishes a task in a particular medium.

the importance of spelling and grammar and focused attention on fixed points of view. The electronic age (and by extension the digital age) reintroduced the importance of oral discourse, encouraged a kaleidoscope of messages and opinions, and increased the speed with which news reached the public.

The media researcher Michael Joyce agrees with McLuhan regarding the transformative power of technology, and describes changes in writing that have been brought about by the hyperlinked nature of the Web. Writing was once a matter of determining a singular *linear* structure for print, but is now a *spatial* activity.[50] Because the reader can improvise the sequence of information in a hyperlinked, online environment, every single content component has simultaneous relationships to many other components, not just to the preceding and subsequent paragraphs. In McLuhan's sense, online text is a mosaic—not the linear release of information we find in books, but a whole made up of an infinite number of diverse parts in ever-shifting relationships. Structuring a document as a traditional outline is therefore less well suited to the Web than working from a three-dimensional model of nodes and connecting lines. This spatial quality of the contemporary act of writing raises interesting questions about the design of digital writing spaces and how the current collecting behavior of computer users, in which files are grabbed and recombined from many sources for later use, can be reflected in the design of digital tools.

surfaces and structures

The qualities of surfaces also contribute to our interpretation of meaning. For example, we assign significance to the attributes of paper (its weight, texture, color, and opacity) as well as to how ink sits on its surface. Silk-screen printing feels different from offset printing. And we are more likely to save something printed on heavy, glossy stock—for example, a museum catalog—than something printed on newsprint. Our sense of its value is tied directly to the quality of surfaces that carry the information and our perceptions of their material worth.

While printed typography signifies something quite different from screen-based media, we also find differences in our perception of various types of projected surfaces. McLuhan wrote on this topic, describing the hypnotic aspects of television (and the computer) as resulting from the way in which our eyes and brain respond to "light-through" images in contrast to the "light-on" images of print or film.[51] McLuhan suggested that unlike film, which is composed of a series of still frames, television is an actively reconfiguring image, a "ceaseless forming contour" that is involving because it demands our constant participation to complete the image.[52] And whereas a film begins behind the viewer and is projected to a screen in front, "the TV projection begins behind the screen and winds up literally on the viewer's face."[53] It is compelling because it invites us to enter the action and engages us in perpetual participation. While it is unclear what type of brain research led McLuhan to these conclusions, we can attest to the mesmerizing effects of television and computer screens. We have all watched young children sit too close to the screen to discern real content, yet remain absorbed for hours in the light-through experience.

What is apparent is that designing for a dynamic surface, a visual space that can change its state of being, is different from designing for static, print-based media. In their earliest technological iterations, computer displays replicated print. We referred to screens as "pages" and arranged typography in columns and layouts, erasing one display and replacing it entirely with another, much as we do when turning the page of a printed book. As the capabilities of the technology grew, film became the metaphor for computer media; the qualities of time and motion constituted new variables in the graphic designer's expressive repertoire, allowing us to manage complex information by releasing content incrementally over time and with specific temporal behaviors.

As we will discuss in chapter 7, however, the current question is whether the dynamic surfaces of interactive media, in contrast to motion graphics, represent an extension of the traditional domains of graphic design and filmmaking or define a very new challenge to longstanding principles that guide the creation of form. Are they simply surfaces on which we organize information content and visual elements, or are they much deeper windows into people's emotional and cognitive engagement with the world? Is it our job to design only the visual attributes of objects with which people interact (the look of interaction) or to provide conditions and tools that support their self-defined experiences (the behavioral **AFFORDANCES** of interaction)? If our goal is the former, we focus on the attributes of the representation, on its visual characteristics, the ordering of its content, and its inventory of features. But if our intention is to design for experience, we focus on the attributes of the interaction, on the capabilities of the user to act on his or her motivations, to control outcomes, and to apply or extend the system in the service of personal and social needs.

Formats and the structures that contain representations also carry meaning and influence our behavioral expectations through their material nature. For example, we have a general notion of what constitutes something we call a "book": a hinged cover with multiple pages, read sequentially from left to right. As a schema, we know what is expected of us behaviorally when confronting this object. We have some idea of its organization—that it will contain a title page, some introductory material, and chapters or some equivalent division of content. Our past experience tells us there is usually a one-to-one relationship between text and images within the pages and that we are expected to discover these relationships by reading the text in a linear fashion.

Although we can stretch the limits of this organizational structure as designers, there is a point at which a book is no longer a book and becomes something else. The structural changes in the large books by Boom and Mau push that envelope (SEE FIGURES 3.13–3.14). In many ways they take on the characteristics of the Web through their invitation to read out of sequence, demonstrating that as new technologies emerge they influence their predecessors.

A magazine has a very different structural nature from a book. Its design format begs us to scan and to assemble meaning by looking quickly at pictures, captions, and headlines, deciding to read the main text only after determining which of the many articles interest us. We know that it is composed of non-sequential narratives that may be read in any order without significant differences in our understanding of their meaning. We also recognize that advertising material originates from a source that is different from the editorial content and interrupts the flow of reading.

AFFORDANCE

James J. Gibson's term for the quality of an object, environment, or technology that allows someone to perform an action. Technology can be enabling or constraining in terms of such "action possibilities."

Despite their increasingly high production values, magazines also tend to occupy a less noble role in our culture than books. We typically view them as ephemeral objects that contain information that is of more short-term consequence in our lives than the information in textbooks, great literature, or important works of non-fiction. Because we are less likely to keep magazines than books, we tolerate and are actually attracted to greater novelty and superficiality in their material nature, knowing that their content and physical qualities are simply products of a particular moment in time. For collectors of older periodicals, it is precisely the temporal associations with the material nature of the publication that are appealing.

The publication *Nest: A Quarterly of Interiors* stretched the material boundaries of the traditional magazine format (SEE FIGURE 3.15). During its brief history, which ended in 2004, the magazine produced issues with magnetic patches, tongue depressors, scalloped die-cut borders, and individually spattered covers. Never taking itself too seriously, unlike the more august *Architectural Digest* or the sophisticated *Interiors*, the magazine reveled in its material role as ephemera. Self-described as "where high-style London and Paris interiors meet igloos and prison cells on equal terms . . . where those who look and those who read meet on equal terms,"[54] the magazine used material means to reinforce its distinction from other interiors magazines on the newsstand and to subvert the traditional glossy, two-dimensional surface and the sense of thousands of identically reproduced copies. *Nest* established as its identity the constant reinvention of format within the technological context of magazine design. Its self-defined

THE DIMENSIONS OF CONTEXT

role in an environment of endlessly repeatable mastheads, type choices, and colors was to introduce new materials and processes with each issue.

technological affordances

The technology by which visual messages are created, reproduced, and distributed defines more than their material nature. Technologies have affordances, characteristic capabilities or functions that enable or constrain certain types of interactions among audiences, content, environments, and the originators of messages. Books have the affordance of self-pacing; film does not. Websites have the affordance of instant information updating and user-generated content; silk-screened posters do not. Word processing has the affordance of allowing different authors to work on the same document in different locations at the same time; calligraphy does not. Such affordances determine how easy or difficult it is to distribute certain kinds of message, who receives them, what they mean, and how recipients are able to respond.

For example, the affordances of offset printing dictate that all copies of a single edition be identical and that content producers demonstrate certain qualifications and resources to publish. The time necessary to print information and the processes for disseminating it determine the length of time between its conception and eventual reception by audiences. On the other hand, the programming code of digital media makes it possible to vary electronic documents in one or more ways for each recipient, and anyone with minimal software skills can post information on the Web with no one's permission. Unlike print, the time between electronic message origination and dissemination can be measured in seconds, rather than days and weeks.

The affordances of the Internet also allow users to navigate seamlessly among linked sites created by different content producers, so that it is often unclear that they have left one source and arrived at another. Information on the Internet is dynamic and changeable at any time, affording time-sensitive updates but providing users with little assurance that information on a site, once seen, will be the same when they return. The order in which users view information is self-determined and interactions with sites can be tracked, analyzed, and inform future engagement with the same or other content. And because anyone with software expertise can publish online, confidence in the credibility of Web information is in direct proportion to the frequency of bad experiences.

Marshall McLuhan summarized the impact of technology on culture in his phrase "the medium is the message," asserting that the "personal and social consequences of any medium . . . result from the new scale that is introduced into our affairs by each extension of ourselves, or by any new technology."[55] Think, for example, of the time when long-distance conversations took place only through surface mail or the telephone. But today

3.15 *NEST* MAGAZINE COVERS, 1997–2004

The graphic identity of this magazine, edited by Joseph Holtzman, was defined by the constantly changing material qualities of its covers.

we are reliant on e-mail, and any network downtime places a company at a serious disadvantage in the competitive business market. The frequency of business interactions increased exponentially with the advent of e-mail, to the extent that some companies have developed protocols for limiting the amount of time employees devote to sorting useful messages from ones that require no action. On the other hand, our general threshold for the formality and spelling accuracy of business correspondence has declined. We are far less critical of errors and, in some instances, we accept e-mail or text messaging shorthand in lieu of standard English. Historians lament the loss of letter-writing as a record of past events, and many of us have difficulty in determining which version of a document we have saved. On a personal level, we often use e-mail as a substitute for conversations that would be less comfortable or convenient on the phone, and we are quicker to respond without thinking in digital form; writing and mailing handwritten letters took time, during which many tempers cooled. And because electronic files can be traced or observed by third parties, our sense of privacy is challenged. In other words, the introduction of e-mail technology forever altered many practices in how we go about our lives and what things mean.

Beyond its precision or ability to mimic historical form-making processes, digital technology also has affordances that reflect certain formal biases. Adobe InDesign, for example, uses the modernist grid as the basic format for layout. By setting margins and gutters (measurements demanded by the software and depicted on the screen layout), the user enters text and image into pre-determined divisions of space. Adobe Illustrator, on the other hand, opens with a blank field in which type is not represented as a set of boxes to be filled. Therefore, the kinds of typographic composition that are encouraged by the two software programs differ. It is possible to work against these affordances, to circumvent the functions that are foregrounded in the design of the interface (by setting InDesign columns at "1" and margins at "0," for example), but their presence is evidence of a technological bias in the software for certain kinds of form. Further, the perspective of the software developer is reflected in the information requested of the user. In asking for the width of margins instead of the width of the typographic columns, for example, the software reflects its lack of concern for legibility, which normally results from the number of typographic characters per line and increments of leading, not from the size of an arbitrary space left over after margins have been set.

What all of this means is that technology is not neutral. It embodies values, both in how it is constructed and in the decision to deploy it. As such, it refers to its history of use and the practices that surround it. The observation that "the computer is just a tool" is missing the point. It is a tool with a *point of view* and with the ability to change user behavior and our expectations of information.

Additionally, as technology becomes more immersive—exists more as a convincing simulation of some reality—it is no longer a tool or a medium in the same sense as pen and ink. It represents its own world, one with implicit and explicit rules, communities of practice, and transformative power over what and how things mean. The technological responsibility of the graphic designer is therefore not simply to master software programs, but to understand the technological context as enabling or constraining cognitive and social behaviors that have a direct impact on the success of communication.

THE PHYSICAL CONTEXT FOR DESIGN: EVERYTHING IS RELATIONAL

The importance of the physical context for design is obvious. The material surfaces on which messages reside; the distances between viewers and designed objects; the attributes of the surrounding environment that compete for viewers' attention; and the **LEGIBILITY** and **READABILITY** of form—these are just a few aspects of the physical context that govern the effectiveness of design.

We all experience the frustration of digital displays that are too small to read, menus that are too large to be used when sitting opposite a dinner partner, and identification signage that is lost in a sea of screaming messages. And sometimes the consequences of a designer's failure to consider the physical context of information can result in more than frustration. The instrumentation on potentially dangerous medical equipment, package warnings about product use, and text in a primer for children learning to read—if not designed appropriately, all can produce catastrophic outcomes that last a lifetime.

It would be comforting if the complexity of these physical issues could be reduced to a set of rules that predict results—the optimal point size for type or the most legible color combinations for computer screen displays, for example. And it would be reassuring to have an inventory of the various physical conditions that affect the usability of design solutions. There are books and workshops that attempt to provide a one-size-fits-all solution, which respond to a climate of increasing accountability. It is not uncommon, for example, to find human-factors experts who claim that "white space is not good" or that web-screen navigation "should always be arranged in an inverted 'L' because users cannot find it otherwise."

The research that informs these claims is, however, sometimes suspect, and such variables are, by their very nature, **RELATIONAL**. The effect of one variable may depend entirely on the presence or absence of another variable. Some studies, for example, tell us that serif type is more readable because the horizontal nature of the serifs facilitates the left-to-right eye movement of reading. At the same time, other studies confirm the ultimate legibility of sans serif. And just what serif or sans-serif typeface at what point size and leading (line spacing) are we talking about? (SEE FIGURE 3.16.)

Perceptual psychology offers theories that suggest some design solutions may be better than others in various respects. Yet such studies rarely account for the *situatedness* of design problems, for the specific attributes of the context and audiences with whom a design must work. In one study, for example, visual comparisons of a donkey and a toaster at different sizes are used to test for the viewer's speed of recognition of actual sizes of the same objects and their relative distances apart when judging scale. Placing images of donkeys and toasters on blank sheets of white paper hardly replicates most conditions in which making quick judgments of relative size matters. And the content and

LEGIBILITY
The degree to which typographic forms and layouts are decipherable, based on their appearance.

READABILITY
The degree to which typographic forms and layouts are easy or desirable to read, based on their appearance.

RELATIONAL
The idea that judgments about how design performs (its legibility, readability, expressiveness, reproducibility, and so on) depend on the particular combination of formal variables, audience, and setting.

Bauer Bodoni Regular   Helvetica Bold

This text is set in 10/12 point and the headline is set in 24 point Bauer Bodoni Regular. Because the typeface has a small x-height (the height of lowercase letters in relation to capital letters) and because of the thick and thins in the strokes of letters, its visual impression is one of delicate text surrounded by generous white space. Therefore, it requires less additional space between lines of type for comfortable reading than the Helvetica Bold setting in the paragraph to the right.

This text is set in 10/12 point and the headline is set in 24 point Helvetica Bold. Because the typeface has a large x-height and because of its bold strokes in relation to the enclosed white space, its visual impression is one of sturdy text surrounded by little white space. Helvetica, therefore, requires more additional space between lines of type for comfortable reading than the Bauer Bodoni Regular setting in the paragraph to the left.

When the linespacing is increased and point size is reduced, as in this 9/13 point paragraph, the legibility of the typeface for reading large amounts of text improves. And because Helvetica has a large x-height, it can be set at sizes smaller than Bodoni and be equally readable. For these reasons, it is difficult to use a single set of rules for the legibility of type.

contrasting shapes of the two objects are so incongruous that it is hard to believe that they represent any likely comparative task in real life. These types of study therefore have little transferability to real design situations unless they are tested in the actual circumstances of use.

On the other hand, the emerging design research culture in universities shows promise for building more relevant theories of the perceptual implications of design form in various physical settings and for confirming or denying designers' intuition about what does and does not "work." For example, research by the design professor Dennis Puhalla addresses how people assign hierarchical significance to text on the basis of projected color in such software programs as PowerPoint. Puhalla's work stops short of recommending particular color combinations in favor of the more useful discovery that contrast in intensity (brightness or dullness) and value (lightness or darkness) is significant and that hue (the particular color, such as blue or green) is not.[56] This finding is of far more use in that it identifies a general principle for making decisions in individual situations and addresses a specific, recurring context (digitally projected text). There is a difference, therefore, between studying a phenomenon (such as color) and studying its application in a context.

In general, communication that succeeds in gaining audience attention exhibits some visual, auditory, kinesthetic, or temporal contrast with its physical setting. A well-known design educator used to preach, facetiously, to students, "If you can't make it good, make it big . . . if you can't make it big, make it red." Yet there are clearly times when visual restraint creates the most contrast. The storefront signage in a commercial strip and the supermarket ads in the newspaper provide ample evidence that when all messages "scream,"

3.16   TYPE SAMPLES

Both headlines are set at 24 point and body copy at 12 point. Because the serif Bodoni has a much smaller x-height (the height of lowercase letters) in comparison to the generous proportions of the sans-serif Helvetica, it requires less additional vertical space between lines of text to make it legible.

THE DIMENSIONS OF CONTEXT

no one will be heard, and that too much contrast creates a pattern of visual clutter in which the boundaries and meaning of a single message are lost in the chaos. These relationships must therefore be crafted individually and take into consideration an environment that competes for people's attention.

physical embodiment

Design also addresses the physical context in the sense that it deals with meanings that arise from our own physical place in a setting. Many of our metaphors for talking about the virtual space of the Internet, for example, involve references to our spatial locations in a physical context: the "information highway"; "site"; "address"; and the concept of "going to" somewhere (when changing content or source) are not literal but figurative references to bodily movement through a physical world.

Some technologists have compared our perception and navigation of cyberspace to the way in which we interpret and move spatially through the built environment. The work of the urban planner Kevin Lynch in his book *The Image of the City* (1960) is often cited in this context. Lynch studied people's conceptions of the urban environment and found recurring similarities, regardless of the city in which they lived. Urban dwellers organized their conceptual map of a city into districts, nodes, edges, paths, and landmarks.[57] *Districts* are areas that have some identifiable character and that we may enter. Some cities, for example, have a warehouse district or an arts district. This is not a political designation as much as a perception that a particular area of the city has distinctive functional or visual features that define it in contrast to other areas. *Nodes* are destination points, places to and from which we travel. We can also enter a node (for example, when we go to a city park or visit a collection of shops on a city block). Lynch describes an *edge* as a boundary between two areas of the city. It may be well defined by a wall, railroad tracks, or a major highway, or it may be fuzzy as we move from one district to another. We may or may not be able to enter an edge. *Paths* are the channels along which we move and they connect nodes. *Landmarks* are visible reference points but we do not enter them. They may be viewed from a variety of angles and are used in orienting our movement.

If we were to draw a diagram of an information search on the Internet, we could think about the collection of sites defined through a keyword by a search engine or a content area within a site as a district. A node would be a specific site or a particular document within a site. Edges would be the embedded links that take us to related content without engaging in another keyword search—in some ways, edges define conceptually "adjacent territory." Landmarks would be the keywords through which we search. Their repetition in each entry provided by the search engine simulates different points of view around which our search can be oriented. What is not visible in cyberspace, however, is the path that connects two nodes. With a click we instantly arrive at the second site, having no sense of how we "got there." Several software programs attempt to reveal the path (Acrobat, PowerPoint, and InDesign, for example, display linear sequences of pages on the screen when the user is working) and the log or history of movement over time is recorded as URLs in Internet use.

At present, most of these metaphors are text-based, but there is some belief that a spatial metaphor for virtual navigation could be more helpful and intuitive than one based in language.

In *The Body in the Mind* (1987) the philosopher Mark Johnson writes about **EMBODIED** or image schemata. These are structures of physical activity through which we organize experience in our minds.[58] Johnson describes the work of the linguist Susan Lindner, who formulated a small number of prototypical schemata as diagrams. Lindner's diagram for "out," for example, is a confining circle with an arrow exiting from the contained area [SEE FIGURE 3.17]. We understand this concept (moving away from containment) through our earliest bodily experiences, none of which is dependent on culture for its meaning. For example, as toddlers we break from the confinement of a crib, the enclosure of a parent's arms, or the restraint of a highchair. Johnson and Lindner believe that these early physical experiences allow us to grasp such linguistic metaphors as "out of office," "shouting out," and "coming out." As we mature, our abilities expand from simply processing concrete stimuli to thinking and communicating through abstraction. Lindner and Johnson suggest that these are not independent operations but that language is embodied by our past physical experiences.

It is possible that such schemata also extend to the interpretations of visual and spatial compositions. The landscape architect Lawrence Halprin designed the Franklin Roosevelt Memorial in Washington, D.C. Occupying 7.5 acres (3 hectares), the memorial is composed of four outdoor "rooms," each tracing an aspect or period of the former president's life. Visitors move physically through time and the story of his life, in contrast to the more static, singular presentations of most memorials and monuments. The visitor's bodily passage out of containment in one room into the next corresponds metaphorically to the changes in Roosevelt's life.

The Vietnam Veterans Memorial in Washington, D.C., designed by the architect Maya Lin, lists names in chronological order of death, starting at the central corner of the memorial and moving outward. It is said that this design is also a physical gesture—that of the dead reaching out to embrace the living who have come to view the memorial.

It is therefore evident that the physical nature of artifacts and environments has special standing in our cognitive, social, and cultural interactions with the world. Designers take action by making real things through which people achieve goals in their exchanges with other people and places. And the concrete attributes of these objects have important consequences that extend beyond function.

EMBODIMENT

Mark Johnson and George Lakoff used this term to refer to the idea that cognition and language are shaped by physical experience—that is, by bodily interactions with a concrete world.

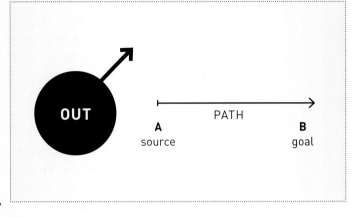

3.17   IMAGE SCHEMATA
Based on the work of Mark Johnson and Susan Lindner

The theory of image schemata suggests that we have common physical experiences that are culturally neutral. These experiences underpin our use of metaphors, which, by contrast, are culturally determined. Above are the schemata for the physical experiences of *in* and *out*.

THE DIMENSIONS OF CONTEXT

THE ECONOMIC CONTEXT FOR DESIGN: EXPANDING THE DEFINITION OF "COST"

It is difficult, in a general survey of design theory, to address the breadth and depth of the economic context for design and to summarize the complex role design plays in the economic health of specific companies. The history of design has been one of service to commerce, as well as to culture, and design is accountable to a range of economic priorities and fluctuating conditions. Several university programs focus on design as a business operation and a number of professional associations offer training in **DESIGN STRATEGY**. Recent books by business leaders acknowledge *design thinking* as a competitive edge in the marketplace. And new areas of practice, such as service design, emerge as companies recognize the ability of designers to plan and innovate.

There are, however, contemporary trends that raise questions about how we understand the range of economic concerns that face today's designers. In 2005 the Pulitzer Prize-winning journalist Thomas Friedman published *The World is Flat*, in which he asserted that technological and economic shifts in the distribution of production and manufacturing have leveled the global playing field. We need only look at the number of jobs once held by Americans that are now done by people in India and China to understand the increase in globally co-dependent economic relationships that defines contemporary business.

In an article for *Atlantic Monthly*, however, the economist Richard Florida argued that Friedman got it wrong, that the world is spiky, not flat. Florida describes hills and valleys in the distribution of economic potential and cautions that we cannot think of countries as homogenous in either their cultures or opportunities. He offers three types of place in the world that have less to do with geopolitical boundaries and more to do with potential in the confluence of resources: those that can attract global talent and create new products; those that manufacture the world's goods and support its innovation engines; and those with little connection to the global economy and few immediate prospects.[59]

Under Florida's perspective, it becomes apparent that designers must often choose between working at the peaks for centers of innovation or applying their talents toward helping those in the valleys. The methods are often the same, regardless of the economic context, but the scale of socio-economic realities often calls for different outcomes and requires collaboration among people with different incentives, cultural behaviors, and values.

strategy

How objects look and work is certainly part of the competitive advantage that design brings to the top ten percent of the world's market for design. But there are less obvious ways in which design functions as an extension of the business context and influences the quality of goods and services and the costs consumers pay. For example, a well-known electronics manufacturer was having trouble with expensive service calls. Forty percent of the calls resulted in "no service necessary," simply because customers could not understand how to install their new television sets. The company asked design consultants to redesign user manuals to address the problem. The design team studied the situation and

DESIGN STRATEGY

A segment of design practice that helps companies and organizations to determine what to make and do, how to innovate, and how to implement processes for the benefit of the consumer as well as the producer.

discovered that the company expected one-color printed manuals to describe the connection of several wires, all of which were black, and buttons, all of which were exactly the same shape. There was no way to illustrate in pictures or to describe in words which wire or button was to be used.

More revealing, however, was that the people who designed the television sets were in the product-design division of the company and the people who designed the manuals were located in the service division—and they never spoke to each other. The consultant's recommendation was to move the manual designers into the same division as the television designers so that they could design products and manuals simultaneously, thus avoiding formal attributes of the televisions that were impossible to describe in one-color printing. In this example, the design solution involved a change in corporate structure and a very simple change in form, both of which had big economic benefits in reduced service calls.

One economic role for design is therefore to develop business strategies that improve goods and services for consumers while fostering responsibility and innovation within companies.

consumption

Much has been written about the economic context for design from another perspective—that of its complicity in fueling **CONSUMPTION**. The German critic Walter Benjamin (1892–1940) studied the shopping arcades of nineteenth-century Paris. He wrote of the urban spectacle of department-store windows and advertising (which continues today in our contemporary malls), indicating a link between economic enterprise and patterns of social behavior. The historian Stuart Ewen (see also p. 47) discussed "form following value" and the illusion of upward mobility that comes from owning objects associated with a particular socio-economic status that we may not have achieved.[60] And the French critic Jean Baudrillard (see also p. 23) talked about a consumer society that envisions wellbeing as "measurable in terms of objects" and "growth" as equivalent to affluence.[61] Some of these ideas will be explored in later chapters, but at this point it is sufficient to say that design and mass media are essential to a capitalist economic system that assigns social value to the consumption of material goods.

The economic consequences of design therefore reside not only in its ability to execute a successful business strategy or to provide good service but also in the social perceptions of value engendered by an economy based on consumption.

sustainability

There is also a direct link between patterns of consumption and our views regarding the appropriate use of resources—an issue that has received considerable attention in recent years. Public policy in Germany now requires that every mass-produced object includes a plan and cost for its reuse. The information designer Richard Saul Wurman once estimated that the typical Sunday edition of *The New York Times* consumed 3,900 tons (3,538,000 kilograms) of newsprint and that the annual consumption of ink used to print the paper, if it were milk, could supply every citizen of Wichita, Kansas, with 2 gallons (7.5 liters) per

THE DIMENSIONS OF CONTEXT

week for a year.[62] He also estimated that 55 percent of the space in an average edition at that time was consumed by advertising, not by news.[63]

There are many resource implications in various forms of printed waste. The big message in these statistics, however, is that the cost of a publication resides not just in the bill paid by the client, but also in the relationship between information and material lifespan long after the message has been delivered. A resource-driven view of design would therefore ask, "How much stuff is necessary to do the job, and is the job worth doing in the first place?"

It is easy to think of design as a discipline removed from its economic context, as above the fray of economic competitiveness and service to private enterprise. It is encouraging that today's students are anxious to help good social causes and cultural agendas and that they see design as empowering ideas that might otherwise never reach public consciousness. But it is also important to understand that *all* design is social production; that advertising does as much, or more, to define who we are and what we believe as any "socially oriented" poster or media spot. Design can leverage its position in commerce to present positive images that consider long-term consequences for society as well as short-term profit for clients. Good design may be good business, but it is also accountable to the social agenda.

SUMMARY

While each design challenge resides within a context, how we define the scope of possible forces that vie for the designer's attention is significant. The first task of the designer, whether presented with a fully formed problem-statement or not, is to determine which aspects of context are most important to the achievement of the communication goal. Designers must often rank equally pressing performance demands that are in competition. In general, a designer must think at the level of systems and information lifespan, even when designing products and components. The nature of contemporary life makes it unlikely that the consequences of design action, however small, will be confined to the success or failure of communication objects alone.

Context has various dimensions: cognitive, socio-cultural, technological, physical, and economic. A variety of theories drive design decision-making with respect to these dimensions and it is the responsibility of the designer to be well informed and to hold a perspective on these issues. As the means for making and reproducing form become increasingly accessible to audiences through computer software, the role of the designer is now to bring expertise to the management of the complex forces at play in any communication context.

It has been suggested by the design historian Lorraine Wild that the interest in graphic design theory—most evident in the typographic experimentation of the 1980s and development of mature design histories in the 1990s—was as influential as technological innovation in changing the course of contemporary design. Such theory spawned critical discourse and writing that were in stark contrast to the picture-and-caption approach of many earlier design publications. It therefore made possible the development of a segment of scholarship that was devoted exclusively to design. This introspection marks the evolution of design from a trade to a profession and a discipline of study.

While this self-consciousness was focused generally on the work of its own time, often borrowing core ideas and values from fields outside design, it also called into question the theoretical underpinnings of earlier design movements. The ideas of post-modernism, for example, could not be understood without examining how they differed or evolved from those of modernism. We are fortunate that many early modernists wrote manifestos and published treatises that provide insight into the analysis of their work. And the growth of design writing in recent times has deepened our understanding of how designers make sense of what they do.

This theoretical lineage in design practice can be traced to the beginnings of industrialization, which established a consumer society and the development of a mass media necessary to advertise the expanding inventory of products. While the history of design prior to the late nineteenth century holds some relevance for our own form-making, and certainly reflects the broad array of philosophies and ideologies that preceded industrialization, most of our contemporary assumptions about design coincide with its origins as a modern practice.

Part 2 of this book therefore traces relevant theories from the beginning of the twentieth century to the present day. Chapter 4 examines the study of language by early semioticians, including Ferdinand de

part 2

theory from 1900 to the present

Saussure, Charles Sanders Peirce, and Roland Barthes. Chapter 5 explores several tenets of modernism, sampling a variety of movements and their underlying principles. Chapter 6 introduces the complex theories of post-modernism and draws heavily on writings in architecture and cultural theory. Chapter 7 ends the book with discussions of the twenty-first-century shift from designing objects to designing experiences.

As in Part 1, this section identifies seminal readings by the original authors. Some of these essays and books are translations and use discipline-based phrasing and terms that may be unfamiliar to design readers. The following chapters therefore attempt to distill key concepts and to place such writing within a broader framework of ideas.

the language of

the visual world 4

The study of language holds particular significance

for graphic designers, whose work involves the combination of visual and verbal elements according to social and cultural conventions. This concern for meaning and how it is made and interpreted is as fundamental to graphic design practice as are the aesthetics of form. Any text on design theory must therefore include explanations of how language and meaning-making work.

SEMIOTICS, SEMIOLOGY

The study of signs, particularly their production and interpretation in the context of communication and social interaction. Ferdinand de Saussure and Charles Sanders Peirce, the founders of semiotics, sought to define what constitutes a sign and the laws that govern its use. Later work expanded the focus of the discipline to include all sign systems, not just words. Under Roland Barthes, images, gestures, sounds, and fashion were studied in semiotic terms.

SEMIOTICS, or **SEMIOLOGY** as it is often referred to in Europe, is the study of the life of "signs." The discipline developed in the early twentieth century through the writings of linguists, anthropologists, and philosophers. In contrast to nineteenth-century scholars, who were interested in where words came from and how they changed over time, semioticians expressed concern for the patterns and functions of language in everyday use and for the fundamental processes by which meaning is established and maintained. Working at about the same time, early twentieth-century artists, designers, and typographers, in search of an appropriate visual language for the ambitious social agenda of the new century, brought material form to similar ideas about the relationships among culture, politics, language, and knowledge.

Although semiotics is most often associated with the work of its founders, Ferdinand de Saussure and Charles Sanders Peirce, it is an ongoing project of investigation in which scholars build upon the theoretical work of others while also taking into account the shifting social landscapes of their own times. For this reason it is difficult to connect the work of individual semioticians to specific movements and objects in the history of graphic design, or even to isolate certain scholars exclusively as semioticians. Semiotics is neither a style nor a singular ideology—it is a discipline of study. This book therefore describes overlapping work by a diverse group of people whose ideas about language contribute to the intellectual climate in which design was and is practiced.

The earliest efforts to frame meaning-making in graphic design in semiotic terms date to the early 1970s. Thomas Ockerse and Hans van Dijk, professors of graphic design at Rhode Island School of Design (RISD), have dedicated much of their academic careers to building a semiotic theory of design that attempts to address not only the critical analysis of existing design but also generative approaches to making new work. Proponents of the ideas of Peirce, Ockerse, and van Dijk structured RISD's curricular experiences around Peirce's typology of signs and his notion of the *interpretant*, which they described as the context, condition, or function of signs.

The design historian Johanna Drucker positioned her discussion of early twentieth-century typography—an area often slighted by art historians as a footnote to discussions of painting and sculpture—as the material manifestation of semiotic theory. In *The Visible Word* (1994) she explains the period of typographic experimentation between 1909 and 1923 as an outgrowth of ideas that were circulating in linguistics and anthropology, as much as in visual art.

THE LANGUAGE OF THE VISUAL WORLD

At Cranbrook Academy of Art, Michigan, in the 1980s, under the leadership of Katherine and Michael McCoy, post-structuralist investigations responded to the legacies of semiotics and structuralism. Graphic and product design work published in *Cranbrook Design: The New Discourse* (1991) documents the efforts to translate theories of language and literature into material form. Many Cranbrook graduates of this period entered influential design practices and teaching, continuing their interests in visual language through their professional work or through writing and the work of their students.

The aim of this chapter is to describe the theoretical underpinnings of linguistic approaches to design, and to provide a brief chronology of their development.

FERDINAND DE SAUSSURE: THE BIRTH OF SEMIOTICS

At the turn of the twentieth century, two scholars, one in Europe and the other in America, launched investigations into the nature of representation and the relationship between language and knowledge. Ferdinand de Saussure (1857–1913) was a Swiss linguist teaching in Lausanne; his American counterpart was Charles Sanders Peirce (1839–1914), a professor of philosophy and logic.

We know of Saussure's theories not primarily through his own writings but through a posthumous publication, *Course in General Linguistics* (1916), which was compiled by his students from lecture notes. Saussure's approach to the study of language focused on the exchange of meaning between individuals and on the commonalities across languages, rather than on the eccentricities arising from their specific cultural origins.[1] He viewed all languages as systems of dynamic relationships, the basic unit of which is the sign. This outlook was in marked contrast to that of his nineteenth-century predecessors, who studied particular languages as compilations of words, each with separate meanings resulting from an historical lineage of change and somewhat detached from their use in day-to-day communication.

Language, according to Saussure, should be viewed not only in terms of its parts (words) and their histories, but also in terms of the relationship between those parts. It should be studied as a structured system, as we experience it in the present, in the act of communicating. He believed that any language is complete at any given moment, regardless of its place in an evolutionary history: the speaker of a language is confronted with a current state in which the lineage of the word is neither apparent nor relevant to the current communication.[2] For example, knowing that the word "mop" comes from the Latin word for "napkin" (*mappa*) is not important or necessary if we are concerned about cleaning up a spill on the floor. It is important, however, to understand through the structure of a question whether we are asking someone for a tool ("mop" as a noun) or for an action ("mop" as a verb)—the answer determines who will be doing the mopping. This focus on the relationships among parts is a particular approach or method for the study of language that later became known as **STRUCTURALISM**.

STRUCTURALISM

A methodological approach to the interpretation and analysis of human activities (including cognition, behavior, language, and culture) that focuses on the relationships of contrast among elements within a conceptual system, not solely on the elements themselves.

Saussure's notion of the linguistic sign was as a combination of a *concept* and a *sound-image*. He did not think of this as a one-to-one correspondence between a thing and its spoken name but as the imprint the sound makes on our senses. We can think in language (without speaking out loud) because we have a mental impression of how a word sounds. Saussure viewed the sign as sensory and material only in this respect.[3]

But Saussure's primary contribution to the study of language was his definition of two components of a sign: the **SIGNIFIED** and the **SIGNIFIER**, terms he eventually used to replace concept and sound-image. The signified is the person, thing, event, place, or concept called forth by the stimulation of the signifier. The signifier is the sound or word (or image, in the case of graphic design) that recalls in our mind the signified, even in the absence of the real thing. Using the example from chapter 2, our mental concept of a farm animal that gives milk is a signified that is prompted by a signifier, such as the word "cow" or a photograph of a black-and-white Holstein. Saussure tells us that the relationship between the signifier and signified is entirely arbitrary—nothing about the word and sound of C-O-W resembles the animal itself; it is, instead, a collection of correspondences between letters and sounds that have been established only through the social conventions of the English language. We must be taught that C-O-W stands for the animal we know as "cow," and if we speak a language other than English, we may find no resemblance between C-O-W and the corresponding word in that language (for example, the Spanish word for "cow" is vaca). Also, the letters C, O, and W may appear in many other words with other meanings that have nothing to do with a "cow" (see p. 35).

Further, while the photograph of a Holstein (a signifier) bears some physical resemblance to a real cow, it is not a cow, nor is it exactly the same as our mental concept for "cow" (a signified). We had to learn that shapes on a two-dimensional piece of paper configured in certain ways stand for "cow." And we see only a limited number of cow-like qualities in the photographic sign, whereas our mental concept of a cow may include more than appears in the picture: how it smells, moves, and sounds, for example, or how our grandfather's old Bessie behaved in the barn. And if the photograph of the Holstein is to serve as some representation of "livestock," "dairy," or "farming," then the relationship between the cow in the photograph and its meaning is no less arbitrary than the relationship of letters to what those words stand for. It is only through some cultural consensus or experience that a picture of a cow can represent more complex concepts. The photograph is therefore no less arbitrary a representation than the word—it is through convention or cultural agreement that its meaning is established.

This separation of the physical representation (signifier) from our mental idea of the thing it stands for (signified) seems simple to us today. In fact, it is fundamental to the work of graphic design. Designers determine the appropriate signifiers for another's message content with the goal of producing the corresponding signifieds in the minds of audiences. Had Saussure not made this distinction (a concept he called *duality*), however, it would not be possible to discuss the visual, spatial, temporal, auditory, or kinesthetic

SIGNIFIED

One of two components (with the signifier) of a sign. The signified is the concept for which the sign stands.

SIGNIFIER

One of two components (with the signified) of a sign. The signifier is the sound or image that represents the concept. The relationship between the signifier and the signified is arbitrary (i.e. a matter of cultural consensus regarding the correspondence between the two, rather than the result of a natural relationship).

THE LANGUAGE OF THE VISUAL WORLD

attributes—the material qualities—of the signifier or their contributions to meaning as distinguished from the mental concept for which the signifier stands. Theoretically, typographic form—letterforms and all their possible variations (typeface, weight, size, and so on), their composition on the page, and the material qualities of ink on paper or pixels on screen, for example—would be considered irrelevant to the meaning of the text were the signifier not seen as distinct from the thing for which it stands. The designation of the signifier as a discrete component of language makes it possible to discuss writing as different from speech, visual signs as different from verbal signs and, consequently, form itself as a critical contributor to meaning.

Johanna Drucker affirms the importance of Saussure's contribution in her analysis of early twentieth-century typography. She says that although writing was an indispensable tool of linguists in transcribing the spoken word, especially in the phonetic recording of exotic or primitive languages that did not possess written form, the inscription of language did not undergo analysis before Saussure:[4] "Forms of writing and their material properties went unacknowledged by a phonological science focused on the spoken word; in some cases, writing even presented a threat by virtue of its inability to be quantified."[5]

While Saussure did not analyze writing in his own work, he did acknowledge the graphic representation of language, the need to study it, and reasons for its ascendance over the spoken word. Yet he described the difference between studying external linguistic phenomena, such as writing, and internal thought processes, as "thinking that more can be learned about someone by looking at his photograph than by viewing him directly."[6]

Saussure did describe what he believed to be the only two systems of writing: the **IDEOGRAPHIC** system, in which each word is reduced to a single sign that is unrelated to the sounds of the word itself (for example, Chinese); and the **PHONETIC** system, which attempts to produce a sequence of sounds that makes up a word (for example, English). The former tends to lose its symbolic meaning over time (most contemporary Chinese people do not really understand the origins of specific ideographs in their language), yet Saussure believed that the mental substitution of the ideographic word for sound was less problematic for a theory of language than a phonetic system. The same Chinese ideograph (pictorial character) can stand for the concept, regardless of how the word is pronounced in various dialects.[7] This belief should not be confused with a general assumption that we have a greater consensus about the meaning of pictures than we have about the meaning of words. Saussure's ideas about ideographic form focused on formal languages, codified across time, at the level of a system.

The dominance of writing was attributed by Saussure to its appearance of permanence and stability (in contrast to that of sound); its importance as manifested in a set of formal written codes, such as dictionaries, books of grammar, and rules of usage taught in schools; and its documentary position in debates concerning the accuracy of language.[8] While his arguments supported the need to study language as speech, Saussure inadvertently established a foundation for separating the written from the spoken word. In so doing, he opened the way for questions about how the attributes of graphic representations of language may influence meaning. Although he did not address writing in his own analysis,

IDEOGRAPHIC WRITING

A system in which each word is reduced to a single sign that is unrelated to the sound of the word itself.

PHONETIC WRITING

A system in which there is a direct correspondence between symbols and sounds.

and demoted it to the lesser role of recording speech,[9] his deconstruction of the signifier and signified was contemporaneous with visual experiments by designers and artists that focused on the political and social significance of material form.

langue and parole

LANGUE

Ferdinand de Saussure's term for the abstract system of signs, governed by rules for their combination in expressing ideas. According to Saussure, it is the differences between signs that make them meaningful and it is the system of grammar that allows people within a cultural group to use them to communicate.

PAROLE

Ferdinand de Saussure's term for the individual aspect of language or an individual utterance in a specific context.

SYNTAGMATIC AXIS, SYNTAX

The horizontal relationship between words in a sentence. The syntax of a sentence is the specific arrangement or ordering of words, according to the rules of grammar within the language system. Meaning is established not only by the choice of the word, but also by its position within the sentence. The relationship between words on the syntagmatic axis is diachronic.

DIACHRONIC

Over time. In writing and speech, one word follows another in time.

Saussure's work was groundbreaking in another respect. Whereas traditional notions of language addressed an assemblage of words, each with separate meanings that underwent change over time, he viewed language as a dynamic system in which meaning was constantly subject to the structural relationships within the system. These structural dimensions of language he called **LANGUE** and **PAROLE**.

In Saussure's terms, langue is the set of abstract rules within the language system that governs the combinations of signs—a group of general linguistic conventions adopted by a particular social or cultural group that allows them to construct and exchange meaning among their members. Grammar is an example of langue. Although the grammatical rules may vary from language to language regarding, for example, where the subject of a sentence is positioned with respect to its object, all languages have such rules.

Parole, on the other hand, is the individual utterance made by a single member of that linguistic group in a specific, concrete situation—an individual act of discourse among many of infinite variety. Grammar controls how these utterances are put together, but individually each has its own meaning established by the specific choice of words, the implied tone of voice or style, and the setting in which it occurs. These two dimensions, langue and parole, are in play every time we communicate through language.

The relationship between rules and utterances can be explained in another way. The meaning of words in a sentence is revealed over time, whether in speech or writing. Saussure refers to this collection of signs in sequence as the **SYNTAGMATIC AXIS**.[10] The meaning of any single word depends on its horizontal position in relation to the other words in the sentence; the set of rules governing that position or **SYNTAX** is grammar. Consider the example below:

The dog bites the man.
subject → verb → object

The set of linguistic rules for speaking and writing in English tells us that "dog" is the subject of this sentence and "man" is the object. This convention (the syntagmatic relationship between subject and object, separated by an action verb) communicates, without ambiguity, who bites whom. The relationship is horizontal and **DIACHRONIC** (one word follows another in the sentence in spoken or written

THE DIACHRONIC STRUCTURE OF GRAPHIC DESIGN

Well-designed books exhibit the syntagmatic, diachronic structure described by Saussure in his study of language. In other words, how the sequence of pages play out over time is significant, not random, and may be attributed to the structural relationship among parts of the story or the larger visual concept of the book design. The book designer Keith Smith describes the role of horizontal syntax in his book *Structure of the Visual Book* (1993), an analysis of the physical form of page sequences, as well as the composition of text and images within single compositions. In an explanation of *pacing*, he demonstrates that patterns in writing can be extended to the visual structure of the book. Contrasting a *sequence* (in which there is a deliberate rhythm established from page to page) with a *series* (in which rhythm is confined to the composition within the borders of individual pages), Smith encourages a vocabulary of book design that assigns meaning to the transitions between visual elements, not just to running text and compilations of images.[11] Through a series of diagrams, he illustrates how the variables of rhythm, referral (one image recalling or foreshadowing another elsewhere in the sequence), and inflection (degrees of visual emphasis) can define the visual pacing in book design.[12]

In the top sequence of images, the layout of pages denies pacing. The spreads are equal in emphasis and interchangeable in their position within the sequence. They constitute a *series* in which the horizontal structure contributes little to the overall meaning. In the bottom layout, the positions of subordinate and dominant images (those with lesser and greater visual impact) both preview and recall

time). Meaning therefore results from the position or order of the words in the sentence, not just from the choice of the words themselves. The rules governing this relationship between subject and object with respect to this kind of verb are generally consistent in English, regardless of the specific sentence. This is an example of langue. There is no chance that we would read this sentence and imagine a man's teeth clamped to the hind end of a schnauzer—grammar, not the words themselves, prevents us from making that interpretation.

Saussure's notion of syntax also holds relevance for the organization of images in visual or pictorial space, as well as for typography. (See box: "The Diachronic Structure of Graphic Design.") In visual terms, we often refer to the

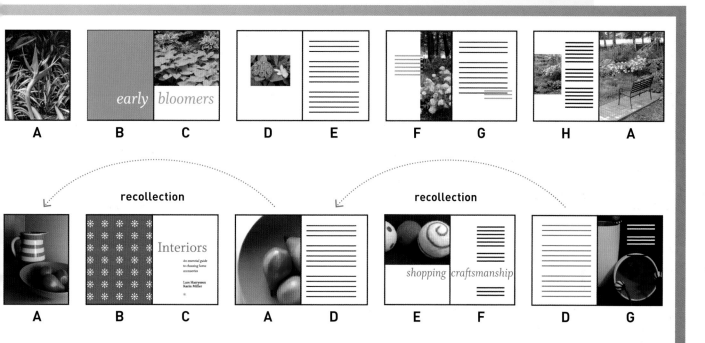

objects or events in the overall story. In this case, position is significant: where images appear and their relative emphases (inflections) are visual extensions of the narrative—the layout signals places where the text changes in its tone or focus. The visual syntax is therefore constructed to enhance meaning, not just to create visual interest.

Langue and the syntagmatic axis are also critical to the interpretation of comics. Scott McCloud illustrates these relationships in *Understanding Comics* (1993). A single scene is read as a series of events taking place over time. Most people are familiar with the conventions that govern comics. The relationships between a sequence of individual actions within the same frame are therefore not misunderstood as happening simultaneously but are recognized to be taking place over time. Because we

understand the grammar of comics (its langue), and despite the content and dramatic changes in the angle of view from which scenes are drawn (its parole), we are able to assemble these frames as a single narrative. Our mind fills in the transitions and missing action between frames, preventing us from reading this depiction as merely a series of unrelated scenes and actions.[13]

Although the conventions defining a grammar of visual form are less clear than those governing verbal language, the previous examples illustrate that compositional structure is significant in the construction of meaning; the ordering of form carries some burden for communication; and that meaning inheres in *relationships*, not just in the inventory of subject matter represented by the elements or images themselves.

ordering or arrangement of elements as *composition*. How we arrange images and typographic elements on a page, order pages within a book, link screens within a website, or sequence scenes within a film influences what we think they mean. Design can succeed in its choices of image content, but fail in its visual organization of those same images.

the assault on syntax

Common to many of the early modernist movements in art and design was the belief that the transformation of symbolic systems was a political and social act, that a new aesthetic language would result in a changed and better future for the world (see p. 136).[14] If the conventional correspondences between meaning and form were arbitrary to begin with, as the early writings in semiotics professed, then they were subject to renegotiation. And that renegotiation could take place through the visual media of art and design. The material nature of artistic form could therefore transform the most basic notions of how and what things mean. While many visual experiments were carried out on aspects of daily life (housing, factories, furniture, advertising, literary and political magazines, and so on), most of these artists and designers aspired to a poetic visual language that surpassed utilitarian or merely functional exchanges of meaning. If a piece of furniture, a political treatise, or a building could embody the qualities of poetry, then it could instill in the activities of everyday living the transcendent status of art. Life would be better—more harmonious, more consciously lived—as a direct result of the visual and spatial attributes of the things around us. Much of the avant-garde design work in the early decades of the twentieth century therefore undermined the conventional order of visual things with the goal of achieving such a world.

The Russian film theorist and director Sergei Eisenstein (1898–1948), for example, created films that used the sequencing of images (the *syntagmatic axis*, in Saussure's terms) to maximum expressive effect. For Eisenstein, the basic unit of the film was the *cell*, a single photographic shot that was later assembled with

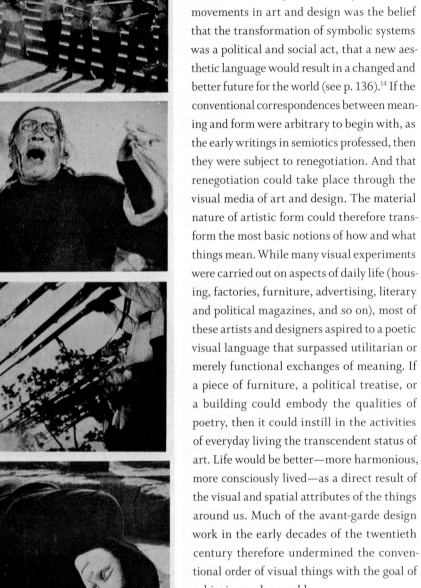

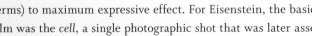

4.1   SEQUENCE ON THE ODESSA STEPS FROM *THE BATTLESHIP POTEMKIN*, 1925
Sergei Mikhailovich Eisenstein (1898–1948)

Eisenstein mastered what he called the *collision montage*, an intentionally jarring juxtaposition in the frame-to-frame relationship within a film, which produces a different interpretation from the meanings of the singular images or a continuously shot scene.

THE LANGUAGE OF THE VISUAL WORLD

others into something he called a **COLLISION MONTAGE.** He believed that an intentionally disruptive nature in the sequence of images within a film, in the cell-to-cell relationships, was more powerful than the content and form of any single image (SEE FIGURE 4.1). Eisenstein photographed objects and scenes from many points of view, under different lighting conditions, and with a variety of gestures by the actors. He then assembled the optimal sequence in editing. The filmmaker understood that a *third meaning* arose from the juxtaposition of any two images, and that such meaning differed from the content of the individual images themselves. Eisenstein's film experimentation preceded the publication of Saussure's work in semiotics. It is clear nevertheless that he grasped the principle of the syntagmatic axis as a sequencing of signs that is meaningful precisely because the components are different and arranged in a particular order. Early twentieth-century viewers, not familiar with such editing techniques, were under the illusion that Eisenstein's films were documentaries of continuous action, rather than a compilation of staged scenes. Today we take such editing for granted as an expressive contribution by the filmmaker.

COLLISION MONTAGE

Sergei Eisenstein's term for the frame-to-frame relationships within a film that are achieved through editing and that are intentionally jarring in order to amplify emotional impact. A break in continuous action or point of view used to heighten the visual contrast for dramatic effect.

4.2 *APRÈS LA MARNE, FROM LES MOTS EN LIBERTÉ FUTURISTES*, 1914
Filippo Tommaso Marinetti (1876–1944)
British Library, London

4.3 *ZANG TUMB TUMB*, 1914
Filippo Tommaso Marinetti (1876–1944)
British Library, London

On the printed page, the exuberant compositions of the Italian futurist Filippo Tommaso Marinetti (1876–1944) (SEE FIGURES 4.2–4.3) blew apart the traditional linear structures of typographic layout and demonstrated his interest in "speed, simultaneity, and sensation."[15] These concepts were consistent with modern ideas about the new twentieth century and the growth of industrialization. Drucker describes Marinetti as also introducing "mathematical and diacritical marks [the small notations on letterforms that tell us how to pronounce a word] into the sequence of alphabetical symbols as part of his attack on ordinary syntax."[16] These marks expressed his fascination with the machine—changing the appearance of verbal language to something more mechanical—and reinforced his aim to subvert the romantic author, who the futurists believed was hopelessly tied to a sentimental past, by breaking the normal reading order of text.

Futurist and Dadaist compositions sought to redefine the reading experience with the intention of "waking up" audiences to a more critical reading of text (SEE FIGURES 4.4–4.6). While sometimes loosely "illustrating" the subject matter of the text through the manipulation of purely typographic form, these early twentieth-century typographers and poets focused on breaking the socially determined structure and rules of verbal language. In the case of the Dadaists (see pp. 165–66), the disruption of typographic conventions was

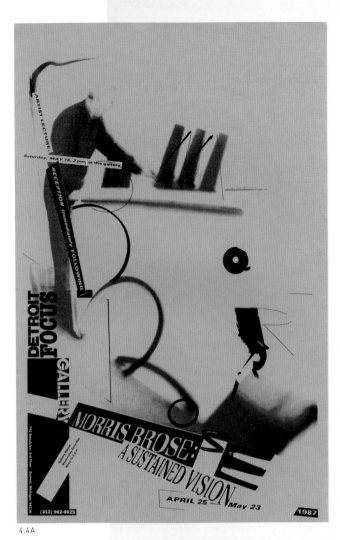

4.4A

4.4B

4.4 (A–B)
A *MORRIS BROSE: A SUSTAINED VISION*, 1987
Ed Fella (b. 1938)
Exhibition poster for Detroit Focus Gallery

B COVER FOR *DADA NO. 7*, MARCH 1920
Francis Picabia, (1896–1963)
University of Iowa, Dada Archives

4.5A

4.5B

4.5 (A–B)
A *TORCHSONG*, 1984
Neville Brody (b. 1957)
Magazine advertisement for performance

B COVER FOR *CLUB DADA*, 1919
Raoul Hausmann (1886–1971)
British Library, London

4.6A

4.6   (A–B)
A   *WORDS*, 1988
Phil Baines (b. 1958)
Text by David Blamey

B   *L'ANTITRADITION FUTURISTE:*
MANIFESTE = SYNTHESE, JUNE 1913
Guillaume Apollinaire (1880–1918)
Bibliothèque Nationale de France, Paris

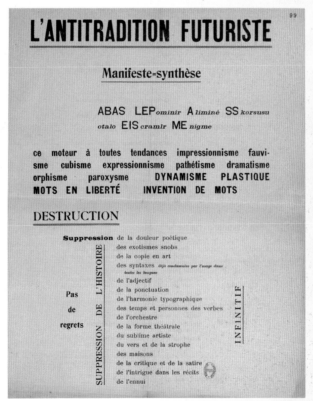

4.6B

Experimental typography of the early and late twentieth century shared similar concerns for the disruption of conventional syntax. The intention was to redirect the reading experience, and subsequently the reader's attention to ideas, through spatial arrangements that defied the typical linguistic ordering of letters and words. In both time periods, such work reacted to long-established systems of typographic layout and obvious visual hierarchies among information components.

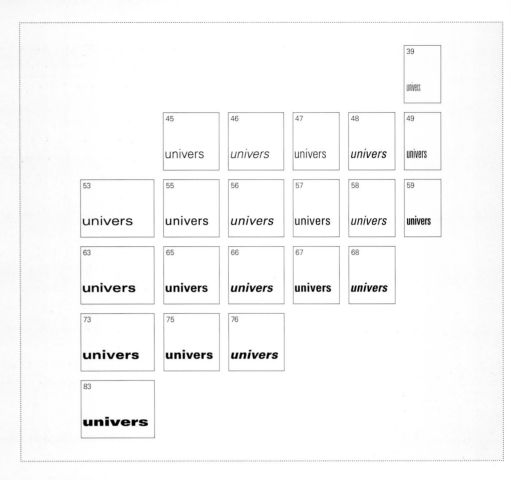

4.7 UNIVERS TYPE FAMILY, 1954
Adrian Frutiger (b. 1928)

Univers is typical of the type families
used by the International Typographic
Style of the 1950s to 1970s. Individual
members of the family are distinguished
by incremental variations in proportion
and weight, designed to achieve contrast
among information units when used in
the same document.

The International Typographic Style, also
referred to as "Swiss Design," formalized
the rules for good typographic form in the
middle of the twentieth century. Using
photography, typographic contrast within
a limited number of typefaces, and a clear
hierarchy among elements, designers
emphasized neutrality and formal systems
over the content of any individual message.

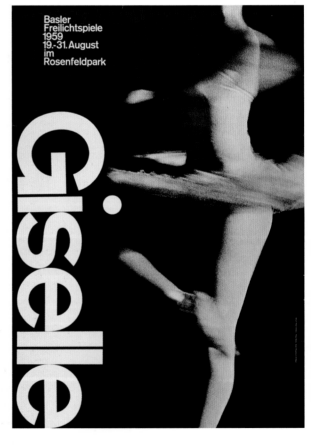

4.8 *GISELLE, BASLER
FREILICHTSPIELE*, 1959
Armin Hofmann (b. 1920)
Photolithograph
Museum für Gestaltung, Zürich,
Graphics Collection

intended to outrage an overly complacent upper class. The futurists (see pp. 150–51) were less antagonistic in their behavior but clearly believed that the visual form of language should be an expression of new, modern times, not a reflection of another social reality.

The typographic and image experimentations of the 1980s and 1990s [SEE FIGURES 4.4-4.6] had a similar aim to undermine the conventional grammar of elements on the page. But in this case their target was the formal systems of late modernist design, which emphasized rationality and the logic of mathematics. The International Typographic Style was developed in Switzerland in the 1950s and continued in popularity through the 1970s. Swiss Design, as it was also referred to, formalized rules for the visual organization of elements within compositions (see pp. 157–58). Grids controlled the proportions and alignments of photographs and text, dividing the page mathematically into positive elements and negative white space (see p. 147), with the aim of achieving a unified composition. A limited palette of highly refined typefaces [SEE FIGURE 4.7], organized into rational systems of proportions and weights, regulated typographic variations. The system ensured visual harmony among diverse elements within the composition and a clear hierarchy among information components. A poster for a ballet, however, looked much like the identity of a high-end furniture company or an announcement for a conference [SEE FIGURES 4.8-4.9]. Such modernist approaches privileged the authority of the writer and presumed that a single interpretation of his or her text was possible. The role of the designer was therefore seen as translating such meaning into visual form, using typographic contrast and the grid to direct the reader's experience. Astute audiences recognized virtuosity in this work when the typographic notes were played well. But so dominant was the langue or grammar of form at this point in design history that it appeared to offer little opportunity for designer variation in the parole of individual solutions and responses to very different problems or content. In many cases, the system for arranging elements overshadowed the particular meanings of the elements themselves.

Experimental compositions of the late twentieth century toppled these conventional hierarchies among typographic components. By placing elements in confrontational relationships [SEE FIGURES 4.10-4.13], rather than in obvious rankings of importance, designers acknowledged the role of the audience in the construction of meaning, and the potential for multiple interpretations through the viewer's engagement with text and image.

4.9 EXHIBITION POSTER FOR THE ALLIANZ HELMHAUS ZÜRICH, 1954
Richard Paul Lohse (1902–1988)
Museum für Gestaltung, Zürich,
Graphics Collection

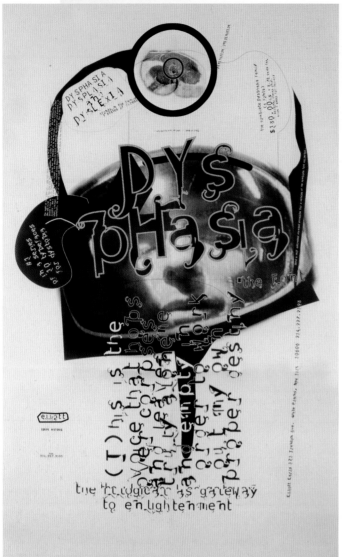

4.10

4.11

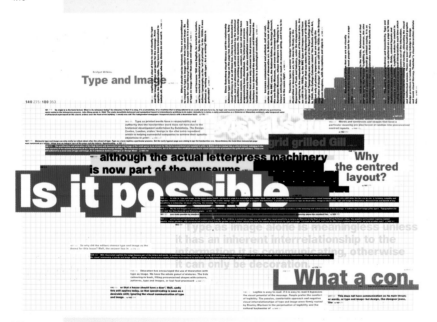

4.12

By the end of the century, many
designers longed for a more expressive
visual vocabulary and found new
inspiration in the formal potential of
digital technology and post-modern
writing that challenged the possibility of
singular meanings.

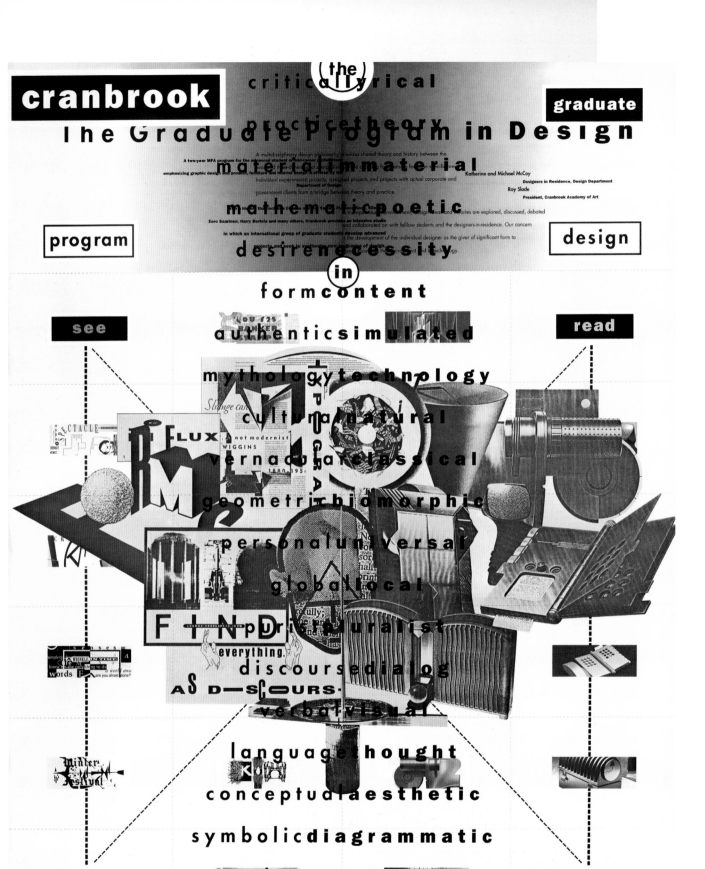

4.13

In contrast to modernist assumptions that meaning could be imposed on text and images by the author or designer, expressed through a tight system of visual theme and variation, these compositions offered ambiguous and pluralistic meanings. The rationalist confidence about finding answers to information problems presumed by the late modernist syntax gave way to works that reveled in the challenge of questions, in the decentering of meaning and the reading experience. The Cranbrook Academy of Art professor Katherine McCoy and student David Frej described the outcomes of such experiments in the article "Typography as Discourse" (1988):

> *Objective communication is enhanced by deferred meanings, hidden stories and alternative interpretations . . . . It is an interactive process that heralds our emerging information economy, in which meanings are as important as materials.*[17]

These late twentieth-century experiments launched post-structuralist interpretations in design (see p. 182) and continuing challenges to what many viewed as the tyranny of modernist syntax.

design parole

Saussure also inadvertently established the foundation for recent typographic explorations of style as the locus of meaning. He explained that, in addition to the ordering of words within the sentence, we make specific choices of words from a collection of possible words for the person, thing, or concept we wish to represent. This collection of associated words constitutes what he called the **PARADIGMATIC** or **ASSOCIATIVE AXIS**.[18] The relationship, in this case, is vertical and **SYNCHRONIC**: all of the possible word choices are available to us simultaneously and we interpret the meaning of the sentence, not only by focusing on the one chosen word, but also by knowing what other choices were available and not chosen.

person

boy

guy

dude

male

The dog bites the man.

In this example, the choice of "man" as the object of the sentence was made from among other reasonable word options that have roughly equivalent but subtly different meanings and that could occur at that particular location in the sentence. Knowing that "boy" was an option not used, we make the judgment that the person being bitten is an adult. Although we know his gender by the choice of "man" rather than "woman," the author does not obviously foreground gender, which could have been the case had the word "male" been chosen. If the slang term "dude" had been selected, the author might have added information about himself or herself to the meaning of the sentence.

THE LANGUAGE OF THE VISUAL WORLD

This is an example of parole—a concrete, individual use of particular words at a particular time. All possible words that could be used to designate the object that could reasonably appear in the same position in the sequence of words in the sentence are mentally available to the reader at the same time. The differences in their meanings do not depend on their horizontal position within the sentence and the choice of one over another is seen as significant.

Although the post-modern designers of the late twentieth century, mentioned earlier, drew their primary inspiration from a variety of theoretical sources, we can see Saussure's idea of the associative axis in their work. The typographic systems of late modernism had reduced words to pure function. Their form was stripped of meaning, other than that of their role within a highly regulated hierarchy. Typeface design was valued for its potential to establish carefully calculated contrast and harmony in order to maintain that hierarchy. The best faces, in late modernist terms, were those that were neutral, that had no obvious cultural or historical associations. Unlike the early avant-garde typography at the start of the twentieth century, late modernist work rarely combined typefaces in the same work, and if it did, it used faces with visually compatible qualities, such as x-height (the height of lowercase letters) and proportion (SEE FIGURE 4.14).

Typical typographic assignments in college design classes, such as variations on Yale professor Dan Friedman's famous "weather report" exercise, asked students to create multiple versions of the same content using only one

4.14 *PICCOLO TEATRO DI MILANO*, 1964
(above and opposite)
Massimo Vignelli (b. 1931)
Lithograph

4.15
YALE WEATHER PROJECT
Compositions based on an assignment
developed by Dan Friedman, faculty at
Yale University

typographic variable at a time—such as weight, size, proportion, spacing, and so on (SEE FIGURE 4.15). Although the American approach to typographic modernism showed less allegiance to rules than the European version, the goal in these exercises was still to manage contrast and hierarchy within a limited palette of choices: to explore rhythm, coherency, convention and unpredictability, and legibility and readability in layout within certain typographic constraints.

Similarly, the number of type families discussed in textbooks on typography, well into the 1980s, typically favored representatives of five historical classifications of type (old style/Garamond, transitional/Baskerville, Egyptian/Century Expanded, modern/Bodoni, and sans serif/Univers or Helvetica). This restriction subtly suggested to students that compositions using these typefaces could meet the late modernist requirements of "good form." Generations of design faculty debated the merits of limiting students to these exemplars or letting them recognize the superiority of classical fonts after mucking around in an unedited collection of commercial options.

In later investigations designed to open meaning to a wider range of expressive options and to acknowledge audiences' complex histories in a visual world, post-modern designers appropriated **VERNACULAR** typefaces and layout strategies. The aim was not to illustrate words or reinforce their literal meanings (for example, Western-themed content set in a typeface that looks like a wooden fence, or neon type for an article on the urban environment). Instead, it was to attach additional meanings to the word, some that were even inconsistent with their verbal associations, thus creating a collision of cultural signifiers not exclusive to the literary content of the text itself. In this way, form brought its own associative axis to the overall meaning of typography, which was placed in juxtaposition to that of verbal language (SEE FIGURES 4.16-4.18). The often hand-generated and "crudely" designed vernacular faces were in stark contrast to the typographic precision and refinement of late modernism. They recalled the history of communication, distinctions of social class and settings, and associations with how and for whom they were produced. They were anything but neutral in their meanings.

Encouraging such departures from modernist form, the development of computer technology and software programs, such as the font-design program Fontographer, broke the stranglehold that

VERNACULAR

The everyday language of ordinary people that is characteristic of a region or culture. In the context of design, "vernacular form" refers to the visual language produced by people who are not trained in design and contains connotations of a particular culture, place, or use.

4.16   ADVERTISEMENT FOR FRENCH PAPER COMPANY
Charles Spencer Anderson (b. 1958)

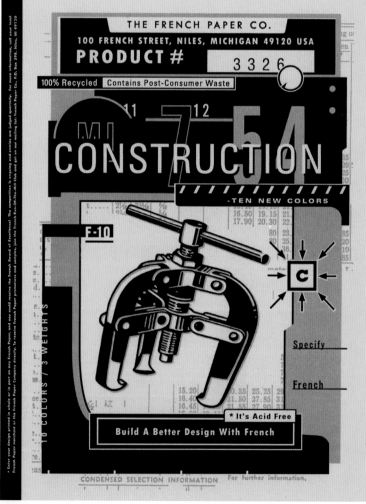

4.16

THE LANGUAGE OF THE VISUAL WORLD

4.17 (above and below)

4.18

4.17 TRIPLESTRIP TYPE
DESIGNS, 1996
Sibylle Hagmann (b. 1965)

TripleStrip alphabets are influenced
by letterforms created by expert and
amateur sign painters. These letters
appear on billboards and store fronts. The
unconventional font family embodies
a fusion of many different letterform
characteristics, often containing
symbolism and humor found in the urban
environment of the American West.

4.18 FLUX MUSIC FESTIVAL
POSTER, 1997
8vo, Hamish Muir (b. 1957)
Tephra type design

In the last decades of the twentieth
century designers used vernacular
typefaces to carry historical and
cultural messages that were distinct
from the literal meaning of words.
These forms alluded to the social
character of their original contexts
and use and were in stark contrast to
the refined precision and neutrality of
mid-century modernist forms.

large type foundries held over available form. The computer could imitate historical and found form and distribute it to thousands of other machines in a fraction of the time it took to develop a font in pre-digital times. The semantic associations of vernacular form acknowledged more diverse audience experiences than the high culture of fine arts and corporate sponsors, who were supporters of late modernist design. In true post-modern spirit, the meanings of typographic compositions were free-floating and pluralistic, borrowing from the diversity of the popular culture experience as a means for expanding the parole of typography.

We can also think about the choice of images as an expression of Saussure's associative axis. A poster for a Seattle film festival by designer Vittorio Costarella from the design studio Modern Dog [SEE FIGURE 4.19] features a movie camera rendered by hand. In evaluating the meaning of this image, a representation of independent filmmaking, we know that the concept of filmmaking could have been depicted using a photograph of the same camera, a tightly drafted mechanical drawing of the object, or any other element related to film and its audience. We understand that typesetting would have produced more finely crafted typography than hand-drawn letterforms and that higher production values—the use of four-color process printing, for example—were available to the designer. All of these possible visual attributes are accessible to us at the moment of interpretation and constitute Saussure's associative axis. Therefore, the designer's choice to use a handcrafted image and typography, as well as silk-screen printing, is read as significant. These choices lead us to interpret the poster as advertising independent films, not slick Hollywood blockbusters.

Our understanding of the meaning of a particular image, therefore, has to do with knowing the members of the appropriate group of associated ideas and attaching significance to one particular choice over others. Fashion magazines, for example, are persuasive precisely because we can imagine the alternative images that could have been used. Any woman could be used as a model if the role of the fashion photograph were only to feature a particular dress. But the role of the photograph is to persuade female readers that owning and wearing the dress will make a woman beautiful, sexy, powerful, edgy, or any other intended, desirable quality. To accomplish this, the woman in the photograph must exemplify the appropriate attributes—she must be interpreted as "a beautiful woman," for example, to the exclusion of other types of women and to the exclusion of those aspects of her own identity that have nothing to do with her beauty. Her perceived beauty is in relation to all the other ways in which she could look and all other types of women who could have been photographed.

A post-modernist critique would go further to say that, as consumers, not only do we wish to achieve beauty through the purchase of the dress, but that repeated exposure to this type of sign also makes us value that manufactured image of perfection over the other possible ways for women to be, despite our inability to achieve it; that we not only distinguish a difference between this and other signs, but also attach social status and value to that difference. In fact, the recent decision in Milan to ban underweight models from its fashion shows was countered by research that said women actually prefer to see clothing on skinny models, even though they know they will probably never become as thin themselves.

THE LANGUAGE OF THE VISUAL WORLD

4.19 RAINY STATES FILM FESTIVAL
POSTER, 1997
Vittorio Costarella for Modern Dog
Design Co.

Later critics used Saussure's concept of parole to categorize different types of literature. Poetry, for example, is a category of *literary parole*. We understand something about the particular character of poetry and, in general, a poet's intentions, that is different from other kinds of writing. A writer's choice to use poetic form, rather than another literary genre, such as short-story prose, functions as a dimension of its meaning. It sets up expectations for its readers that are not present if we think we are reading the short story.

The fashion image also represents a class of images with something in common, in the same way all poetic compositions are distinct from other types of writing. It is an "utterance" among all the possible types of photography. Through lighting, pose, gaze, and other conventions of an artificial reality, we recognize it as distinct from news, snapshot, portrait, documentary, and fine art photography (other members of the associative axis). These images can undergo considerable transformation and still be identified as fashion photography.

We may also think of some types of design work as counterparts to types of literary parole. We are able, for example, to sort a group of objects into the category of "corporate design," based on the way they look and how they are structured. Corporate work, while it may respond to a variety of stylistic trends, subject matter, and communication intentions, usually employs a general approach to visual language (typically within the legacy of modernist approaches to graphic identity) that is recognizable to us as distinctly different from objects of popular culture. It speaks with a particular "voice" through the selection and use of typefaces, structure of content, and choices of and approaches to imagery. We may even be able to identify certain materials (types of paper, page sizes, and so on) as being distinctly "corporate," despite variety in the visual messages themselves. Because we are able to do this, we assign meaning to the choice to look "corporate" and also take note when a business chooses to look "not corporate."

The significance of Saussure's work, then, resides in the idea that language operates on the basis of relationships: first, on the relationship between the signifier and signified, and then on relationships among the rules of the system by which distinct signs are combined and separate from one another. His description is one of the dynamic uses of signs in which the tensions among these rules and elements are always in play.

CHARLES SANDERS PEIRCE: A PRAGMATIST'S APPROACH

Charles Sanders Peirce represents the American branch of early work in semiotics. Although Peirce was a philosopher, he was a pragmatist and believed that logic and science were sufficient in letting us know what and how to think. Unlike Saussure, his primary interest in language was as a mode of information and thought, not as social interaction. Peirce believed that **SIGNIFICATION**, or the consumption of signs, is essentially a mental process, and that meaning resides in the mind, not in the objects themselves. Peirce called this process **SEMIOSIS.**

SIGNIFICATION

Charles Sanders Peirce's term for the consumption of signs: a mental process in which meaning is actively determined and resides in the mind of the interpreter, not in objects themselves.

SEMIOSIS

The process of meaning-making through the interpretation of signs.

A sign (representamen) stands for something (object) to somebody (interpretant) in some respect (ground).

Peirce's doctrine of signs defined four conditions that must be present for something to constitute a sign. First, the sign must represent an object (a person, thing, or idea); all signs must be about something.[19] Peirce calls this aspect the *representative condition*. Second, a sign must represent something in some sense or capacity (its ground).[20] He refers to this as the *presentative condition*. Third, a sign must determine an *interpretant*, a translation of the original person, thing, or idea into some equivalent in the mind of the interpreter.[21] Peirce calls this the *interpretative condition*. And finally, if the first three conditions are met, there must be a fundamental relationship between them, one that cannot be reduced to any simpler form, through which meaning is mediated.[22]

If we return to the example of Costarella's poster for the Seattle film festival (SEE FIGURE 4.19), we can analyze it in terms of Peirce's four conditions. First, the image in the poster represents a movie camera. There is a connection between the real object and the visual representation of that object in the poster. Next, the drawing itself presents a particular quality, a certain set of characteristics that are selected from among other ways for the camera to be illustrated or other aspects of the camera that could have been shown. It is a drawing that captures the form of the object but that is not overly concerned with technical accuracy. Many details are missing and some are replaced with the typographic elements of the poster. This is its *ground*, the presentative basis on which it stands for a camera. Then, through a mental process informed by our prior experiences, we interpret this as a camera with these qualities. Our interpretation has both depth (taking in all the qualities or characteristics of the representation necessary to understand it as a camera) and breadth (all the possible references made by the presence of those camera-like qualities). Finally, if the representation had a more tenuous connection with the object—if it was simply a gestural line that resembled film moving through a camera—or the rendering quality of the illustration was so general that it could be any mechanical object, the interpretation could easily be inconsistent with the intended object and the meaning of the poster would be lost. But because these three conditions have been met and are congruent, we process the relationship among them as congruent with our mental concept of a movie camera. The physical sign on the poster matches or recalls the thought-sign in our minds.

There is, however, a deeper reading of this sign, a second-level signification that arises from the choice of the camera, rendered in this particular way, as a sign for independent filmmaking. Not only is the camera a camera, but the style of the representation (the hand-drawn lines) also emphasizes its "edginess" as a presented quality over other possible qualities. We interpret that notion of "edgy, creative filmmaking" as affiliated with a particular category or type of filmmaking among all kinds of films (the big-budget Hollywood blockbuster, home movies, journalistic news footage, and so on). In this way, the connection of the representation with a concept we call "filmmaking," the individualistic quality in its presentation, and our ability to process these characteristics in association with a concept we know as "independent filmmaking" result in the image functioning appropriately as a sign for the film festival.

This example illustrates the fact that Peirce's concept of the process of signification privileges materiality in ways that Saussure's did not. Peirce was interested in the fundamental nature of signs and how they function in a concrete world. Unlike Saussure's signified/signifier relationship, in which meaning depended almost entirely on the position of a word within a linear text, Peirce's model considered the broader notion of context as influencing interpretation and the material nature of the sign as having consequences for our behavior. The duality of the sign, as both an object in the concrete world and as a mental artifact, is fundamental to Peirce's work.[23] For this reason, Peirce is generally favored as a theoretical reference, over Saussure, by designers who work with image- and time-based signs.

a taxonomy of signs

Peirce's most notable contribution to semiotics is his taxonomy. This describes natural groupings of signs that behave in analogous ways, and their classification, in terms of different relationships between the signifier (the *representamen*) and the object for which it stands. His designation of sixty-six aspects of signs (usually organized as triads according to function) is in contrast to the work of Saussure, who saw only one kind of sign (the combined signified and signifier).

The aspect most frequently referred to by designers is Peirce's second triad, which deals with relations of *performance*. These types of signs involve actual entities in the real world and are based on the context and background of the interpreter. Within this triad, Peirce described signs that are: *iconic*, having physical features that resemble the objects they stand for; *indexical*, functioning as signs by virtue of some cause/effect connection or by pointing to the objects they stand for; and *symbolic*, performing as signs because of some arbitrary rule or habitual association between the sign and the object.[24]

ICONS, which share some likeness with the things they stand for, are interpretively efficient from a designer's standpoint and require little or no formal learning on the part of the audience. Instead, understanding arises largely from matching the sign visually to something that shares its physical properties. In semiotic terms, a photograph is iconic: once we know how to interpret shapes on paper as meaningful, the content of the image typically resembles the things for which it stands. In earlier times, graphic icons made it possible for pre-literate societies to transmit their values and histories, as well as to support their day-to-day activities. For centuries the church told stories through allegorical paintings that communicated religious lessons for living a moral life. In cultures where only the most privileged could read, pictorial shop signage identified the activities and goods that were contained within. Much of the work we associate with graphic design today (logos, glyphs on signage, information graphics, and so on) relies on iconic form.

Peirce's concept of **INDEX** is a bit more elusive. An index points to something or describes a causal relationship. For example, smoke is an index for fire and a siren is an index for the response to an emergency. In this way, an index is one step removed from the actual goal of the representation. While the representation is not entirely random, it is probably something we have learned as an association through our life experiences. Electrical appliances, for example, used to display the words "on" and "off" next to the power switch, but today the more typical representation is "0" and "1," an index to the binary code that runs digital technology. Radios and audio equipment once had knobs that we rotated to control volume. Today, digital audio equipment no longer functions through this mechanism, but so powerful is the indexical association of a knob with volume control that many manufacturers retain the form. Typeface design may be indexical. Script typefaces, for example, reference handwriting better than a

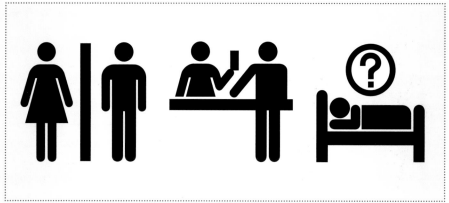

4.20   AT&T LOGO, 1983
Saul Bass (1920–1996)

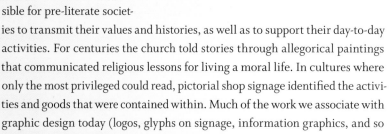

4.21   SIGNAGE SYMBOL SYSTEM FOR AMERICAN INSTITUTE OF GRAPHIC ARTS AND THE U.S. DEPARTMENT OF TRANSPORTATION, 1974
Roger Cook (b. 1930) and Don Shanosky (b. 1937)

The modern attempt to develop a picture language that transcends the cultural limits of verbal language began with the work of Otto Neurath in the 1930s and continued in the designs of Cook and Shanosky for AIGA and Otl Aicher for the Munich Olympics in the 1970s (see page 157). In the 1990s, the Women's Design + Research Unit commented on the attempt at cultural neutrality through its adornment of an otherwise "objective" depiction of women.

THE LANGUAGE OF THE VISUAL WORLD

4.22 (A–C)
PUSSY GALORE IN ALL OF HER
GUISES, 2008–10 (based on a typeface
originally designed in 1994)
Women's Design + Research Unit (Teal
Triggs, Liz McQuiston, and Sian Cook)

roman font, such as Times. It has also been suggested that serifs are indexical references to a time when ancient stone typographers ended a stroke of the letterform with a tap of the chisel to align the tops and bottoms of letters in a single word or line of type.

In contrast to the cognitive efficiency of icons, the meaning of abstract **SYMBOLS** must be learned, often through some formal exposure to the symbol over time. The late modernist proliferation of abstract logos in the 1970s, for example, placed the additional burden of such education on the shoulders of companies seeking to identify themselves in the competitive marketplace. Favoring simple geometric or alphabetic shapes with strong figure–ground relationships (SEE FIGURE 4.20), graphic designers struggled to capture the long list of attributes assigned to the company by corporate executives in tiny marks that may be only ½ inch (1.3 cm) in size. After a decade, the number of recognizable differences among the millions of logos was negligible for many consumers. To expand the symbolic opportunities and reflect the increasing diversification of business, these same executives renamed their companies, often through consultation with design strategists who assist businesses in reinventing themselves. In many cases, the new names were as abstractly symbolic as the marks that previously identified the corporation: International Harvester, once a manufacturer of farm equipment, became Navistar, and the Standard Oil Company became Exxon. Such examples illustrate the difficulty of building awareness for a symbol and its meaning, of making a connection between the signifier and a very specific signified when its physical attributes or name provide no reference to an audience's prior experience with the concept.

Peirce's classification of sign types is not mutually exclusive—we can have iconic symbols or indexical icons. For example, the iconic images of men and women in Cook and Shanosky's system for the American Institute of Graphic Arts and the U.S. Department of Transportation, designed in 1974 (SEE FIGURE 4.21), bear some resemblance to the physical attributes of human beings, with women differentiated from men by dress. In these images, we can also see the legacy of attempts to create an international system of wayfinding for travelers by Otto Neurath and Rudolf Modley in the 1930s and 1940s, whose goal was to make verbal language unnecessary (SEE FIGURES 5.31–5.32). When we see these icons on the door of a restroom, we are not confused that the purpose of the room is to store piles of men or women. Instead, their repeated use to designate a particular room-function has taught us that when they appear there are gender-specific restrooms present. In this way, they are also indexical.

The application of these male and female icons acquires additional meanings over time, through use and through the contexts in which they appear. When taken out of their typical setting, they still retain the meanings acquired

SYMBOL
Charles Sanders Peirce's term for a type of sign in which the relationship between the sign and what it stands for must be learned and is governed by a code or cultural convention.

through their history in signage and statistical charts, and it is sometimes impossible for us to separate them from their original sources and intent. In some repurposed uses, however, as in a call for papers originating from Teal Triggs's Women's Design + Research Unit (SEE FIGURES 4.22A–C), the residual meaning supports commentary: it not only separates the work of the organization as being for and about women, but it also subtly comments on a system that defines women primarily by their clothing. It serves as a symbol for how women have been defined by designers and as a simple iconic description of gender.

In *Design Writing Research* (1996), the design curator and author Ellen Lupton goes a step further in her analysis of Cook and Shanosky Associates' wayfinding system. Lupton points out that if the icon depicts service, the person being served is usually male and the person providing the service is usually female (SEE FIGURE 4.21).[25] The seemingly objective qualities of the icon are actually socially symbolic in their gender references as applied within the system.

As discussed, Peirce provides the theoretical grounding for a discussion of material form. His main focus of attention, unlike Saussure's, is on the concrete attributes of the sign, which he links to their role in the construction of meaning.

ROLAND BARTHES: A BRIDGE TO POST-STRUCTURALISM

The investigations of the French literary critic and theorist Roland Barthes bridged *structuralist* and *post-structuralist* approaches to the semiotic analysis of subjects as diverse as writing, photography, and fashion (see also p. 42). Barthes's ideas about language and criticism reached maturity in his book *Writing Degree Zero* (1953). Building on the structuralist theories of Saussure, Barthes's seminal essay focused on classical French writing style. He professed that no form of writing is a free expression only of the writer's subjectivity, but is the product of larger social and ideological values. In fact, Barthes viewed writing as all style and never free of ideology; each literary work signifies literature in general, in addition to whatever content is contained within its text.[26]

Barthes also shared the structuralist interest in **MYTH**, extending his analysis to images. In his consideration of a cover of *Paris Match* from 1955 (SEE FIGURE 4.23), Barthes described the denotative content of a young, black French soldier (signified by his uniform) saluting a French flag that is outside the picture frame. The image, according to Barthes, also suggests that the great French empire is supported by black and white alike and is not a colonial oppressor in equatorial Africa (the French occupied colonies in western, northern, and central Africa until 1960), as was alleged by detractors of the time. It is this second-order reading of the sign that transforms the literal, denotative meaning (a saluting soldier) into myth and abstraction (that of an imperial, colonizing France supported by black French citizens). Barthes lamented this appropriation of a denotative sign for another communication intent, calling it a "theft of language."[27] Its dishonesty is in trying to "pass off an arbitrary sign as a natural, analogical one."[28] Barthes resented the insertion of political content into an objective representation of fact.

MYTH

A term used by Roland Barthes to describe how bourgeois society imposes its values on others. The myth depends on connotations that are not factual (denotative) descriptions of things, but are values assigned to something (such as an image) as a second-order reading of the object that is made to appear natural. For example, according to Barthes, the image of a young black soldier saluting the French flag that was shown on the cover of an edition of *Paris Match* in 1955 propagated the myth that the colonization of Africa by France was supported by everyone—black and white alike.

For Barthes, to read is to be complicit in this myth-making process. He believed that there is no innocent reader. For the audience of the time to interpret this image as "French imperiality," the soldier must be saluting the French flag, rather than an officer; the reader must perceive his allegiance to the country, not to commands from an authority figure. Similarly, to understand the myth-making in the photograph aligning George Bush's head with those of other presidents at Mount Rushmore, discussed earlier (SEE FIGURE 2.13), we must view the South Dakota monument as more than just a pleasant location for a speech.

Barthes described myth as a vehicle of the **PETITE BOURGEOISIE** in 1950s France, as a covert manipulation of codes. Despite their lack of actual wealth, the petite bourgeoisie maintained their position as a social middle class through representations that depicted a material world to which they had no real access. For example, the poorly paid office worker sees himself sunning on the Riviera; the low-wage secretary imagines herself as the bride in an opulent wedding or a fashion trendsetter in designer clothes. In selling consumers the myth of higher social status, commerce speeds up the consumption of goods and secures the continuation of existing social positions by making it impossible to attain what is desired. The actual ability to acquire things that fit with our perception of "right and inevitable" values and social status always seems slightly out of reach.[29] We continue to consume in order to achieve the social status we imagine as an appropriate and achievable personal identity.

That these representations constitute a system is also important to Barthes. There is a structural relationship between culture and the material aspects of society, and we understand the network of connections through sign-to-sign relationships. For example, Jacques Tati's comic film from 1967, *Playtime*, is a commentary on modernism told through a loose storyline about a group of tourists in Paris. In a short but recurring scene, people pass through a glass door to the lobby of a modern but anonymous highrise. Each time someone opens the door, a different example of historical French architecture is reflected in the glass (the Eiffel Tower, the Arc de Triomphe, Notre Dame). Tati uses

4.23   COVER OF *PARIS MATCH* NO. 326, 1955

The semiotician Roland Barthes's analysis of this cover spoke to the post-modern notion that images can function as myth. In an environment of public debate over the colonization of equatorial Africa, a young French soldier confirms the "rightness" of French rule. If a black patriot shows respect to the French flag, then how can the country's occupation of an African nation be seen as morally wrong?

PETITE BOURGEOISIE

The lower-middle social classes (between the working class and the upper class) in the eighteenth and nineteenth centuries. Marxist theorists use the phrase to refer to shopkeepers and professionals who are not engaged in production, but who may employ workers and benefit from their labor. The term is also sometimes used derisively to refer to levels of taste and habits of consumption that are failed attempts to imitate the upper class.

4.24   SCENE FROM *PLAYTIME*, 1967
Jacques Tati (1907–1982)

these images as subtle though geographically impossible reminders that the characterless modern building is in a city with a rich architectural heritage (SEE FIGURE 4.24). Had he not provided this juxtaposition, the content of the scene would not have been about modernism—the building would have been simply the setting for other action. But by alluding to past architecture, Tati calls our attention to the larger system of architecture and tells us it is the tourists who are inconsequential to the meaning of the scene. Further, by reflecting ornament and historical significance that are particular to Paris, the filmmaker forces us to confront the architectural anonymity of the modern glass box. Another recurring object in the film is a travel poster that appears in a variety of interiors: the name of the city on the poster changes with each scene, but the modern skyline of the city is identical from poster to poster.

Between 1957 and 1963 Barthes's ideas about systems were expressed in his writings through an analysis of fashion. This marked his move to a post-structuralist understanding of the sign, in which social values extend purely functional meanings. He identifies the various structures within the fashion system. There is a *real garment*, which he refers to as the technological structure. There is the *visual representation of the garment* in magazines, which he links to an iconic photographic structure, and the *written garment*, as described in advertising copy.[30] Barthes refers to the technological structure, the real garment, as a "mother tongue" but sees the other two structures as "translations" that intervene in the original speech of garments to communicate values that encourage purchase.[31] Real clothing is practical (it protects, adorns, and so on) but the image garment and written garment constitute supercodes, which are imposed on and overtake the real garment.[32] As such, they arrest the real reading of the clothing (its physical qualities and materials) in favor of an emphasis ("the flirty hem" or "rugged attitude," for example). The limits of

In Tati's critique of modern life, movie viewers are reminded of the traditions of French architecture through the reflection of famous buildings from the past in the glass door of a curtain-wall highrise. Each time the door opens, a different French monument appears in the glass. Through his post-modern commentary, Tati reminds us that modern architecture turns its back on a rich visual lineage that is distinctly French and about more than function. The director further reinforces these concepts through a recurring poster that shows the same highrise, each time with the name of a different world city beneath it, implying that modern buildings are interchangeable and lack any cultural specificity.

THE LANGUAGE OF THE VISUAL WORLD

written clothing are no longer material limits, but limits of value.[33] By describing the hem as "flirty" the copywriters tell us that we will be sexy by wearing it; they appeal to our social desires, not just to our functional need to protect the body through clothing. Barthes says the photographic image replaces the dress and makes purchase unnecessary. We can "intoxicate ourselves on images" alone, imagining ourselves as the model.[34] But the written garment steps in to encourage the purchase. The system is complete.

Barthes will also be discussed in chapter 6. His ideas concerning the role of the reader in the interpretation of text influenced a number of graphic designers at the end of the twentieth century and offer an interesting bridge between the structuralist work of his predecessors and the richness of post-modern criticism, especially in France.

SUMMARY

Semiotics is the study of the life of signs and was developed in Switzerland by Ferdinand de Saussure and in America by Charles Sanders Peirce at the start of the twentieth century. This work was consistent with avant-garde art and design efforts to challenge prevailing ideas about the structural relationships between form and meaning. If the relationship between form and what it means is arbitrary (merely a matter of cultural agreement), then it is open to renegotiation as a means of social reform. These ideas also played a role in the experimental typographic work of designers in the 1980s.

While Saussure was concerned with language in the act of communication, Peirce saw language as a reflection of the human mind. Both agreed that a sign is something that stands for something else, in some respect, to someone. Saussure identified two components of language, the signified and signifier, which opened the door for a discussion of the contribution of form to meaning. He further articulated the difference between langue (the rules governing the linguistic system) and parole (the individual use of language in specific contexts). These have direct parallels in design: both syntax, or the ordering of elements within a composition, and the choice of particular visual elements among all available options within a context shape the meaning of a designed object.

Peirce described the conditions necessary for something to perform as a sign, and developed a taxonomy of sign types. His triad of icon, index, and symbol is particularly relevant to design, and examples can be found throughout history.

The French semiotician Roland Barthes holds particular significance for designers because much of his writing addresses the visual world. His discussion of photography as paradoxical—being at the same time the denotative production of a machine and the connotative result of lighting, pose, and so on—laid the groundwork for later post-modern ideas about value signs. And his analysis of the fashion system illustrates how printed communication extends the meaning of the garment in an attempt to fuel consumption.

modernism

5

Any discussion about the history of design involves the question of perspective. Should we follow an art-historical canon, working from the idea of connoisseurship to highlight exemplary objects and their famous makers? Or should we privilege other critical filters that place the interpretation of design theory in larger social, technological, and economic contexts?

The short tradition in graphic design history generally favors the first approach: a chronological unfolding of important stylistic movements as identified through seminal objects and important contributors to the practice. This approach extends the traditional domain of art history, in which design was previously secondary to fine art. But it also tends to fuse discussions of history and criticism in works the meanings of which are framed only by their own times and a few stellar makers. The risk in this approach lies in seeing design simply as a sequence of discrete object styles or as the product of individual genius, rather than as overlapping responses to changing conditions that acknowledge and generate certain outcomes for audiences and the culture at large. Further, an art-historical approach often fails to address forces for which the designer is simply an instrument of expression or the cultural means for making visible some social, technological, or economic change.

Sidestepping some of these pitfalls, the following discussion places a number of common modernist themes within larger social contexts in an attempt to achieve a richer understanding of theory. The goal of this chapter is not to present a chronology of modern design or to provide an exhaustive inventory of the theoretical differences underlying particular stylistic movements. The aim is to illustrate how design ideology arises from social conditions and from the trajectory of ideas across time.

In this chapter we face the particular problem of **MODERNISM**, a complex term that is used to denote a range of design responses that includes the rebellion of avant-garde typographic experimentation in the early 1900s, in addition to the well-established practices of **CORPORATE IDENTITY** toward the end of the twentieth century. While these diverse styles all owe something to ideas circulating in the modern world, they are far from alike in form or intent. It is therefore important to describe how circumstances for the designer changed during the twentieth century to produce these contrasting responses.

A NEW CENTURY

Conditions in the late nineteenth and early twentieth centuries were dramatically different from those of preceding times. Scientific progress and cheap energy, matched by centuries of accumulated capital for investment in the market economy, brought unprecedented refinements to agricultural and manufacturing technology.[1] Machines did the work that had once been accomplished

MODERNISM

An array of cultural movements in the late nineteenth and twentieth centuries that responded to new economic, social, and political conditions and the growth of industrialization, mostly in Western countries. Modernist ideas can be traced to the Enlightenment, an "age of reason," marked by the rejection of superstition and religion as dominant forces in culture.

CORPORATE IDENTITY

The persona of a corporation, usually expressed through its name, logo, typefaces, and supporting visual applications, which are guided by a manual of style.

by human and animal labor. Public attention focused on speed and precision, as well as on the increased availability and lower cost of manufactured goods.

Unlike the times when a single artisan or craftsman controlled the design and hand-production of an object from start to finish, the machine-powered age required planning and collaboration among many people for making something in mass quantities. The assembly line fragmented the production process into discrete tasks for which individual workers held only a fraction of the knowledge and skills necessary to bring products to market. It standardized form so that the same object could be made repeatedly with identical effort and quality by a large number of workers. The new trend was for companies to centralize work under one roof and to focus their production on a limited range of goods. The division of work that separated management from labor reinforced the longstanding distinctions between **SOCIAL CLASSES** in urban factories and commercial centers around the world. At the turn of the century there was very little about the world of work that resembled the past.

The rhythm of life changed for workers and their families as a result. Their days, previously structured by nature and the demands of farm life, were now accountable to the pace of technology. The need to keep expensive machinery running and to sustain factory production and the flow of investment capital altered the pace of work. It was important to maintain accurate timetables and to account for production output. Automation often forced workers into monotonous routines, only to produce profit for someone else. Children, whose work in the fields had been matched to their limited physical strength, now labored in the same factory jobs for the same hours as adults.

5.1 *YOUNG SPINNER IN THE WHITNEL COTTON MILL*, 1908
Lewis Hine (1874–1940)
Library of Congress, Washington, D.C.

A century of dramatic population growth and advances in manufacturing technology had therefore transformed a culture of farmers and craftsmen into a **CONSUMER SOCIETY**. People no longer produced what they needed to live on their own land. Commercial towns mushroomed throughout Europe in the nineteenth century. London, for example, grew from 900,000 to 4.7 million residents between 1800 and 1900.[2] By the second decade of the twentieth century, most people in Europe and the United States were town dwellers.

Such expansion was not without consequences. Filth, disease, poverty, and visible differences in how the social classes lived and worked were evident in most industrial towns. While some governments feared that the uneven distribution of wealth in cities would foment revolution, other people saw opportunities to right the injustices of oppressive social and economic conditions.[3] Upton Sinclair's novel *The Jungle* (1906), for example, took on working conditions and corruption in the American meatpacking industry. Laws to prevent the abuse of child labor were in place in England by the middle of the nineteenth century, but other countries were slower to respond.[4]

Industry required unprecedented numbers of laborers and frequently found its workforce in poor immigrants seeking higher wages and refuge from political upheaval in their home countries. Cities in the United States and Europe teemed with people who sought new beginnings. Despite their optimism for a fresh start, immigrants found that their native languages often failed them outside their ethnic neighborhoods. City life, unlike rural life, presented new demands for social interaction and unfamiliar ways of doing things. Survival, in its most basic form, depended on interpreting the complex interplay of unfamiliar visual and spatial cues in the workplace and the urban environment.

Out of these circumstances arose new missions for design: the growth of advertising to support a burgeoning world of goods and new lifestyles; searches for the appropriate expression of a new age and form that transcended specific cultural experiences; and a social conscience that viewed design as capable of building a utopian future from an environment of social and political chaos. Intellectuals and activists who emphasized a radical idealism hoped to rebuild society through sheer willpower, and apart from the traditional interests of the economic elite. These missions generated new types of form and the very idea that form could drive social outcomes.

STRIVING FOR OBJECTIVITY AND LOGIC

We can trace the earliest intellectual origins of modernism to the Enlightenment, an "age of reason" that emerged in Europe at the end of the seventeenth century. Overturning centuries of belief in tradition and superstition under oppressive monarchies and the church, the progressive movements of the Enlightenment embraced **OBJECTIVITY**, rationality, and order. Enlightenment thinkers placed their faith in the order of mathematics, the predictability and rigorous methods of science, and a belief that complex things could be understood through the orderly study of their fundamental components.

OBJECTIVITY

The ability to view something with accuracy and neutrality, as it actually exists.

The work of early modernist designers was also grounded in the notion of social progress that had developed in the Renaissance. If the future was no longer seen as the inevitable outcome of something determined by the supernatural, then people could influence the content and quality of that future—it could be different from and better than the present. Further, art and design could play some part in making that future come about, because form no longer owed any allegiance to the past or to some higher power. How things looked was seen as a visible instrument of change.

The twentieth-century workplace was also subject to new objective measures of success. **TAYLORISM**, developed and promoted by the mechanical engineer F. W. Taylor, determined the optimal method for performing a manufacturing task, trained workers in standardized jobs, and rewarded increased production output through incentives.[5] This practice produced a logical division of labor, a value system that prized efficiency above all things, and a seemingly objective culture of performance measurement that was consistent with a mechanized view of the world.

TAYLORISM

A twentieth-century approach to determining the optimal method for performing a manufacturing task. Developed by the mechanical engineer F. W. Taylor.

In this rational, optimistic view of the future, technology was fundamental and equivalent to notions of linear progress. The machine was the epitome of functionality and was developed through sequential improvements. Mass production was possible only through planning and **STANDARDIZATION**; it required organization and collaboration within the workforce. No longer could a craftsman or artisan "make it up" as he went along in the process of producing something—the workers' days were ordered by technology and accountable to goals larger than their own.

the technological image

In this machine-centered environment of mass production, the application of technology to image-making was the next logical step. Photography, fully developed by the end of the nineteenth century, was a medium that was consistent with an objective view of the world and the public's appetite for images of a new age. The representation of places and events was no longer subject to the individual, edited interpretations of illustration; the stylistic mannerisms of drawing; or the longer exposures of the **DAGUERREOTYPE** (SEE FIGURE 5.2), which made it impossible to capture the movement of busy urban life. Early photographic studies, such as those by the English photographer Eadweard Muybridge (1830–1904), reveled in the ability to freeze time and record phenomena of the material world for further study (SEE FIGURES 5.3–5.4). Muybridge's famous studies of animal locomotion, for example, were efforts to prove scientifically that all four hooves of a horse leave the ground when the horse is in motion (they do).

Other photographers were fascinated by the technical and formal possibilities of the photographic medium itself. The Hungarian Bauhaus designer László Moholy-Nagy (1895–1946) created **PHOTOGRAMS** (SEE FIGURE 5.5), which involved placing objects directly on photographic paper, then exposing them to light. The results were compositions that resembled medical X-rays, an objective recording of the shape and density of the source material. **RAYOGRAPHS**, by the American Dada/surrealist photographer and painter Man Ray (1890–1976), also used negative imaging but recorded the position of objects over time through multiple exposures.

The American photographer Alfred Stieglitz (1864–1946), who was one of the earliest to use photography as an art form, always insisted that a photograph should look like a photograph. He believed that the image should be straightforward, reflect its mechanical production, and remain free from the

5.2 *U.S. CAPITOL BUILDING, c.* 1846
John Plumbe Jr. (1809–1857)
Daguerreotype
Library of Congress, Washington, D.C.

Because of its long exposure times, the daguerreotype was ineffective for capturing the movement of everyday life. Sitters had to remain still for long periods of time and it was impossible to record the hustle and bustle of busy cities. The process was far better suited to architectural studies.

5.3 *ATHLETE. BACK SOMERSAULT,* FROM *THE ATTITUDES OF ANIMALS IN MOTION,* 1878–79
Eadweard Muybridge (1830–1904)
Library of Congress, Washington, D.C.

STANDARDIZATION

The process of developing and agreeing upon uniform technical specifications, criteria, methods, or practices. The assembly line and mass production required the standardization of components so that work could be accomplished through a division of labor.

DAGUERREOTYPE

A nineteenth-century photographic process that used silver-coated copper plates, which were exposed to light and developed using mercury vapor. These fragile metal images required long exposure times (twenty to thirty minutes) and were susceptible to scratching and oxidation.

PHOTOGRAM

A photographic image made without a camera by placing objects directly on a photo-sensitive surface and then exposing them to light. Areas covered by the objects appear white, while the exposed background is black.

RAYOGRAPH

A photographic image made without a camera by placing objects directly on a photo-sensitive surface, exposing them to light and then shifting the composition for additional exposures. Objects of different densities record at different values from white to black. Rayographs were developed by the American painter and photographer Man Ray.

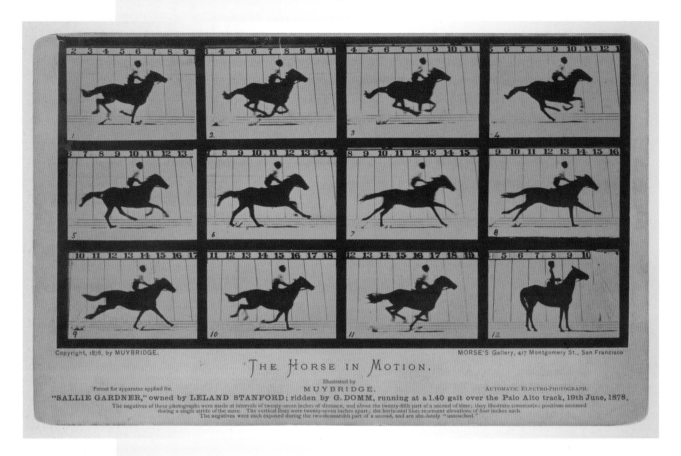

THE HORSE IN MOTION.

Illustrated by
MUYBRIDGE.

Copyright, 1878, by MUYBRIDGE.

MORSE'S Gallery, 417 Montgomery St., San Francisco

Patent for apparatus applied for.   AUTOMATIC ELECTRO-PHOTOGRAPH.

"SALLIE GARDNER," owned by LELAND STANFORD; ridden by G. DOMM, running at a 1.40 gait over the Palo Alto track, 19th June, 1878.
The negatives of these photographs were made at intervals of twenty-seven inches of distance, and about the twenty-fifth part of a second of time; they illustrate consecutive positions assumed during a single stride of the mare. The vertical lines were twenty-seven inches apart; the horizontal lines represent elevations of four inches each. The negatives were each exposed during the two-thousandth part of a second, and are absolutely "untouched."

5.4 *THE HORSE IN MOTION*, 1878
Eadweard Muybridge (1830–1904)
Library of Congress, Washington, D.C.

5.5 *PHOTOGRAM*, 1926
Laszlo Moholy-Nagy (1895–1946)

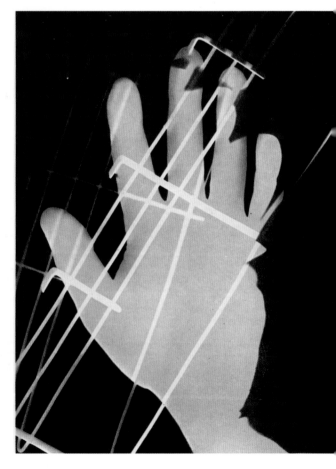

New ideas about image-making grew with technological advances in photography at the beginning of the twentieth century. Muybridge's time-based images of animal and human locomotion were considered by many to be scientific studies, even though Muybridge considered himself an artist and edited the sequence of images. Moholy-Nagy's photograms were produced by placing objects on photographic material and exposing them to light without the use of a camera. He believed in a "new vision" and that photography "could create a whole new way of seeing the outside world that the human eye could not." Stieglitz captured the conditions of modern life, arguing that photography should avoid the romantic artifice that had defined painting in the nineteenth century.

5.6 *THE STEERAGE*, 1907
Alfred Stieglitz (1864–1946)
Collection Harry Ransom Humanities
Research Center, University of Texas, Austin

aesthetic treatments and critical standards of other art forms. Unlike many photographers of the time, Stieglitz did not manipulate the image in printing to heighten its artistic qualities in ways that resembled drawings and paintings. His subject matter frequently captured the activities of everyday life and the qualities of the urban environment at the start of the twentieth century. Stieglitz's images were not about the stylistic obsessions of wealthy patrons or the picturesque. They were a record of the times: horse-drawn trolleys waiting at a New York terminal on a winter day, or a crowd of poor travelers in steerage on a ship crossing the Atlantic (SEE FIGURE 5.6). Through his magazine *Camera Work*, and later in his gallery, Stieglitz established a unique role for photography in modern America—that of expressing the character of life in modern times.

With a similar interest in capturing life at the turn of the century, the photographer Lewis Hine (1874–1940) documented the American worker and child labor in factories and sweatshops (SEE FIGURE 5.1) throughout the country. Hine was trained as a sociologist, worked as a schoolteacher in New York, and was committed to social reform. From 1908 to 1912, working as a photographer for the National Child Labor Commission, Hine recorded the abuse of young children by American industry. Later, during the Great Depression (the late 1920s to the early 1940s), he worked for the Works Progress Administration, photographing the impact of industrial changes in patterns of American employment.

Displaced workers were also the subject of Hine's contemporary, the New York-educated photographer Dorothea Lange (1895–1965), who worked for the Farm Security Administration in the 1930s. Married to a Berkeley professor of economics, Lange photographed the poverty and displacement of sharecroppers and migrant farm workers during the Depression. She distributed her images for free to newspapers around the country (SEE FIGURE 5.7).

5.7 *MIGRANT MOTHER*, 1936
Dorothea Lange (1895–1965)
Library of Congress, Washington, D.C.

Photography played the important role of documenting the changing social conditions of modern experience. Hine and Lange created images of American labor that, while emotionally powerful, avoided the sentimentality of earlier times. These images served as objective evidence of the circumstances in which Americans labored in the first decades of the twentieth century, but they were also compellingly persuasive in bringing attention to the need for social reform.

The power of these images as authentic representations of early twentieth-century life resides not only in their mechanical means of production, but also in the photographers' choice to forgo both sensationalistic journalism and the artifice of prevailing artistic conventions. These are poignant but straightforward images, seemingly objective realities without obvious references to their makers. Even when focused on the ultimate persuasive purpose to bring about reform, as in the case of Hine's work, the photographs reflect the eye of the social scientist. Hine captioned these images with the same objective voice:

One of the spinners in Whitnel Cotton Mill. She was 51 inches high. Has been in the mill one year. Sometimes works at night. Runs 4 sides, 48 cents a day. When asked how old, she hesitated, then said, "I don't remember," then confidentially, "I'm not old enough to work, but do just the same." Out of 50 employees, there were ten children about her size.[6]

The use of photographic images in advertising, journalism, fine art, and the depiction of everyday life grew as the century progressed, and the photograph gained particular status in illustrating modern culture to the people who lived in it. Through its technological production, the photograph carried the imprimatur of "objective truth," of its maker having "been there" and recorded the state of affairs accurately.

In the 1920s and 1930s, however, avant-garde artists and designers used the documentary standing of photographic images not only to represent the emergence of a modern world, but also to challenge its realities.[7] The **PHOTOMONTAGE**, a composite picture made of images from more than one source, often different in scale and points of view, ruptured the illusion of a continuous life. Designers foregrounded objects of industry and consumer society, political figures, and scenes from cultural events in compositions that emphasized their importance in modern times, countering the objective narrative form of journalistic photography and rational, naturalistic representations of physical space. Avant-garde designers employed this hybrid imagery as a way of representing a "culture of fragments,"[8] a social reality that was not as easily represented by straightforward photography (SEE FIGURES 5.8-5.9).

PHOTOMONTAGE

A composite picture made up of images from more than one source and from multiple points of view.

The photomontage took on greater political significance during war, especially in Europe, as the illusion of photographic objectivity gave way to the power of propaganda and persuasion. The Dadaists used photomontage to protest about what they believed to be the causes of World War I (SEE FIGURE 5.10). Although members of the rebellious group disputed who really invented the form, the Dadaist Raoul Hausmann (1886–1971) described photomontage in a lecture he gave in Berlin in 1931:

[The] photomontage was as revolutionary as its content . . . . [The Dadaists] were the first to use photography as material to create, with the aid of structures that were very different, often anomalous and with antagonistic significance, a new entity which tore from the chaos of war an entirely new image; and they were aware that their method possessed a propaganda power which their contemporaries had not the courage to exploit.[9]

The constructivist Varvara Stepanova (1894–1958) also saw the camera as a tool that was well suited to a new social agenda in Russia following the October Revolution (1917) and to theories that explored the relationships between the material properties of objects and perceptions of their roles in defining space. In 1928 she wrote:

The mechanical complexity of the external forms of objects and of our whole industrial culture is forcing the artist concerned with production—the constructivist artist—to move from the imperfect method of drawing to the utilization of photography.[10]

5.8   POSTCARD FOR THE ALL UNION OLYMPIAD, 1928
Gustav Klucis (1895–1938)

ДА ЗДРАВСТВУЕТ КРАСНАЯ АРМИЯ—
ВООРУЖЕННЫЙ ОТРЯД ПРОЛЕТАРСКОЙ РЕВОЛЮЦИИ!

5.9

5.10

5.9 *GLORY TO THE RED ARMY*, 1933
Vasili Elkin (1897–1991)
Collage

5.10 *CUT WITH THE KITCHEN KNIFE THROUGH THE LAST WEIMAR BEER-BELLY CULTURAL EPOCH OF GERMANY*, 1919–20
Hannah Höch (1889–1978)
Photomontage

5.11 *THE RESULTS OF THE FIRST FIVE-YEAR PLAN*, 1932
Varvara Stepanova (1894–1958)
Photomontage

5.12 *WHITE SEA CANAL*, 1933
Alexander Rodchenko (1891–1956)
Photograph

The photomontage combines images from more than one source, often creating unnatural scale relationships and multiple points of view for greater visual impact. These images were used by the modernist avant-garde to present a "culture of fragments," an assembly of different aspects of modern and political life in a single pictorial space.

Stepanova goes on to cite her work with her husband, the photographer Alexander Rodchenko (1891–1956), in a book for the Russian poet Vladimir Mayakovsky (SEE FIGURE 5.11), as "the first great work in photomontage."[11] She divides the technique into three historic phases. The first phase combined many images in a single composition, using the graphic surface as a "connective medium." In these compositions, elements of different sizes and sources coexist on a two-dimensional plane, flattening the space. The second phase moved to the composition of the individual photographs themselves as studies in space. We can see this interest in the dramatic compositions of Rodchenko's photographs (SEE FIGURE 5.12)—the subject matter of the image seems less important than recording a point of view, a sensory awareness of the photographer as having been in a particular place at a specific time. Stepanova describes this approach as increasing the documentary role of the photograph. In the final phase, she asserts, photography is the only medium that can provide the artist with "the traditional method of drawing while allowing him to fix and record the reality around us."[12]

5.11

5.12

So, even when the early modernists compromised the traditional spatial integrity of the photographic image by its recombination with other images or a less conventional viewpoint, the goal was an objective depiction of reality, whether physical or social.

geometry and abstraction

Photography was not the only medium in which artists and designers found a new expressive language that was compatible with the modern industrialized world. Many modern movements (cubism in France, futurism in Italy, and suprematism and constructivism in Russia) were experiments to define new roles for the pure sensory experience of abstract visual form. Rejecting the illusionistic visual conventions of the nineteenth century as irrelevant to the conditions of a new age and as too closely associated with elitist visions of high culture, these artists and designers created new, never-before-seen relationships between form and function.

Just as Stepanova's and Rodchenko's photomontages challenged the artificial systems of Renaissance perspective, which attempted to replicate a natural view of the physical world through a mathematical system of vanishing points, other artists of this period defined space through the sensory qualities of color, line, and shape; and by the size, intensity, and position of shapes within the flat plane of the composition (SEE FIGURE 5.13). This kind of space was dynamic and based on concrete perception, not on an artificial system of rules, and mirrored a new unity of art and life that required no acculturation to the conventions of representational art. The work of the Russian suprematist painter Kazimir Malevich (1878–1935), for example, was linked to new scientific theories of relativity and interactions between space and time. Energy and movement were created by the weight (saturation) of a color, which responded in a manner consistent with the physical laws of gravity.[13] Forms appeared to have trajectories, to behave in space according to their size, shape, and mass, and to command a presence that was consistent with their roles in the visual hierarchy of the composition.

Designers therefore found in abstraction: an embodiment of the values of scientific reasoning and objectivity; the language of technology; the properties of non-representational, sensory experience; and a semblance of elemental order in a world of political and social chaos. Simple geometric shapes were interpreted as having the underlying logic of the material world. They were seen as essential forms that owed nothing to the eccentricities of culture or to the whims of individual artistic experience. Such forms established a fundamental relationship

5.13 *PROUN 12E*, 1923
El Lissitzky (1890–1941)
Busch-Reisinger Museum, Harvard University

Suprematist paintings invited direct experience of the concrete world, in contrast to the artificial illusion of physical objects that is found in nineteenth-century still life, landscape, or portrait painting. This experience was defined by the sensory qualities of shapes and colors and the arrangement of abstract form in space. The elements of the composition do not "stand for" something; they are to incite responses in the viewer that are unfiltered by traditional artistic conventions, such as linear perspective and chiaroscuro shading.

between the viewer and object that was unobstructed by the conventions of high art and **STYLE** and that was therefore accessible to the masses. In this sense, modern art and design were socially motivated—through pure, objective, sensory experience they were thought to transcend the boundaries of class and politics.

standardization

Geometric form also lent itself to **STANDARDIZATION**, which was increasingly necessary as factories and building construction flooded the market with components that had to work together. There needed to be logic in how things were made, a system for reconciling the work of individuals in the production of manufactured goods.

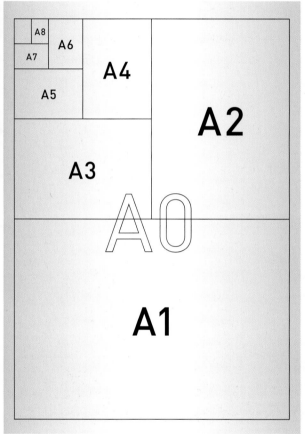

The Swiss, already known for their precision of craft, embraced the idea of standardization and had a profound impact on modernist theories of typographic design. The German printer Jan Tschichold (1902–1974), for example, brought his modernist experiences at the German Bauhaus to Switzerland in 1933. He wrote and published articles on typography that became the basis of modern Swiss design and the later International Typographic Style (see pp. 115, 157–58). In a guide from 1932 for typesetters and designers, Tschichold lauded the aesthetic merits of the German DIN "A" series (SEE FIGURE 5.14), a standardized format for sizing paper based on a single aspect ratio of the square root of two: if the page is divided exactly in half, the result will have the same mathematical proportions as the full sheet. This aspect ratio was eventually adopted as an international standard (ISO) and still determines paper sizes in countries outside North America today.

Tschichold also encouraged the adoption of rules for the unity of design across components of a typographic system through his work with Penguin Books in the 1940s. Standardized divisions of space on covers, consistent relationships of text to margins to page size, and a limited palette of typefaces established a repeatable visual identity for the publisher's titles (SEE FIGURES 5.15–5.16).

5.14   DIN PAPER SIZES, "A" SERIES
Introduced in Germany in 1922.
A0 measures 1189 × 841 mm
(approximately 46¾ × 33 in)

In his most famous book, *The New Typography* (1928) (SEE FIGURE 5.17), Tschichold praised the circle and the square, testimony to the importance of geometry in his work.[14] His aim was not that these abstract shapes should stand for something but that they should serve as pure experience of the forms themselves and as a unifying factor in compositional organization. He wrote:

[The aim of the art of today] is utmost clarity and purity. It makes use of exact geometric forms and so achieves an aesthetic paraphrase of our technical-industrial times. Just as exact geometric forms hardly ever appear in nature, so the colours of new painting are not derived from nature either.... In our new art we have ended the conflict between 'being' and 'seeming,' for both are identical. The new painting shows clearly what is: an unrepresentational, pure, painterly harmony.[15]

STYLE

A distinctive form or prevailing mode of expression. Often associated with an era or a culture and having less to do with the subject matter of the communication than with how it is represented.

STANDARDIZATION

The process of developing and agreeing upon uniform technical specifications, criteria, methods, or practices. The assembly line and mass production required the standardization of components so that work could be accomplished through a division of labor.

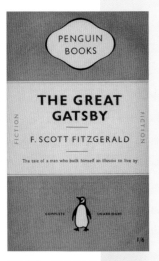

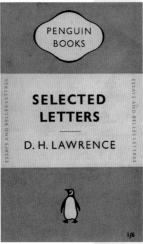

5.15   PENGUIN BOOK COVERS, 1950
Jan Tschichold (1902–1974)

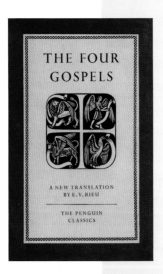

5.16   COVER FOR PENGUIN
EDITION OF *THE FOUR GOSPELS*, 1952
Jan Tschichold (1902–1974)

5.17   ADVERTISEMENT FOR *DIE
NEUE TYPOGRAPHIE* (*THE NEW
TYPOGRAPHY*), 1928
Jan Tschichold (1902–1974)

The jacket image 5.18 shows:

Thomas Morus .... **16.** Jahrhundert
Bellamy .... **19.** Jahrhundert
Illing .... **20.** Jahrhundert

Werner Illing **utopolis**
Roman

Illing
**uto-
polis**

Werner Illing

utopolis

Phantastischer Zukunftsroman

Ein Schiffbruch verschlägt Hein und Karl in das Land der freien Arbeitergenossenschaft von Utopien, die nahezu die vollkommene sozialistische Gemeinschaft verwirklicht hat. Sie erleben hier am praktischen Beispiel, wie weit selbst der organisierte europäische Proletarier noch mit der Anschauung und Denkweise der bürgerlichen Welt verbunden ist. Als der Arbeiterstaat durch den verbrecherischen Anschlag einer kleinen Kapitalistengruppe in höchste Gefahr gerät, gelingt es Karl, einen wesentlichen Beitrag zur Rettung beizusteuern.

Der Verfasser hat es vermieden, seine Utopie mit lehrhaften theoretischen Ausführungen zu belasten. Die Handlung ist abenteuerlich-spannend und hält sich bewußt innerhalb der Grenzen des Möglichen. Nur so gelang es, aus dem Wunschbild einer denkbaren Zukunft die Gegenwart satirisch und kritisch herauszuspiegeln. Der Roman ist mit einem Humor geschrieben, der das Buch in den Vordergrund des literarischen Interesses rückt.

»... eine einfache, aber eindringlich gefaßte Gesellschaftssatire voll des großen Atems der Menschlichkeit.«   »La Nouvelle Revue Critique«, Paris

»... Dem Verfasser kommt es darauf an, dem Leser den Gegensatz zwischen kapitalistischer Gegenwart und einer möglichen besseren und schöneren Zukunft zum Bewußtsein zu bringen. Und wir entnehmen dem Buch die Nutzanwendung: das Zukunftsbild, das uns der Dichter entwirft, braucht keine Utopie zu sein. Freilich müssen wir darum kämpfen.«
»Arbeiter-Jugend«, Berlin

„Ein Zukunftsgemälde einer freien Gemeinschaft Utopien mit der Hauptstadt Utopolis. Von erfinderischer Phantasie mit allen technisch-mechanischen Fortschrittsmöglichkeiten ausgestattet • In vielem ist das Buch Gegenwartssatire am Stoff einer imaginär erschauten Zukunft. Illing hat Phantasie, einen einfachen, bildhaft genauen, unprätentiösen Stil und als Bestes eine gute, tatwillige Gesinnung."   **Die Literatur.**

In Ganzleinen gebunden 4.30 RM

5.18   JACKET FOR *UTOPOLIS*, 1930
Jan Tschichold (1902–1974)

The Germans developed mathematical standards for the sizes of publications, now referred to in Europe as ISO (International Organization for Standardization) standards. Tschichold embraced this geometry in his system for the typography, layout, and colors of Penguin Books. On bookstore shelves, the family of books could be identified as belonging to Penguin, and the design of each book was no longer dependent on the aesthetic choices of individual designers.

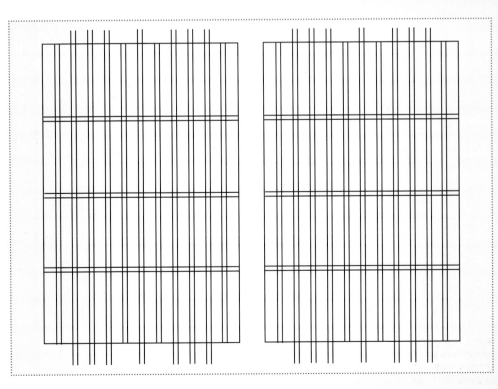

5.19   GRID

Designers use modernist grids to create unity among elements in multi-page publications. The grid defines possible sizes for images and text, proportional relationships, and alignments that bring harmony to disparate elements in the same visual space. Consistent placement and hierarchy among information components maintains continuity for the reader from spread to spread and from issue to issue of the same publication. Throughout design history, designers have based grids on perceptions of optimal proportions—such as the golden section, in which smaller divisions of space are proportionally identical to the dimensions of the larger space. Document-design software programs, such as Adobe InDesign, are based on the grid, and therefore embed modernist design principles in their features and functions.

Tschichold is here referring to the fact that modern art and design no longer depended on artistic conventions that "seemed to stand for" sensory experience in the real world, such as mechanical perspective or painted highlight and shadow. Instead, the use of **ABSTRACTION** eliminated such artifice, and the experience of space, weight, motion, and color was the result of direct perception, unimpeded by our intellectual understanding of representational systems that mediate our true experience of the world. As long as such representational systems are in place, said Tschichold, real harmony is not possible.

Strongly influenced by Russian constructivism, Tschichold's typographic compositions stressed contrast (among sizes, weights, and groupings of type) and asymmetry (SEE FIGURE 5.18). The goal was to integrate the elements and their backgrounds, to create an intentional distribution of negative "white" space that commanded the same attention as the positive typographic forms on that surface. Here again we see the modernist concern for abstraction as direct experience (for the most essential logic of form), even when dealing with the representation of verbal content.

This sensibility dominated art and design for much of the twentieth century. Decades after Tschichold's writing, the Swiss designer Karl Gerstner expanded the logical division of space on the page as permutations of mathematical formulae (SEE FIGURE 5.19). Gerstner, who is best known for his book *Designing Programmes* (1964), argued that the more elaborate the system, the greater the artistic freedom. But such freedom was always accountable to the mathematical origins of form that, through common increments of measurement, guaranteed visual harmony among the components.

The modernist preoccupation with logic and geometry can also be found in the corporate identities of the later twentieth century. Once again, a system dictated how the various parts would come together. Abstract logos frequently exhibited strong reversals of positive/negative space within simple geometric shapes. Often reducible to circles, squares, or triangles, and integrated with typography, they reinforced a mathematical logic through their application. Placement on letterheads and forms dictated the acceptable letter formats for typists. Manuals elucidated the rules of the system, often detailing measurements for each printed application. In contrast to the complexity of heraldry and the typographic eccentricity of hallmarks, these minimalist identities lived comfortably on standardized sizes and surfaces and represented the forward-thinking qualities of the companies for which they stood. They presented an objective, rational system for making visual decisions, so that work produced under different designers looked the same and projected a precise, consistent visual representation of the company to the public (SEE FIGURE 5.20).

Late in the twentieth century, these monolithic, rules-based identity systems would be challenged by a more kinetic approach in which individual designers were encouraged to create infinite combinations from a loosely determined palette of colors and shapes (SEE FIGURE 5.21). These later identities were established on the basis of an attitude or personality—a unique character among a vast landscape of more neutral forms—and led the way to what we now know as branding. In this sense, the abstract language of elemental modernism had

ABSTRACTION

A reduction of the content or concept of something to its most essential form. Twentieth-century artists and designers used abstraction to free visual language from the illusory conventions of art of the past, such as perspective, and to focus on the pure perception of concrete visual phenomena.

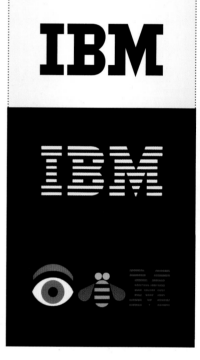

5.20   IBM CORPORATE IDENTITY, 1956. Paul Rand (1914–1996)

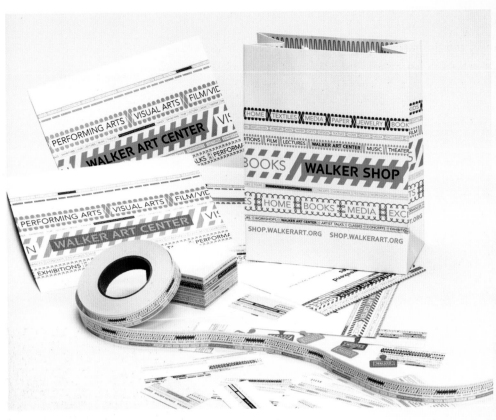

Early corporate identity programs guided design decisions through style manuals that gave detailed specifications for the typefaces, colors, measurements, and placement to be used for all elements. Today, many identity programs use a "kit of parts" approach that gives designers more freedom in adapting elements to the specific nature of messages and contexts. Designers reinforce the "brand" in the overall character of the work, but applications evolve over time in response to the differences in context.

5.21 (A–B)

A WALKER ART CENTER IDENTITY, 2005
Andrew Blauvelt (b. 1964) and Chad Kloepfer (b. 1976). Typeface design by Matthew Carter (b. 1937)

B WALKER CHANNEL ON iTUNES U, 2008
Justine Heideman (b. 1981)

become a formula against which to build contrast, despite modernist efforts to transcend style.

SEARCHING FOR THE UNIVERSAL

Modern design ideologies therefore shared a belief in underlying principles of form (structural relationships, in the linguistic sense) that transcended specific cultures and contexts. If direct, sensory experience of this abstraction exists outside the influence of cultural conventions, it could be seen as **UNIVERSAL**, as fundamental to human existence. And if such forms are essentially human (hard-wired into our brains and not by-products of different life experiences), then it was through form that design could further the humanistic social agendas of the early twentieth century and escape the cultural superficiality of style and historicism.

While we can find strong confirmation that universal form was the goal of most modernist movements, it is particularly evident in the work of artists and designers of the futurist movement in Italy and de Stijl in the Netherlands. The Bauhaus embraced the tenets of modernism but was slightly different from other early twentieth-century movements in its nationalistic agenda to rebuild German industry. In the 1930s and 1940s, efforts to codify universal form as a language were apparent in the work of Otto Neurath and Rudolf Modley (see pp. 156–57). This led to similar efforts in the second half of the century by Otl Aicher and the design office of Cook and Shanosky (see pp. 127–28). In the

UNIVERSAL

An unchanging entity or quality that transcends the individual, culture, or time. Under modernism, it was thought that there were universal metanarratives— enduring abstract ideas that ordered and explained historical experience and knowledge.

1950s the International Typographic Style developed in Switzerland and shaped the practices of late modernism throughout the remainder of the century.

lévi-strauss and the structural analysis of myth

The twentieth-century concept that there are universal principles and codes that owe nothing to cultural experience was bolstered by activity in anthropology and sociology. For example, the modern structuralist analysis of myth by the French anthropologist Claude Lévi-Strauss (1908–2009) furthered the belief that universal, elemental form was possible. Studying myths in various cultures, Lévi-Strauss found the same basic elements in stories—variations on a limited number of themes that had nothing to do with their cultural origins. He believed that, like language in general, myths gain meaning only when these basic thematic units are combined according to a set of universal rules that guide their ordering. The true meaning of the narrative, therefore, resides well below the surface of the story, in its fundamental structure, not in its obvious subject matter.

For Lévi-Strauss, these relational structures are inherent in the human mind and determine how we classify and organize reality. For example, myths frequently involve binary oppositions, as in good and evil, dark and light, or air and water. He believed that these are the same contradictions of daily life that we try to resolve in our minds. The myth simply mirrors our own universal experience of being human. Lévi-Strauss is credited with the notion that people in so-called "primitive" and "advanced" societies use the same intellectual *bricolage*, or mythical thought, that pieces together stories from the elements at hand, but within a limited repertoire of themes.[16]

He also asserted that repetition of these relationships within the single myth is necessary to reveal their universal nature; the key elements are repeated with slight variations in each layer, spinning the story outward but echoing the same basic structure.[17] This structuralist view of consciousness is less concerned with the particular individual who does the thinking, or what he or she thinks about, than with the nature of consciousness itself, with the way of mentally processing or making sense of the work that is universal and fundamentally human.

the plastic universal of futurism

These ideas were consistent with those of avant-garde European designers, who for political and social reasons rejected the romanticized, individualized visual language of the previous century. In 1909 the Italian poet and editor Filippo Tommaso Marinetti (see p. 111) declared the formation of the futurist movement on the cover of the French newspaper *Le Figaro*. In regularly published manifestos beginning in 1910, the futurists proclaimed that the experience of living in a new century should be captured in art and design by **DYNAMIC SENSATION**, as an expression of the transformation of social and economic structures of the past into new ones as the universal essence of the modern experience.[18] The futurist notion of the **PLASTIC UNIVERSAL**, a set of mostly geometric forms that embodied modern life, was a rebuttal to the idea of individual, subjective observation. Futurist typographic compositions were filled with representations of sound and movement and arranged in ways that destabilized the traditional

DYNAMIC SENSATION

The futurists' term for the idea that objects and forms are in constant motion and in constantly changing relationships with each other and their environment. This concept reflects the futurists' interest in speed and the machine.

PLASTIC UNIVERSAL

The futurists' term for a set of mostly geometric forms that embodied modern life and that were to be experienced directly, without the illusionistic conventions of previous artistic approaches.

interpretations of text (SEE FIGURES 4.2–4.3). The printed page was experienced in the shared present, not in terms of culturally specific ways of treating type, and its elements were designed to confront the reader with the universal sensibilities of distinctly modern times.

For the futurists, the modern experience was also a technological one, a universality of the machine and function. Typographic form captured mechanical repetition, frequently through patterns of diacritical marks and mathematical symbols, and made use of ruled lines and shapes as elements that alluded to typesetting and mechanical production. But as the historian Christopher Crouch points out, futurist declarations of the universality of dynamic sensation presented an inherent dichotomy.[19] If circumstances are dynamic, they cannot, by definition, be stable; and if they are unstable, how can they be codified in a universal style? In other words, the goal of universality bumps into the problem of time.

5.22 *DE STIJL*, 1917
Cover designed by Theo van Doesburg (1883–1931) and Vilmos Huszár (1884–1960)
British Library, London

the universal elements of de stijl

The modernist de Stijl movement in the Netherlands was also based on a search for universal elements and principles of form. De Stijl artists, designers, and architects explored a visual language reduced to its most essential components, consisting of straight lines, right angles, and primary colors (red, blue, and yellow) with the addition of black, white, and gray. Unlike the Dadaists and the futurists, whose aim was often to disrupt the conventional perceptions of form and space, the "content" of de Stijl design was viewed as the harmony that could be revealed only through abstraction, not through references to objects in the natural world.

The goal of the loosely organized members of this movement was to create a new way of living, a social outcome through physical form. The de Stijl artists and designers, led by the Dutch designer Theo van Doesburg, who had a history in the Dada movement, saw writing and graphic design as a way of promoting these ideas. Like the futurists, de Stijl designers used the small magazine as a forum for publishing their thoughts (SEE FIGURE 5.22). A de Stijl manifesto of 1918 stressed the symbolic relationship between art and life. The aim was to gain in life a precision found in the machine (as expressed through geometry) and to overcome the political and social chaos of the times. In stripping visual form of all but its most basic elements, the de Stijl designers hoped to "purify" the vocabulary and grammar of the arts, to free it from the unique perceptions of the individual artist or viewer, as well as from any given time or specific version of reality.

The Dutch position on universality and individuality is not surprising, given the neutral status of the Netherlands during World War I and concurrent interests in theosophy (a nineteenth-century school of religious thought that

5.23 DUTCH CABLE FACTORY
CATALOG PAGE, 1928
Piet Zwart (1885–1977)

5.24 *MECANO* MAGAZINE, 1922
Theo van Doesburg (1883–1931)

The visual language of the de Stijl movement—geometric forms, primary colors, straight lines, and right angles—is evident in works by different artists and designers, including Mondrian in painting, Rietveld in architecture and furniture design, and Van Doesburg and Huszar in graphic design. Such forms were considered universal, with the power to bring harmony to life through their visual purity.

5.25 SCHRÖDER HOUSE, 1924–25
Gerrit Rietveld (1888–1964)
Utrecht, the Netherlands

aimed to unify world religions under a single belief system) and Esperanto (a language that was created in the nineteenth century to act as a universal written and spoken language). Dutch designers considered the turmoil of war as a struggle to destroy the individualism associated with the old world. They turned their backs on the notion that art, politics, and society were about the temperament and personal stories of individuals. Far greater importance was placed on universal principles, for which time and context were irrelevant, and on shared values and codes. Harmony and balance between the individual and the universal were seen as the desirable outcomes of such struggle. As with Lévi-Strauss's myths, visual and spatial forms were not tied to the particular instance of their use, but were subject to universal laws for their combination and recombination.

The similarities in form in the works of de Stijl artists and designers reveal a common belief in essential form. The architecture of Gerrit Rietveld (1888–1964), the paintings of Piet Mondrian (1872–1944), and the designs of van Doesburg show loyalty to principles held by all members of the movement. Like Lévi-Strauss's notion that basic structures underlie any myth, regardless of the variations introduced in the specific telling of the story, the work of the de Stijl movement is grounded in a conviction that geometric abstraction transcends the individual experiences of artists and the utilitarian functions of objects. Rietveld uses the same visual vocabulary in his red, blue, and yellow chair, for example, as in the house he designed for Truus Schröder-Schräder in Utrecht (SEE FIGURE 5.25). Panels in the house slide to reconfigure the use of interior rooms. Just like Lévi-Strauss's concept that myths spiral out through theme and variation but remain true to the underlying structure, Rietveld's design is flexible but operates within an established set of rules for harmonious form. Surrounded by traditional Dutch architecture, the Schröder house was a "model for the future, a symbol of a new way of living."[20]

the nationalistic tendencies of the bauhaus

The Bauhaus represents arguably the best known of the early modernist movements in design. Its reputation benefited from a strong organizational structure as a school and a collaborative practice, and from ideas that were spread by its expatriates, who later fled Germany during World War II. The Bauhaus opened in Weimar, Germany, in 1919, rising out of the ashes of World War I. Bauhaus designers sought an expressive visual language to promote the industrial prowess of Germany at a time when the country needed to rebuild its economy. The nation was saddled with reparations as punishment for waging war, and its once-efficient industry had been decimated. Positioned geographically between the Netherlands and the Soviet Union, German designers benefited from proximity to the influences of de Stijl and Russian constructivism.[21] While many other modernist movements of this time were grounded in philosophy and political activism, though, the Bauhaus stood alone in its overriding interest in commerce, industry, and the very practical work of improving the ordinary lives of German citizens. Its agenda was therefore nationalistic—to restore the spirit of Germany—but its strategy was the elemental visual language of modernism.

abcdefghi
jklmnopqr
stuvwxyz

5.26 UNIVERSAL TYPE DESIGN, 1925
Herbert Bayer (1900–1985)

Bauhaus designers had the practical goal of restoring Germany's industrial reputation after World War I, by means of the creation of functional objects that embodied the principles of good design and an authentic use of twentieth-century materials. These principles were propagated through a rigorous and philosophically driven curriculum at the school and brought to the United States when Bauhaus designers fled Germany at the onset of World War II. First-year experiences in today's American and European design schools still show much allegiance to the Bauhaus curriculum, despite its original nationalistic intention to address the prevailing conditions of early twentieth-century Germany.

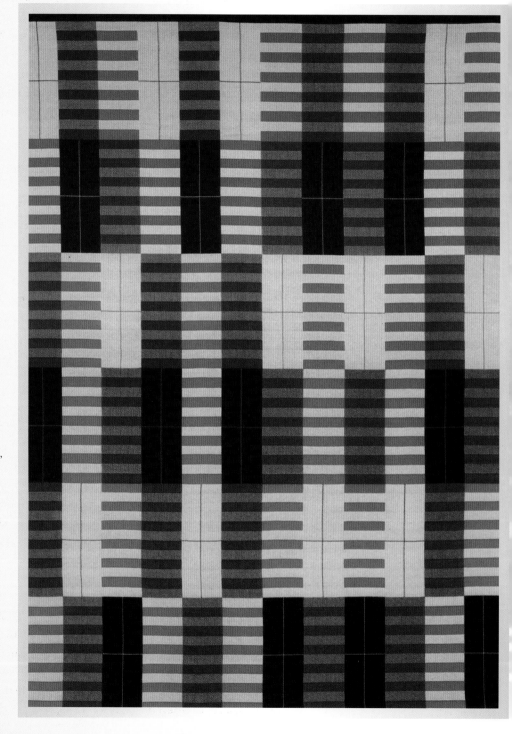

5.27 WALL HANGING, 1926
Anni Albers (1899–1994)

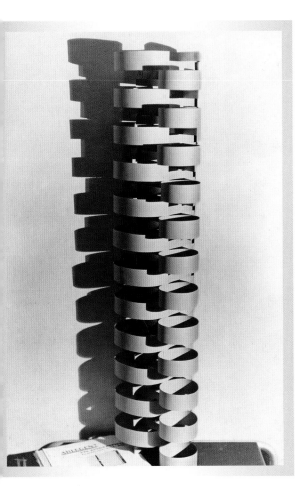

5.28 PAPERFOLDING EXERCISE
FROM THE PRELIMINARY COURSE AT
THE BAUHAUS, 1928
Gustav Hassenpflug (1907–1977)
Bauhaus-Archiv, Berlin

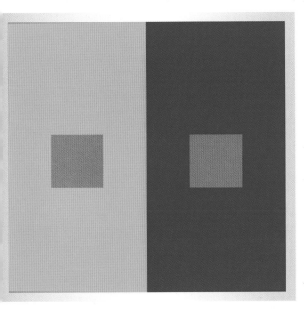

5.29 COLOR INTERACTION
Based on an image in Josef Albers, *The
Interaction of Color,* 1975 edition (first
published 1963)

But this is not to say that the ideas of the Bauhaus lacked theoretical grounding or concepts about universal form. In the 1920s and 1930s, architecture in Germany responded to the New Objectivity, an approach to design that had begun under the Deutscher Werkbund (German Work Federation), a state-supported collective of designers and industrialists that experimented with new materials and methods of production. Encouraged by the German architect and diplomat Hermann Muthesius (1861–1927), a proponent and careful observer of the Arts and Crafts Movement in England, the goal of the Werkbund was a social one—to transform German cities through standardized principles of design and manufacturing that unified form and function for a new style of living.[22]

With its aim of unifying the arts in one combined practice, the Bauhaus shared the Arts and Crafts Movement's values of restoring the quality of production and authenticity of materials to everyday objects. But it also recognized the economic and technological imperatives of the times. A number of key members of the movement had socialist roots and believed that technology served the industrial worker by bringing about a changed world that lacked any concern for class or tradition. Gone, however, were the Arts and Crafts Movement's concern for hand labor and nature as sources of inspiration. These were replaced by the universal language of function, mechanical production, and the visual logic of new materials (SEE FIGURES 5.26–5.27).

The school's curriculum presented an opportunity to propagate Bauhaus principles. It emphasized the goal of universality through exercises in abstraction, such as the experiments in color and materials by the designers/painters Josef Albers (1888–1976) and Johannes Itten (1888–1967) (SEE FIGURES 5.28–5.29). Albers was described as leaving students alone in a room with a single sheet of paper until they stumbled on its structural potential through scoring and folding. His lessons in the interaction of color isolated abstract visual concepts (for example, making one color look like two) as a precursor to their use within specific contexts—an attempt to describe an underlying universal vocabulary of visual phenomena that eclipses cultural circumstances. Again, such understanding was achieved through direct sensory experience, not through the artifice of representational artistic conventions. This pedagogical strategy, later promoted in the United States by expatriated Bauhaus teachers at the start of World War II, formed the basis of design education in the West for most of the twentieth century and still persists at the foundation level in many college and university design programs.

Such ideas as these threatened right-wing politicians and the Bauhaus school was closed in 1925. The Third Reich (1933–45) found the heroic architecture of Albert Speer (SEE FIGURE 5.30) more compatible with its aspirations to create buildings that were distinctly German and expressive of Hitler's sense of Nazi grandeur. The Bauhaus reopened in Dessau later in 1925, closed again in 1932, and after a brief time in Berlin its faculty fled to other parts of the world to escape the political strife in Europe.

the universal picture language of otto neurath

Some modern attempts at universality had very practical missions. Otto Neurath (1882–1945), an Austrian philosopher and social scientist who directed the International Foundation of Visual Education in the Hague, developed an international picture language he called ISOTYPE (International System Of Typographic Picture Education). In a book of 1936, instructing designers, educators, and scientists in the use of ISOTYPE, Neurath states the goal of the system as being "independent of the knowledge of language, because pictures, whose details are clear to everyone, are free from the limits of language .... WORDS MAKE DIVISION, PICTURES MAKE CONNECTION."[23] He saw reading pictures as a universal experience that could be applied to the translation of statistical data, scientific explanations, and the problems of transnational travel (SEE FIGURE 5.31). A true modernist, Neurath's system was a kit of signs that he treated like letters of the alphabet, setting them in lines and in combination with other signs.

Neurath expressed through the system what he believed people understood inherently through observation. He said, "The sign 'man' has not to give the idea of a special person . . . but to be representative of the animal 'man'."[24] Neurath's human icons were formally economical but detailed, their constituent parts combining according to the rules of the system as described in his manual. Neurath's modernist utopian vision was that everyone could learn to read and write his iconic picture language as a reasonable and culturally neutral substitute for verbal language.

In an article in the scholarly journal *Visible Language* in 2008, Jae Young Lee describes Neurath's work as a "rhetoric of neutrality," borrowing from the phrase used by the British typographer Robin Kinross.[25] The ISOTYPE appears to be free from cultural bias, seemingly neutral in its stripped-down visual explanation of statistics and international travel. But as Lee points out, there is a strong rhetorical component in the very notion of representing cultural conditions, and such representations can never be bias-free.[26] Imagine today's Asian population being represented by the conical straw hat of peasant farmers. Lee goes on to cite the rhetoric professor Richard A. Lanham's concepts of "looking through" and "looking at." In the former, the reader goes straight

5.30 HITLER'S REICH CHANCELLERY, 1938
Albert Speer (1905–1981)
Berlin, Germany

(*Opposite*): Modley continued Neurath's work to develop a universal picture language for the communication of information relating to travel, science, and statistics. The same goal of universality is evident in the work of Aicher for the 1972 Munich Olympics, but with growing sensitivity to cultural issues, Aicher's work eliminated obvious references to gender, class, and nationality. He systematized form in ways that were consistent with the principles of late modernism: a standard set of body parts moves on a grid.

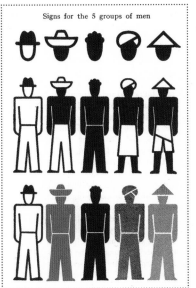

Signs for the 5 groups of men

5.31 IMAGES FROM
INTERNATIONAL PICTURE LANGUAGE:
THE FIRST RULES OF ISOTYPE, 1936
Otto Neurath (1882–1945)

5.32 ISOTYPES, 1930S AND 1940S
Rudolf Modley (1906–1976) with Karl
Kohler, Henry Adams Grant, John Carnes,
and others. As shown in *Handbook of*
Pictorial Symbols, 1976

to the literal content of the sign—the physical form of the text or image is "transparent."[27] In the latter, style or form is a carrier of meaning—the reader considers the surface as well as the content. Neurath's modernist assumption was that the ISOTYPE was free from the cultural bias of style and that readers would "look through" the form to the content.

Neurath's project continued under Rudolf Modley (SEE FIGURE 5.32) and provided the ideological grounding for the work of Otl Aicher's design for the 1972 Munich Olympics (SEE FIGURE 5.33) and Cook and Shanosky's work for the American Institute of Graphic Arts and the U.S. Department of Transportation in 1974 (SEE FIGURE 5.34). While the modernist intention to create universal form shaped the design of all of these solutions, we can see increasing concern across the decades for eliminating cultural references and tightening the rules of the system to promote less variation in interpretation. Modley's work communicated issues of gender, class, and race. In the Cook and Shanosky system, these issues have been ignored or simplified as a singular, anonymous reference to clothing.

the international typographic style

The concept of universal form reached a pinnacle of expression in the International Typographic Style of the mid-twentieth century. Begun in Switzerland in the 1950s under such advocates as Ernst Keller, Max Bill, and Theo Ballmer (many with connections to earlier modernist movements), the style argued for neutrality, clarity, and privileging the content of text over its form. Compositions were characterized by the modernist preferences for asymmetry, geometry, and highly refined levels of contrast (SEE FIGURE 5.35).

Like other modern movements, formal harmony in the International Typographic Style was achieved through a grid—ideal, mathematical divisions of the page that controlled the size and placement of elements (see also p. 147). Consistent with the "Manifesto of Concrete Art," introduced by van Doesburg in the magazine *Art Concret* in 1930, Concrete Art focused on abstraction, free from any attempt to imitate reality or indulge in symbolism. Instead, what was "real" was the pure, concrete experience of line, shape, and color. Swiss designers believed that the use of geometry would liberate art from any allegiance to observed reality or to the symbolism of the past.[28] Such art owed nothing to personal interpretation. Its structure was thought to

5.33 PICTOGRAPHS FOR THE
MUNICH OLYMPICS, 1972
Otl Aicher (1922–1991)

5.34 SIGNAGE SYMBOL SYSTEM FOR
AMERICAN INSTITUTE OF GRAPHIC
ARTS AND THE U.S. DEPARTMENT OF
TRANSPORTATION, 1974
Roger Cook (b. 1930) and Don
Shanosky (b. 1937)

reflect the universality of thought and more general conceptions of the human mind, even when the composition consisted of text and photographic images that carried their own specific connotations.

Sans-serif typefaces and a ragged right (asymmetrical) column style served the precisionist character of Swiss design by maintaining a uniformity of strokes and spaces within and between letters and words. Contrast and hierarchy were achieved through variations in size, weight, and proportion within the same type family, rather than through the combination of different styles. Adrian Frutiger's design from 1954 of a sans-serif type family [SEE FIGURE 4.7], appropriately called Univers, provided maximum opportunity for achieving such contrast through a disciplined, incremental system of typographic variations. Despite changes in stroke widths and counter spaces across the twenty-one variations, each typeface has the same x-height, ascenders, and descenders, allowing it to be combined with others in the system in perfect visual harmony. Numbered categories indicate any family member's place within the system; the first digit represents weight (regular or bold, for example), while the second digit signifies proportion (extended or condensed, for example). Once again, universal logic set the boundaries for formal contrasts.

By the end of the twentieth century, however, it was clear that the issue of style was inescapable. Even in embracing the most irreducible of geometric forms, designers of the twentieth century created distinctive and identifiable forms that can be placed in history and associated with particular aspects of modern culture.

5.35   POSTER FOR THE EXHIBITION NEUES BAUEN (NEW BUILDING), 1928
Theo Ballmer (1902–1965)
Museum für Gestaltung, Zürich, Graphics Collection

The International Typographic Style valued neutrality and clarity in form and message. The grid and typographic systems—designed for measured contrast—were applied in ordered, asymmetrical compositions. Reflecting the voice of the designer mattered far less than the straightforward presentation of content.

THE TROUBLESOME ISSUES OF CLASS AND STYLE

Designers have always grappled with the issue of whose values should be of most concern to them: those of wealthy patrons and clients who can afford design services, or those of everyday people whose quality of life is improved by the products of designers' efforts. Such values are often expressed through style and the choice of materials. In *All-Consuming Images* (1988), the historian Stuart Ewen (see p. 60) traces our modern fascination with style to the fourteenth and fifteenth centuries, when feudal lords established sumptuary laws governing the wearing of apparel. By the 1500s, in some parts of Europe, brocade and velvet were worn only by the nobility.[29] Wealthy homes, says Ewen, were filled with highly crafted, style-conscious furniture and decorative objects designed to communicate the good taste and social status of their owners. Poor homes, by contrast, included just the bare necessities and were usually constructed by local craftsmen using humble materials and construction methods. The growth of mercantile trade expanded the market in objects and the rise of commercial centers over the next century, making it increasingly possible to acquire artistic items for the home and personal use as a confirmation of social standing.

The corollary to style is the concept of **TASTE**, an interpretation "informed by experiences related to one's **SOCIAL CLASS**, cultural background, education, and other aspects of identity."[30] The French sociologist Pierre Bourdieu (1930–2002) studied the notion of taste in the 1970s and argued that it was not inherent in particular people but learned through "institutions that promote certain class-based assumptions about correct taste."[31] He described the correspondence between *goods production* and *taste production*, stating that "a cultural product . . . is charged with the legitimizing, reinforcing capacity which objectification always possesses . . . especially when [assigned] to a prestigious group."[32] So if taste could be acquired through exposure to styles that transform one's own sense of class and that embody the ideologies of their times, then it is easy to understand why modern designers thought that design could achieve positive social effects. By being surrounded by objects that exemplify "good taste," "harmony," or some other desirable social construct, the middle classes could be taught values that were not part of their formal education, upbringing, or current environment. And for the more rebellious avant-garde, form could actually disrupt the ideological comfort of the complacent middle and upper classes, who used stylistic conventions as symbols for the "rightness" of dominant social values.

The public appetite for style was fueled by the mass production of the Industrial Revolution. Nineteenth-century factories and standardization expanded public access to manufactured goods, and changed the value of image. A new "'consumer democracy' . . . was founded on the idea that the symbols and prerogatives of the elite could now be made available on a mass scale."[33] Cheaper and more abundant goods, made possible by mass production, transformed the signification of objects. Now the middle class could afford things that resembled the possessions of the wealthy, however shoddy their construction or use of faux materials. In many cases, the decorative arts became a social indicator. According to Ewen, as technological advancements encouraged the imitation of styles that were previously accessible only to the upper class, appearance emerged as a commodity to be bought and sold.

The craving for elitist images associated with upward mobility, and the unsuitability of such images to the production processes and materials of the machine age, presented challenges to modern designers, as the following

TASTE

Stuart Ewen uses this term to refer to an interpretation informed by experiences related to one's social class, cultural background, education, and other aspects of identity.

SOCIAL CLASS

The hierarchical arrangement of people in groups according to economic or cultural criteria.

discussions illustrate. The Arts and Crafts Movement was a humanist response to such obstacles at the turn of the century. Because style was associated with the aristocracy and wealth, later design movements used modern form to express social unrest. Dada occupied a brief period, beginning in 1916, and had proponents in Switzerland, Germany, France, and the Netherlands. Russian constructivism began around the same time and served a revolutionary spirit that sought the end of a Tsarist monarchy and the inception of an egalitarian society.

In the decades that followed, designers used style to further social agendas. Architectural projects to improve worker housing and the quality of factory environments used a new visual language to advance the utopian ambitions of democracy and socialism.

the public appetite for style

The stylistic transformation of materials and their aesthetic worth was therefore an impetus for modern design. But the task of accomplishing social change by this means was not easy, given the designer's status in nineteenth-century industrialized nations. In London in 1851, the Great Exhibition—often described as the first world's fair—included a staggering display of the latest examples of technology and manufactured goods from the Industrial Revolution. The event symbolized Britain's industrial dominance in the world and the importance of science and technology in nineteenth-century culture. Housed in the Crystal Palace (SEE FIGURE 5.36), a glass and cast-iron structure of nearly 1,000,000 square feet (over 90,000 square meters), the exhibition attracted more than 6,000,000 visitors. But to the lament of many modern designers, it also demonstrated that the greater and more stylistically superficial the machine ornamentation of mass-produced objects, the greater was the public interest in buying them.[34] Manufacturers resurrected motifs from the past, using established stylistic value to sell the mass-produced artifacts of the new technology (SEE FIGURE 5.37). New materials imitated the physical properties and production methods of pre-industrial goods, playing on nostalgia and associations with an upper class that could afford one-of-a-kind, hand-made artifacts in their homes.

The public fascination with acquiring material goods continued and marketing strategies evolved as the consuming public became more savvy. By the end of the nineteenth century, the emergence of the department store had redefined the relationship between women and commercial culture. Bolstered by the success of the Paris Exposition of 1900, where objects of desire triumphed over the more intellectual notion of technological progress, wealthy consumers demonstrated their power to spend on things they wanted, not just on the bare necessities for survival. An emphasis on seeing, often through large display windows, replaced the importance of touch and smell in the open markets of earlier times and prompted the French poet Charles Baudelaire (1821–1867) to write about the **FLÂNEUR**, a detached wanderer who strolled the city and simply observed urban life.[35] In his writings about the style-driven spectacle of commerce and the modern city, the German cultural critic

5.36 THE GREAT EXHIBITION BUILDING, 1851
Joseph Paxton (1803–1865)

The "Crystal Palace" was a showplace for a burgeoning array of products of the Industrial Revolution. These objects replicated styles associated with prevailing notions of "good taste" and wealth. Modern materials of mass production imitated things that had once been made by hand, separating *form* from *substance*.

5.37 CLOCK, 1851
From the official catalog to the Great Exhibition

MODERNISM

Gothic Revival and Neoclassicism were popular architectural styles in the eighteenth and nineteenth centuries. The image of buildings depended less on the rationale of their construction than on the symbolism of their stylistic precedents. An ancient temple was the inspiration for Jefferson's state capitol building, sending a message about the values of the Roman Republic as his model for American government. By contrast, modernist buildings express the structural logic through which they stand up and enclose space.

5.38   THE PALACE OF WESTMINSTER, 1836–68
Sir Charles Barry (1795–1860)

5.39   VIRGINIA STATE CAPITOL BUILDING, 1788
Thomas Jefferson (1743–1826)
Richmond, Virginia

5.40   MAISON CARRÉE, *c.* 16 BCE
Nîmes, France

Walter Benjamin (1892–1940) described the nineteenth-century Paris shopping arcades as "internal streets" for window shopping. Much like today's "mall rats," modern consumers wanted both to see and to be seen, creating an appetite for constantly changing visual appearance, status-conscious style, and the consumption of material goods.

Consumer goods were not the only forms of nineteenth-century design that were subject to public taste. Buildings, once expressions of tectonic forces (columns and load-bearing walls, for example), were wrapped in decorative skins that were more image than structure. Gothic Revival architecture [SEE FIGURE 5.38], for example, flourished in the nineteenth century, evoking an elitist past associated with the monarchy. Neoclassicism [SEE FIGURE 5.39], much simpler in form and popular in the United States, expressed a longing to return to the ideals of ancient Rome and Greece [SEE FIGURE 5.40].

Commercial manufacturing and new construction practices, therefore, often separated *form* from *substance*. Cast iron, a new building material of the Industrial Revolution, could be given any shape and could resemble any of the more traditional building materials, such as hand-carved stone. The cast-iron column, because of its obvious strength and mass production, was used throughout the nineteenth century without regard for visual proportion or expression of its load-bearing function. The architectural critic Sigfried Giedion (1888–1968), in his *Space, Time, and Architecture* (1941), described these buildings as "walls of chocolate works,"[36] which relegated the meaning of style to surface ornamentation and a lack of material authenticity. Giedion went on to attribute such lack of stylistic restraint to public sentimentality about the past:

Perhaps the most characteristic feature of nineteenth-century architecture is its addiction to 'period pieces.' The important buildings, all those edifices from which the spectator imagined himself to gain serious aesthetic impression, appeared in elaborate historical dress....Advances in building technique seemed to have brought with them only the practical problems in using new methods to produce old effects.[37]

form follows function

As a result, for the modernists who sought social progress, "style" was a dirty word—it was something dishonest, not to be trusted, the antithesis of function. Modern designers decried the ornament and form that were associated with historicism, with nostalgia for a specific past and places that no longer existed, and with an aristocracy that was becoming increasingly irrelevant to the political and social agenda. Such decoration was also at odds with the machine-driven economies at the turn of the century. In response to these conditions, modern architects and product designers stripped buildings and objects of their articulated surfaces. The form of modern design revealed the underlying structural and functional principles through which they were organized, just as industrial machines carried no extraneous styling in their functional forms (SEE FIGURES 5.41-5.42).

This polarization of style and function can be found in many modernist writings. The modern architect Louis Sullivan (1856–1924) coined the phrase "form follows function" in a popular magazine shortly before the turn of the century:

It is the pervading law of all things organic and inorganic, of all things physical and metaphysical, of all things human and all things superhuman, of all true manifestations of the head, of the heart, of the soul, that the life is recognizable in its expression, that form ever follows function. This is the law . . . . Is it really then, a very marvelous thing, or is it rather so commonplace, so everyday, so near a thing to us, that we cannot perceive that the shape, form, outward expression, design or whatever we may choose, of the tall office building should in the very nature of things follow the functions of the building, and that where the function does not change, the form is not to change?[38]

An essay by the Austrian architect Adolf Loos (1870–1933), "Crime and Ornament" (1929), went further and declared ornament to be immoral and an obstacle to cultural progress. He wrote, "The evolution of culture is synonymous with the removal of ornamentation from objects of everyday use . . . . The ornament being created now bears no relationship to us, not to any human being, or the system governing the world today."[39] The German architect Ludwig Mies van der Rohe (1886–1969), once head of the Bauhaus and later director of the

5.41   WAINWRIGHT BUILDING, 1890–91
Louis Sullivan (1856–1924)
St. Louis, Missouri

5.42   CROWN HALL, ILLINOIS INSTITUTE OF TECHNOLOGY, 1956
Ludwig Mies van der Rohe (1886–1969)
Chicago, Illinois

Armour Institute of Technology (now Illinois Institute of Technology), was often quoted as saying "less is more," a phrase that came to stand for the late modernist ideal of simplicity in all things.

Such derision of ornament was echoed in graphic design. In an explanation of typography in a special issue of *Typographische Mitteilungen* in 1925, Jan Tschichold stated that "elemental designing excludes the use of any ornament .... The use of rules and inherently elemental forms (squares, circles, triangles) must be convincingly grounded in the total construction."[40] Tschichold saw the use of ornament as "childish naivety," "a giving-in to a primitive instinct to decorate . . . a fear of pure appearance."[41] In the modernist sensibility, such superficial uses of style had nothing to do with the reading experience. Tschichold describes ornamental type as being understood only by its contour, not by the movement of the eye from one piece of text to another by virtue of visual contrast in weight, size, placement, color, and so on.

The modernist movement therefore began with the belief that in style lay wistful longing for a past that was mired in problems of social class, outdated notions of workmanship, and the illogic of forms that were no longer an expression of progress and the modern experience.

the arts and crafts movement

But the shift to modernist values regarding function over style was not accomplished overnight or without more moderate positions on the issues of form. The Arts and Crafts Movement revolted against the churning out of poorly manufactured goods and provided visual contrast to both the excess of earlier styles and the spare, minimalist forms that were to follow. Its artists and craftsmen found delight in simple materials and references to nature. Under the example of William Morris (1834–1896), the initial goal of the movement was to provide fine design for every home. This constituted a critique of mass-produced form and the loss of individuality and **CRAFTSMANSHIP** that was brought about by the Industrial Revolution and exemplified by the exhibitions of 1851 and 1900. Morris, and his often socialist collaborators, valued hand skills because they allowed the intrinsic quality of materials to surface ("truth to materials") and expressed the individuality of workers (SEE FIGURE 5.43)—qualities that were thought to have been sublimated by machine production. Working together, these artists and designers developed a collective style that liberated them from the tyranny of fashion and drew its inspiration from function and forms in nature.

Morris was best known for his fabric, wallpaper, and interior design but he also maintained the craft of fine book design through the Kelmscott Press (SEE FIGURES 5.44-5.45). His designs were reactions to commercial lithography that produced poor imitations of earlier woodcut prints. Influenced by medieval **ILLUMINATED MANUSCRIPTS**, Morris's borders and typeface designs emphasized the long traditions of printing and fine book design. His books were made to be read slowly, to be savored. In a world increasingly defined by sans-serif type and advertising, Morris intended his books to have "a definite claim to beauty, while at the same time they should be easy to read and should not dazzle the eye, or trouble the intellect of the reader by eccentricity of form in the letters."[42]

CRAFTSMANSHIP

An ability of great skill, usually acquired through training. The mastery of materials and tools, combined with knowledge of when to use them to accomplish the best results.

ILLUMINATED MANUSCRIPT

A text adorned with decoration (e.g. ornate borders and elaborate initial letters at the start of paragraphs).

5.43 HILL HOUSE CHAIR, 1902–3
Charles Rennie Mackintosh (1868–1928)
Black lacquered ash

5.44 ACANTHUS WALLPAPER, 1875
William Morris (1834–1896)

In other words, he sought a balance between utility and style, a goal typical of the Arts and Crafts Movement. By contrast, the word "beauty" rarely appears in other modernist writing.

The Arts and Crafts Movement emphasized the beauty of humble materials and also introduced the notion that middle-class ladies and gentlemen could earn money as designers of furniture and textiles without jeopardizing their social standing. But it had little impact on the social lives of the working class it sought to elevate and inspire through well-designed objects and environments. Its processes and organization of labor shared more in common with medieval guilds than with life and work in twentieth-century industrial towns.[43] "What mattered was the harmony between maker and materials, maker and the rhythm of life, maker and the purpose for which the object was intended; art was to do with integrity."[44] Such an approach produced objects that were simply too expensive for all but the wealthy to afford. The original populist mission, to raise the standard of quality and taste in working-class homes, was unachievable in a market-driven economy. And by the end of the nineteenth century, the Arts and Crafts Movement's style had been reduced to an established visual language for home interiors, what the historian Christopher Crouch calls a "superficial coding of rusticity and tradition to provide an escape from the industrial present."[45]

MODERNISM

5.45 FIRST PAGE OF THE KELMSCOTT EDITION OF *THE CANTERBURY TALES*, 1896
Designed by William Morris (1834–1896)
Illustrated by Edward Burne-Jones (1833–1898)
British Library, London

The Arts and Crafts Movement was a design response to the poor quality of mass-produced goods available to the average consumer in the late nineteenth century. Using nature as inspiration, designers espoused "truth to materials" and prided themselves on fine craftsmanship. Although these designers were organized as an artisan guild, the individuality of their work was a primary goal.

style in the service of social and economic change

Suspicion of style was matched by growing mistrust of the upper class and the bourgeoisie, who controlled wealth and the working conditions of the poor. Political and philosophical movements across Europe in the first decades of the new century challenged the longstanding authority of the elite and focused attention on the lives of workers. The legendary chant of Karl Marx (1818–1883) professed that "The proletarians have nothing to lose but their chains . . . . Workingmen of all countries, unite!" and was well known by the end of the nineteenth century.

The Dadaists were among those who were most irreverent toward the socially elite. Founded in Zürich, Switzerland in 1916, the Dada movement quickly spread to other European cities (including Paris, Berlin, and Moscow) and was characterized by its disrespectful, intentionally incoherent attacks on high culture. The Dadaists felt the "low culture" images of commerce—"found" typography and illustrations from advertising and billboards—would agitate their bourgeois audiences into self-reflection. Unsuccessful in building support among the working class, these antagonists alienated many traditional patrons of the arts, deftly using negative publicity and scandal to promote the cause among members of their small group. In 1920, under organizer Tristan Tzara (1896–1963), the group furthered its agenda to undermine the artistic establishment through typographic compositions that defied the prevailing rules of "good" typographic form [SEE FIGURES 5.46-5.48]. While the formal character of Dadaist work shared much in common with the futurists, its purpose was not to celebrate the technological advancements and optimism of a new century. Its aim was to challenge the conventions that defined good taste and the social status quo through chaotic, absurd compositions and performances that often made no sense. Ultimately, the group's success was also its demise. The same antagonism that inspired Dadaist work resulted in bickering and infighting, and the movement fell apart in the early 1920s.

Eventually, the debate about the role of design in the new century shifted. It was no longer a matter of whether design should further a social agenda, but of finding the appropriate aesthetic form and materials for expressing the ideas of democracy and socialism. Workshops and collaborations of artists, writers, and designers formed under a variety of manifestos, each advocating practices "free from middle-class overtones of individualism" and espousing functionalism.[46] Many of these movements believed that good design could raise the standard of living for all, including the working class, but their

The Dada movement used the "low culture" images of advertising, in open defiance of principles of "good form," to attack and antagonize the upper classes and the status quo.

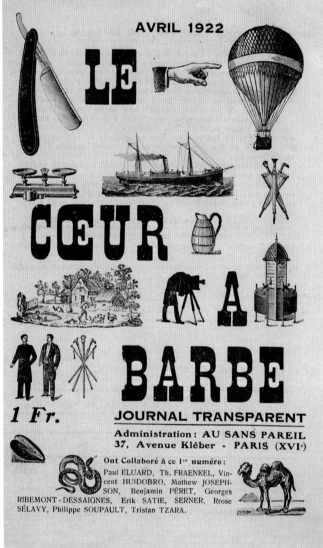

5.46 *LE COEUR A BARBE*, 1922
Tristan Tzara (1896–1963)

5.47 *DER DADA*, NO. 3, APRIL 1920
John Heartfield (1891–1968)

5.48 *DER DADA*, NO. 6, FEBRUARY 1920
Tristan Tzara (1896–1963)

5.49   FAGUS SHOE FACTORY,
1911–13
Walter Gropius (1883–1969)
Alfeld (Leine), Germany

5.50   LOGO FOR FAGUS GMBH,
c. 1911
Max Hertwig (1881–1975)

Gropius's design of the Fagus shoe
factory was both a marketing response
to the stuffy competitor across the
street and an advertising strategy that
anticipated how the building would
look in photographs.

strategies were to partner with industry in such social undertakings by promis-
ing efficiency and an economy of production. New materials that were better
suited to industrial production would replace the labor-intensive ornament and
hand processes of the Arts and Crafts Movement. Rather than fail at unconvinc-
ing imitations of earlier elitist styles, design would celebrate these materials
for their own inherent properties and reflect the machine processes through
which they were formed. The Bauhaus weaver Anni Albers (1899–1994), for
example, wrote of new washable, light-reflective textiles that "would not suf-
focate us with their glamour but would retain the serviceable character useful
objects should have."[47]

The German architect Walter Gropius (1883–1969), founder of the Bauhaus,
had high ambitions for design as a means of economic progress at a time of
widespread anti-German sentiment. His design of 1911 for the Fagus shoe
factory [SEE FIGURE 5.49], with partner Adolf Meyer, epitomized stylistically what
the German factory needed to be in order to succeed in the twentieth century—
a visual exemplar of modern production, but also a reflection of the firm's
personality.[48] The building faced the competing Behrens shoe factory, housed
in a dark-brick industrial building. Gropius designed the Fagus factory's bright
yellow-brick-and-glass structure as a contrast to the older building across the
street, and its facade was as much a marketing image as a functional element of
the building. The owner of the Fagus factory, Carl Benscheidt, commissioned
the Werkbund artist Max Hertwig (1881–1975) to design the company's new
logo [SEE FIGURE 5.50] and to use a photograph of the building in his advertising.[49]
Although the building's design is often cited as a social response for improving
the conditions of industrial workers (by opening factory spaces to light and
air), the architectural historian Frederic J. Schwartz describes its façade as

"flattened and monumentalized," with "the technical information of the elevation sacrificed for the immediate impact of advertising."[50] In fact, the building was primarily administrative. The factory was in an adjacent one-story building. In this way, Gropius understood the link between style and economic progress.

style and the american dream

Things were different on the other side of the Atlantic. What started in Europe as a philosophical debate between old and new ideas about the nature of human experience and the role of art in social progress, emerged in the United States as a pragmatic response to growing commerce and the need to advertise. By the end of World War II, American modernism was all about style. While Europe was rebuilding from the devastation of two world wars, American industrial designers, such as Raymond Loewy (1893–1986), fashioned a romantic vision of speed, travel, and technology in the aerodynamic forms of "**STREAMLINING**." Advertising sold the American Dream of the modern home, complete with labor-saving conveniences, to housewives [SEE FIGURES 5.51–5.53]. And in 1947, the builder William Levitt announced his intention to build a planned community of "ranch" houses in New York that promised a new style of suburban living and low-cost production based on the postwar assembly line. In cities throughout America, modern architects transformed skylines with steel-and-glass skyscrapers that surpassed the height of buildings in Europe, changing the urban landscape forever.

American graphic designers, influenced by European modernists who immigrated to the United States between the two world wars, brought preferences for asymmetrical compositions, mechanically produced imagery, white space, and cohesive typographic systems to their work for government and industry [SEE FIGURES 5.54–5.56], where previously there had been little concern for appearance. Even publications that had little to do with purveying style as a commodity found design important when placed in expert hands. The illustrated diagrams and covers of *Fortune* magazine were in stark contrast to the sober, statistical translations of Otto Neurath in the 1930s [SEE FIGURES 5.31, 5.57]. Many of these immigrant designers (such as Dr. Agha, Alexei Brodovitch, and Will Burtin), as well as the Americans Lester Beall and Cipe Pineles (who immigrated to the United States at the age of thirteen), found work for cultural, design, and popular magazines where modern style was the currency [SEE FIGURES 5.54, 5.57–5.59]. As the century progressed, it was clear that style, even when spare in its formal vocabulary, was something that could not be avoided.

STREAMLINING

Designing the shape of a vehicle to provide the least resistance to air. Streamlined form was popular in the 1930s through the 1950s and was applied to products other than those related to transportation (e.g. irons and toasters).

5.51   GULF OIL ADVERTISEMENT, 1949

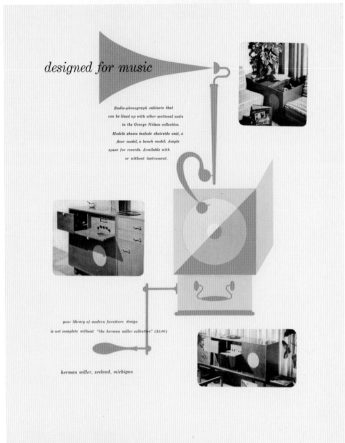

5.52 HERMAN MILLER
ADVERTISEMENT, 1947
George Nelson and Associates

5.53 HERMAN MILLER
ADVERTISEMENT, 1948
George Nelson and Associates

5.54 *SCOPE* MAGAZINE, 1955
Will Burtin (1908–1972)
Published by Upjohn
Pharmaceutical Company

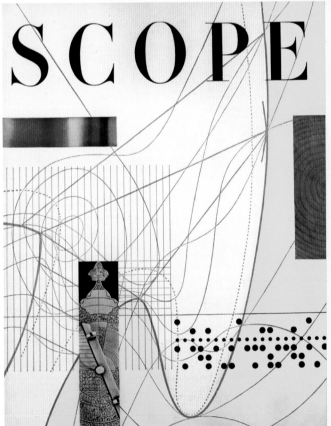

Modernism in America was influenced by designers who fled the chaos of the two world wars in Europe. But American design took on a different character that was born in the conditions of increasing prosperity; it was all about style and fueling consumption. The magazine was a primary vehicle for demonstrating how art and design could further the goals of commerce.

5.55   POSTER FOR THE
RURAL ELECTRIFICATION
ADMINISTRATION, 1937
Lester Beall (1903–1969)

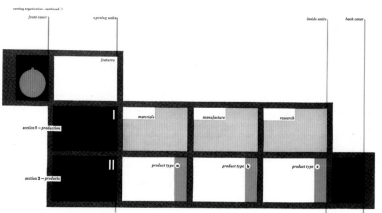

5.56   GRAPHIC IDENTITY FOR
SWEET'S CATALOG SERVICE, 1941
(top right and above)
Ladislav Sutnar (1897–1976)

5.57 COVER FOR *FORTUNE* MAGAZINE, October 1943
Herbert Matter (1907–1984)

5.58 PAGE ON CLOUDS FOR *WORLD GEOGRAPHIC ATLAS*, 1953
Herbert Bayer (1900–1985)

THE GROWTH OF ADVERTISING

This hunger for style was fueled by the burgeoning practice of advertising, the history of which paralleled that of industrialization and an expanding middle class. By the turn of the century Europe and North America had moved from industrial societies—and the idea of working to meet basic human needs—to consumer societies in which the production of goods was focused on feeding desire. Old patterns of life yielded to a culture of consumption. Increasing amounts of leisure time and expendable income for the middle and upper classes, and the lack of a domestically driven routine in urban life, contributed to a culture in which consumption, not work or family, became a social goal.[51]

At the same time, increased production and factory efficiency meant that goods moved quickly into the marketplace. The expansion of railroads extended the reach of manufacturers and fostered the development of a national consumer economy. No longer were available goods only those produced at home. It was necessary to promote the consumption of goods and services in this competitive environment—and the modern advertising profession was born.

Such advertising, and the resulting shift in habits of consumption, would not have been possible without the expansion of the media. New twentieth-century printing technologies made it possible to print more copies more quickly. The linotype machine, which linked the composition of metal type to a keyboard, casting each letter as it was typed, made typesetting faster. Halftone and rotogravure printing improved the quality of magazine images. These publications made it possible to target specific readers with advertising messages and to spread desirable expressions of life in the modern world. With increasingly broader distribution by rail, advertising volume grew exponentially. Magazines, once financed solely through circulation, accepted advertising toward the end of the nineteenth century. By 1920 advertising accounted for nearly two-thirds of all newspaper and magazine income.[52]

Increased consumption was not without its social consequences. The communication professor William Leiss describes the emergence of the "social self" as the personal identities and imaginary states of well-being fostered by advertising, defined by income, and associated with "consumption communities" that showed common expenditure patterns and interests in style.[53] Early twentieth-century culture had replaced the intrinsic satisfaction of work with the satisfaction of consumption—work became simply a means of supporting consumption habits.[54] And consistent with this condition, class was no longer defined by heritage or some other intrinsic quality, but by how wealth and its resulting political power were distributed.

Advertising, according to Leiss, encouraged this distinction by providing lessons for constructing one's social identity, presumably acquired through the consumption of goods. Unlike advertising approaches of the previous century, which typically featured only the object, modern products were shown being used in various settings—both natural and cultural—by an obviously satisfied consumer.[55] The product itself mattered less than the meanings conveyed by the surroundings and the apparent contentment of the model housewife, the businessman, and so on. As a result, advertising transformed objects of use into objects of value.

The fact that these depictions frequently referenced the upper class was not important in terms of whom they reached; they implied the potential of upward mobility through consumption.[56] Advertising therefore assumed a responsibility that was once held by other cultural practices. It transmitted social cues about what constituted a satisfying life and personal fulfillment. And because these messages were not fixed in the activities or attributes of the real world, advertising could shift and fragment the public psyche toward new styles of behavior in ways that were consistent with economic imperatives for consumption.

Mainbocher: His long, slender, fluid evening line—as simple as it is portentous—in pink and white dotted chiffon, bound at the waist with pink grosgrain streamers. Diamond eardrops, Harry Winston.

5.59   PAGE FROM *HARPER'S BAZAAR*, JUNE 1955
Designed by Alexei Brodovitch (1898–1971). Photograph by Richard Avedon (1923–2004)

Leiss describes a shift in the 1920s when advertisers "discovered art," when they realized that people wanted expressive things, organized their possessions into thematically coherent systems, and sought novelty. Design obviously had a role to play in this aestheticizing of products and their promotion through the depiction of desirable futures. And if the economy depended on frequently changing the appearance of products, then something beyond industrial engineering was needed to make such products desirable.

In Europe, the avant-garde movement was engaged in this effort under a philosophy that good design was good for people and capable of bringing about a better world. But things in the United States were different—there was no tradition of product design, beyond that of traditional craft and basic utility. Leiss claims that the literature on this history is consistent: product design in the United States arose from advertising, from the encouragement of industry by advertising to change the appearance and features of goods for high rates of consumption and greater economic gain.[57]

Out of these circumstances emerged the notion of **STYLING** and the conflicting attitudes of early European modernists and American designers. While

STYLING

The surface application of fashionable forms to otherwise functional objects and environments, usually for the purposes of marketing. In the twentieth century, styling became the method of planned obsolescence in American industrial design. Consumers purchased the latest product to signify their participation in the display of the most recent cultural trends, even though older versions of the same object were still serviceable.

European product designers were focused on function, technology, and the social implications of good design, it was "the surface design of American goods that became known universally and associated with the consumer utopia that the United States was perceived to be."[58]

The historian Roland Marchand writes about how early advertisers encouraged manufacturers to organize products into ensembles or collections of related objects that were alike in either function or appearance. Color played a unifying role, connecting one product to another and thus identifying the components of the ensemble. This practice continues today (SEE FIGURE 5.60). Earlier in this book (see pp. 23–24) there is a discussion of Jean Baudrillard's *System of Objects* (1968), which suggests that modern design reduced objects to their functional role within a system and advertised them by encouraging consumers to complete that system through continual consumption. It is difficult today to find a popular product that is not surrounded by extensions of some primary function, by a system of objects that we understand primarily through the medium of advertising.

Advertising still remains a dominant vehicle for shaping and spreading culture. It played a major role in converting an industrial society to a consumer one and in illustrating to the citizens of a new century what progress looked like.

SUMMARY

Although twentieth-century modernism had many philosophical streams, most movements shared a concern for rational order and the objectivism of science, originating in the Enlightenment; universality and the absence of cultural or historical references; and affirmation of the Renaissance notion of social progress. The utopian goals of modern design arose from the conditions of society at the turn of the century. These conditions included the reconfigured lifestyles of urban dwellers, the expansion of industrial production and consumerism, the growing importance of style, and the social and political discontent that erupted in war.

Modernist ideas began in Europe but quickly spread to North America, where they took on a more pragmatic, less philosophical approach to style through the mechanism of advertising. Across the twentieth century, ideas that started as evidence of rebellion and discontent within the European avant-garde—futurism, Dada, suprematism, constructivism, de Stijl, and the Bauhaus—became part of the cultural mainstream, losing some of their socializing functions. By the last half of the century, the International Typographic Style had codified modernist principles in systems of rules for "good form."

5.60   OXO GOOD GRIPS, 1990
Smart Design

This contemporary line of kitchen products is an ensemble. An overarching idea frames the approach to functionally related products, which then gain market share in the product category as consumers discover other members of the ensemble. In this example, OXO's founder Sam Farber wanted a line of kitchen gadgets that would be comfortable for his wife, who had arthritis in her hands. The company later extended its strategy to other products, such as garden tools and dinnerware for young children that adapts to their growing dexterity. Even as the product line expands, the principles guiding design remain constant and are the brand's identity.

post-modernism

6

The concept of post-modernism is not a simple one

and its very definition has a checkered past dating from the late 1960s and the 1970s. For some scholars, the term means the rejection of modernist values and principles, a critique of the notions that designers speak with authority about appropriate form and that universal meaning is achievable. While modernism was characterized by its positive belief in social progress and the goal of objectivity, post-modernism is characterized by questioning these beliefs and the foundations of the social institutions that maintain them.

POST-MODERNISM

A term that is open to debate in a variety of disciplines but that includes descriptions of the conditions of later capitalism and the media saturation of Western societies. Some identify post-modernism as a rejection of the traditional visual forms of modernism, while others focus on its distrust of theories and ideologies associated with how meaning is constructed.

PASTICHE

A mixture of visual references that imitate previous styles or works in a new context; a fragmented experience. *Bricolage* is a related term that refers to the construction of something from a diverse range of things.

POST-INDUSTRIAL

Relating to an economy that no longer relies on heavy industry or mechanical production.

The cultural critic Dick Hebdige describes **POST-MODERNISM** as "modernity without the hope and dreams which made modernity bearable," as a **PASTICHE** or *bricolage* (see p. 150) of free-floating forms the meanings of which are decentered, unstable, and indeterminate.[1] It is modernity without certainty, without clarity of meaning, and without a common social purpose.

Others see all things post-modern as variations of "late modernism" that exist simultaneously with truly modern forms and values. The American architecture critic Charles Jencks describes this view of post-modernism as a combination of modernist techniques and styles (for example, allowing the structural members of a building to be revealed, or glazing the building with transparent walls) with something more sympathetic to the viewer (such as a smaller building scale or humanist references to classical architecture). In "What is Post-Modernism?" (1986) Jencks traced the confusion between post-modernism and late modernism to the fact that both arise from post-industrial society. Just as manufacturing exists alongside the more dominant computer technology and service industries in the **POST-INDUSTRIAL** world, contemporary alternatives to the "impersonal language of modernism" can exist simultaneously with large-scale, reductivist form.[2]

It is therefore difficult to say exactly when post-modern ideas reached the public consciousness. And the ideas associated with modernism did not disappear once critics began discussing the design response to changing social conditions in the middle and late twentieth century. There is no precise moment or event that we can cite as marking the beginning of post-modern thought, yet there was seminal writing that introduced new ideas about design and its role in society as challenges to the modernist paradigm outlined in chapter 5.

6.1   FIRE STATION #4, STREET FACADE, 1966
Robert Venturi (b. 1925)
(Venturi, Scott Brown and Associates, Inc.) Columbus, Indiana

Venturi's "gentle manifesto," *Complexity and Contradiction in Architecture*, prizes architecture that arises from the contradictory cultural references and "messy vitality" of contemporary life. Rather than the rational abstraction of modernism, Venturi revels in what designers can learn from the everyday. His billboard proposal for Philadelphia's bicentennial (see overleaf) refers to objects and places familiar to any resident, and reproduces the vernacular style of sign-painting associated with the medium.

POST-MODERNISM

SIGNS OF DISCONTENT

In 1966 the American architect Robert Venturi delivered a speech that was later documented in a book entitled *Complexity and Contradiction in Architecture* and published as the first in a series of papers on contemporary architecture by the Museum of Modern Art in New York. His "gentle manifesto" confronted head-on the contrasting values of modern and post-modern architecture, even though he claimed to have nothing to do with post-modernism.

In opposition to the modernist quest for simple, rational harmony among the elements of a building, Venturi affirmed his interest in complexity and contradiction, in diverse forms that are broad and dissonant in their connotative meanings. An oversized television antenna (on the top of a retirement home), a computer punch-card (represented on the side of a technology headquarters), the tower of a firehouse (SEE FIGURES 6.1-6.2)—these symbols found their way into Venturi's work as he reveled in the ambiguity of meaning that arose from a clash of specific cultural and historical references (many of them from popular culture), as distinct from the abstraction that interested his modernist predecessors. Venturi sought the tension of something never quite resolved, rather than forms in which intentions and elemental relationships were straightforward and obvious. He described his preference for the "difficult whole," a "messy vitality," rather than a certain unity; a hybridization of forms that celebrated "both/and" rather than "either/or" in their references and meanings.[3] Unlike modernists who wanted to close down possible interpretations to the most irreducible and logical of forms, frequently expressed through geometry, Venturi wanted to open the visual vocabulary of built form to a plethora of meanings that mirrored the complex world in which we live. Whereas modernism sought to bring order to chaos, to sublimate many voices across history under a single objective view, Venturi wanted to reveal a plurality of meanings, to embrace in architecture those contradictions that indicate how culture, language, and meaning-making work.

6.2   HEADQUARTERS OF THE INSTITUTE OF SCIENTIFIC INFORMATION, ENTRANCE FACADE, 1966
Robert Venturi (b. 1925)
(Venturi, Scott Brown and Associates, Inc.) University City Center, Philadelphia, Pennsylvania

Venturi elaborated on these themes in 1972 with the publication of *Learning from Las Vegas*, a book in which he admonished the judgmental modern architecture community to learn from the **VERNACULAR** examples of the built environment, from the commonplace and ordinary. Unlike the modernists, who ultimately stood as critics and arbiters of taste from outside the culture for which they designed, Venturi's work referred to the lived experience within popular culture. In a chapter entitled "A Significance for A&P Parking Lots," he reminded late twentieth-century architects that the modernist icon Le Corbusier "loved grain elevators and steamships" and that the Bauhaus "looked like a factory"; that despite efforts to disclaim all historical and ornamental references, modern architecture began with work in

VERNACULAR

The everyday language of ordinary people that is characteristic of a region or culture. In the context of design, "vernacular form" refers to the visual language produced by people who are not trained in design and contains connotations of a particular culture, place, or use.

"analogy, symbol, and image."[4] Venturi rejected architectural form that was "free from the images of past experience, determined solely by program and structure, and with an occasional assist . . . from intuition."[5] Pointing out the models in fine art, including the pop art movement, which drew its iconography from the commercial world, Venturi urged architects to study highways, billboards, and the persuasive strategies of commerce for images and symbols of the late twentieth century.[6] And what better place to find such inspiration than in the uninhibited visual excess of Las Vegas?

We can find the same interest in popular culture in the work of post-modern graphic designers. A design magazine insert by Thirst designer Rick Valicenti (SEE FIGURE 6.3), for example, focuses on the concept of stereotypes in popular culture (with a play on the dual meaning of "type," as both typography and typology). Valicenti relinquished some control in the design of the insert by encouraging the typesetters to determine the eclectic mix of typographic forms. The verbal dialog of the "manicurist" combines with the visual content of the typography to speak a language or "dialect" that we are able to identify with a specific cultural context, in much the same way as Venturi's proposal for Philadelphia's bicentennial billboards speaks to the sign-painting culture of advertising (SEE FIGURE 6.4).

On the surface, Valicenti's visual representation appears to arise from **LOW CULTURE**, from the vernacular of supermarket ads and commercial packaging that often lack the benefit of "good" design. Although the layout appears somewhat random and without a grid, Valicenti's careful alignment of typographic boxes and control of contrast in typographic size and color produce a result that would not be possible under a less educated eye. In this sense, his work is an image of "low" culture used to make a point about stereotyping, and we understand it in comparison to the "high" culture of late modernism. But Valicenti is actually no less detached from the world of the manicurist than a modernist would be; nor is his work any less an outside commentary on the culture he illustrates than the work of a modernist. Later discussions in this chapter will address this concept more fully.

In contrast to Venturi, Jencks first used the term "post-modernism" in his *The Language of Post-Modern Architecture* (1977). He referred to an end of the modern avant-garde and a return to the traditional role of the architect as someone who communicates with the public.[7] Earlier, in an article published in 1975, Jencks chastised the modern architect who "still believes he is providing universal identity with his articulated forms when he is really just giving

LOW CULTURE

Relating to the taste or means of the general public and the use of forms often associated with contemporary commercial media.

6.3   *STEREOTYPE*, 1990
Rick Valicenti (b. 1951)
Insert for *Step* magazine

6.4   CITY EDGES: PROPOSED SIGNS FOR THE SCHUYLKILL RIVER PARKWAY, PHILADELPHIA, PA, 1973
Robert Venturi (b. 1925)
(Venturi, Scott Brown and Associates, Inc.)
Photo by Tom Bernard

identity within his own limited, historical code and one not shared by the majority of his clients."[8]

In other words, Jencks felt modern architects were deluding themselves by claims of universal form. He argued instead for **PLURALISM**—a variety of styles that arise from the local culture—and that such a pastiche is rich with values and codes that are read differently by viewers. Rather than rejecting history, Jencks promoted the use of classical or conventional architectural elements, which carried both their original meanings as well as new meanings generated by their repurposing in the contemporary environment and in juxtaposition with each other. In this way, he argued that meanings are rich and complex and that a single obvious reading is impossible.

Pastiche also disregards the modernist notions of authenticity and progress. Style is recycled from the past, challenging the "truthfulness" of its form through an intentional undermining of its function: a column that is not load-bearing, a façade with a variety of architectural styles from different time periods and locations.[9] In borrowing, the design raises questions about the original and speaks more about the practice of architecture as an institution in the meaning-making business—about the larger role of architecture in culture—than about the meaning of any specific building or form.

Jencks's writing also referred to **DOUBLE CODING**—the idea that objects can inspire plural meanings, that things will mean different things to different people depending on their own knowledge of visual language. He accepted that modern form can exist outside or alongside other visual traditions and that architecture can therefore actually comment on its modern tendencies.[10]

Graphic design demonstrates a similar ability to make reference to its historical traditions while introducing new ideas about visual language. In 1980, Doublespace designers Jane Kosstrin and David Sterling created the masthead for *Fetish*, the magazine of material culture, from contrasting type variations (SEE FIGURE 6.5)—a subtle nod to the systematically developed sans-serif type families of mid-century modernism. Whereas designers in the International Typographic Style (see pp. 157–58) would have used such variations sparingly to demarcate different types of content within the layout, Kosstrin and Sterling combined extended and condensed forms of different weights within the same word. The result reflected an obsession with the formal qualities of typography, a form consistent with the publication

6.5   COVER OF *FETISH* MAGAZINE, NO. 1, 1980
Jane Kosstrin, David Sterling, and Terence Main (Doublespace)

PLURALISM

A condition in which two or more theories, visual references, principles, meanings, etc., coexist in or are called forth by the same design.

DOUBLE CODING

Charles Jencks's term for the ability of architecture to convey many meanings simultaneously.

signs of discontent

179

6.6 *UNDER THE MOON*, 1988
Nick Bell (b. 1965)
Theater poster

title and purpose as a magazine about material culture. It also focused attention on the prevailing late modernist rules for "good design" by breaking them, although much more radical departures were to follow throughout the decade [SEE FIGURES 6.6–6.8].

These early signs of designers' discontent with modernist values were not carried out in isolation. Post-modern ideas also populated the discourse of literary theory, cultural theory, and philosophy, with strong influences from French writers in the 1970s. These discussions influenced experimental work in graphic design in the late twentieth century, most notably in the graduate design program at Cranbrook Academy of Art, Michigan (see p. 105), where students explored typographic compositions based on post-modern writing about the nature of texts.

Cranbrook Design: The New Discourse was an exhibition held in 1991 of graphic and product design inspired by post-modern ideas [SEE FIGURE 6.8]. The exhibition catalog includes an essay by the Cranbrook alumna Lorraine Wild that describes a student-designed issue of the journal *Visible Language* [SEE FIGURE 6.9] entitled "French Currents of the Letter" (1977–78). The issue contains eight essays on the post-structuralist concept of *l'écriture*, a French term for written or printed text. Consistent with the content, the design of the journal begins with a somewhat conventional layout and progressively undermines the straightforward, apparent meaning of the text as it evolves across the pages of the journal. Just as the theoretical basis of post-modern literary criticism questions the possibility of an innocent reader and the transparency of language (that we can come to a text without being influenced by our prior experience in a world of written texts and that language is a neutral carrier of one universal meaning), so the design of the journal deconstructs the structural relationships

6.7

6.7 EVENTS PROGRAM FOR
LOS ANGELES CONTEMPORARY
EXHIBITIONS, 1988
Jeffery Keedy (b. 1957)

6.8 *CRANBROOK DESIGN: THE NEW
DISCOURSE*, 1990
P. Scott Makela (1960–1999)
Poster

6.9 SPREADS FROM "FRENCH
CURRENTS OF THE LETTER,"
PUBLISHED IN *VISIBLE LANGUAGE*,
SUMMER 1978
Cranbrook Academy of Art students
under the direction of Katherine McCoy

The student-designed journal moves
from a traditional layout at the front to
a deconstructed text in the later essays.

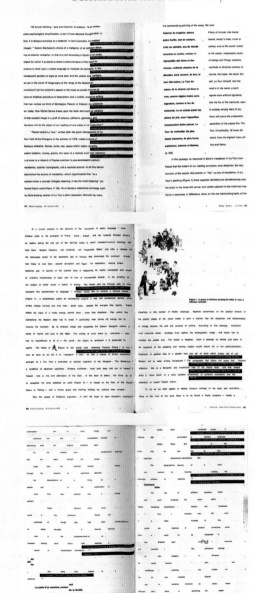

6.9

6.8

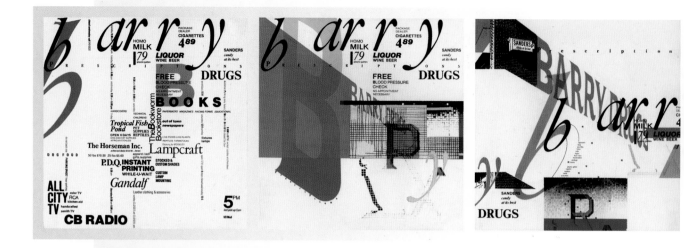

we have come to associate with scholarly journals, making us rethink those relationships within a larger context of literary systems.[11] No longer is the design natural, disappearing under a more privileged notion of writing in which the reader simply passes through the visual surface of typography to get to the literary content it represents. Instead, the meaning of the text expands and is questioned through typographic form that reorders the traditional presentations of language. In this way, the form of the design itself is intended as discourse or discussion about the nature of reading and publication design.

In later years, these ideas about text and its visual presentation would expand through a series of student projects that have been widely published (SEE FIGURES 6.10–6.12). Cranbrook students informed their practice through readings in deconstruction, **POST-STRUCTURALISM**, and reception theory (see box: "Deconstruction"), borrowing ideas from a number of disciplines as the basis of visual work.

But regardless of the source, several major themes emerged from early postmodern experimentation in design and shaped work through the last decades of the twentieth century. Many of these themes persist, in some form, today:

→ writerly rather than readerly text
→ plural rather than singular meanings
→ metonymy rather than metaphor
→ cultural position
→ vernacular, appropriated, and default forms
→ hyperreality and the importance of image

THE READER WRITES THE TEXT

Roland Barthes (see pp. 128–31) was among a number of literary critics whose work influenced designers in the 1980s. In 1970, Barthes published *S/Z*, a structuralist analysis of Honoré de Balzac's novella *Sarrasine* (1830). At the root of this treatise is Barthes's premise of texts as being **READERLY** or writerly. A readerly view of text presumes that the author controls meaning,[12] much as modernism presumes that the artist or designer determines the connotations of abstract visual elements and compositional structures and how they are interpreted. For example, the modernist de Stijl belief (see pp. 151–53) that

POST-STRUCTURALISM

An extension of structuralism that emphasizes plural and deferred readings of text, as well as a reluctance to ground the analysis of text in any single theory of meaning-making. Post-structuralist analyses acknowledge that the reader always has a cultural position and that no reading of text can be "innocent" of the values or biases that come with such a position.

READERLY TEXT

Roland Barthes's term for the idea that the author imposes a singular meaning on the text. This view is consistent with intentional approaches to representation, and privileges the roles of author and maker in design.

6.10   CRANBROOK ACADEMY OF ART STUDIO INVESTIGATION, 1981
Lucille Tenazas (b. 1953)

6.11   CALIFORNIA COLLEGE OF ARTS AND CRAFTS MFA POSTER, 2002
Lucille Tenazas (b. 1953)

6.12   *SEX GODDESS* POSTER, CRANBROOK ACADEMY OF ART STUDIO INVESTIGATION, 1989
Laurie Haycock Makela (b. 1956) and P. Scott Makela (1960–1999)

Cranbrook alumni were able to extend their investigations in professional work following their studies.

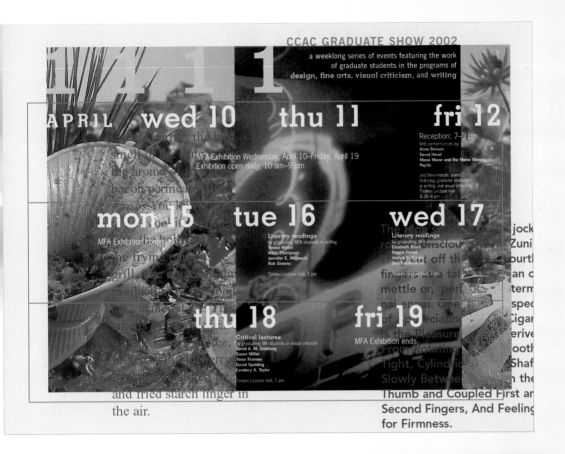

CCAC GRADUATE SHOW 2002

a weeklong series of events featuring the work
of graduate students in the programs of
design, fine arts, visual criticism, and writing

APRIL wed 10 thu 11 fri 12

Reception: 7–9 pm
With performances by
Anna Benson
David Hevel
Meow Meow and the Meow Meows
Pepito

and three-minute slams
featuring graduate students
in writing and visual criticism
Timken Lecture Hall
8:30–9 pm

MFA Exhibition Wednesday, April 10–Friday, April 19
Exhibition open daily, 10 am–9 pm

mon 15 tue 16 wed 17

MFA Exhibition continues

Literary readings
by graduating MFA students in writing
Teresa Walsh
Nikki Thompson
Jennifer E. Majewski
Rob Simons

Timken Lecture Hall, 7 pm

Literary readings
by graduating MFA students in writing
Elizabeth Block
Reggie Forest
Joshua C. Kryah
Dan Encarnacion

Timken Lecture Hall, 7 pm

thu 18 fri 19

Critical lectures
by graduating MA students in visual criticism
David A. M. Goldberg
Susan Miller
Tessa Rumsey
David Spalding
Candacy A. Taylor

Timken Lecture Hall, 7 pm

MFA Exhibition ends

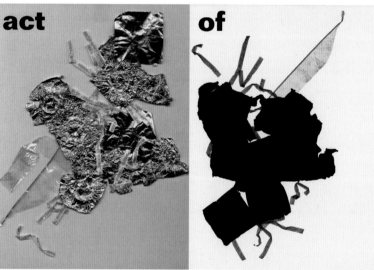

DECONSTRUCTION

Deconstruction is a form of literary and philosophical analysis that arose out of post-structuralism. It is most closely associated with the work of the French philosopher Jacques Derrida (1930–2004). One of its principal theories is that a literary text simultaneously professes and undermines its own authority. Derrida critiqued Saussure's notion of the sign (a unity of the signified and signifier) and structuralism's faith in a fundamental order that lies beneath the surface of texts. He stated that language and meaning have no point of origin and no end; that any meaning always resides, not in the sign itself, but in the difference between the sign and another sign, which may be outside the text. The temporal structure of language, according to Derrida, ensures that the resolution of meaning is always deferred. The sign is in constant juxtaposition to the next sign in the text, as language unfolds, and to signs outside the text, and its final meaning is therefore unresolved. He referred to these notions as *différance*. Text is never continuous or whole in its reading; it is broken into fragments and we reconsider the meaning of each fragment in relation to the others. This process undermines the power of the author. The author (a producer of culture) provides components and the reader (a consumer of culture) recombines them and imposes his or her own meaning upon them as they are juxtaposed with other signs. Any hope of universal meaning is therefore lost.

The architecture of deconstruction in the 1980s was characterized by fragmented form and jagged shapes. It

6.13   SPREADS FROM *SPEAK*
MAGAZINE, ISSUE 16, 1999
Martin Venezky (b. 1957)
Table of Contents
"Act of Contrition" by Brendan Schallert

exhibited an irreverence toward the past that was translated through what the architect Bernard Tschumi calls a "practice of disjunctions."[13] Just as Derrida stated that text defers the resolution of meaning through the constantly changing relationship of signs to other signs outside the text, so deconstructionist architecture looks at the building in relation to the surrounding cultural space. It initiates a critical dialog between the building and the social conventions that frame it (for example, the distinction between interior and exterior spaces or ideals of "good" proportion). Architectural form therefore aims to reveal these binary, oppositional relationships by presenting what is not obvious in the dominant culture (for example, by an unexpected, somewhat dissonant combination of materials to contrast and make apparent the prevailing notions of what "goes together well"). The goal is not simply to rebel against convention but to make us see the convention in the world around us through juxtaposition with its opposite.

Likewise, graphic design in the 1980s challenged the functionalist conventions of late modernism and addressed the binary oppositions in Western thought [SEE FIGURE 4.13], through both process and form. Although work from this period was rarely subjected to the formal ideology found in literary theory and architecture, it could be argued that many graphic designers simply adopted the term "deconstruction" to describe a loosely similar shift in style. Graduate students at Cranbrook Academy of Art and California Institute of

the Arts were, however, familiar with writing in literary and critical theory. The work of this period is characterized by the introduction of objects and form from the culture at large, as a contrast to the highly refined, closed, and formal systems of modernism. Scraps of materials (such as wood laminate and overexposed photographic film) and symbols from popular culture were arranged in compositions that defied any grid or "rightness" of proportion. The processes for their construction were direct—images were torn, collaged, and defaced. Type was frequently set by primitive means (for example, typewriter, "found" type from magazines and newspapers, handwriting, and so on) or displayed all the characteristics of "bad" form (for example, poorly spaced, differently sized letterforms in the same word, irregular baselines).

These fragments, like Derrida's signs in constant juxtaposition, were often not accountable to any visual hierarchy, nor did they have an allegiance to illustrating particular content [SEE FIGURE 6.13]. They were composed, literally, of free-floating signifiers the ultimate meanings of which were constantly deferred and that called into question the claims of logic in modernist work. It is important to view these compositions within the context of a graduate program, where there was no responsibility to a client. The 1980s and early 1990s was a period in which students discovered and built theory. Their goal was to understand design as a field of study.

simple geometry and a limited color palette (primary colors, black, white, and gray) mirror what is necessary for leading a harmonious life is predicated on assumptions: first, that essential meaning can be derived from the abstract form itself; second, that all viewers interpret such form in a similar way; and third, that, surrounded by artifacts that exhibit such form, society will adopt behaviors and values consistent with these interpretations. Under these assumptions, authority is given to the artist/designer to determine what kind of form will produce these outcomes. Further, if we believe that the designer endows the form itself with meaning or creates objects that inherently reflect such meaning by virtue of their form, then the surrounding context and time should have little to do with audience interpretation. According to this view, meaning is stable, regardless of changes in circumstances outside the form itself.

A **WRITERLY** view of text,[14] on the other hand, posits that the reader constructs or writes the meaning as an active participant in the communication process, consistent with the constructionist view of representation (see p. 36). This definition of the reader as a writer of text is fundamental to post-modern ideas of design, as well as to those of literature. A writerly view presumes

WRITERLY TEXT

Roland Barthes's term for the idea that the reader constructs or writes meaning as an active participant in the communication process. This view is consistent with constructionist approaches to representation and supports the position that there are many meanings of the same text.

the reader writes the text

that many possible meanings may arise from one form and that context, time, and the past experiences of viewers—including our own previous readings of the same text—exert influences on interpretations. No meaning is stable and therefore no single truth is possible.

While it is clear that under the writerly perspective we each bring our personal experiences to the interpretation of text, the concern for design is how modulations in the larger culture, or our affiliations with different social groups, influence our construction of meaning. It would be easy to think, by way of a comparison, that words have specific meanings and that such meanings are codified in dictionaries for all time. But closer examination shows archaic dictionary definitions that are no longer used, slang that appropriates existing words for new purposes (dope, bad, ridiculous, and so on), and shifting contexts in which the use of the word is suitable or unsuitable. In this sense, language is alive. The historians Stuart and Elizabeth Ewen cite the migration of words in various editions of *Roget's Thesaurus* as an example. The term "noble" was once a noun that referred to people born with titles. Today, the thesaurus has relocated the word as an adjective under concepts related to dignity, honor, and other personal attributes that have nothing to do with social class or lineage. The conceptual affiliations of this word migrated with changing times.[15]

Likewise, design is subject to reinterpretation and shifting meanings over time. For example, the typeface Helvetica—designed in 1957 by the Swiss typographer Max Miedinger (SEE FIGURE 6.14)—embodied all the attributes valued by modernists in the middle of the twentieth century. It was mechanically and optically precise, coolly detached from any historical references or personalities, thoroughly legible, and in all ways neutral. The Dutch typographer Wim Crouwel, in a film dedicated to the fiftieth anniversary of the typeface in 2007, said in the true modernist tradition that "[Helvetica] should be neutral. It shouldn't have a meaning in itself. The meaning is in the content of the text and not in the typeface."[16]

But over time Helvetica became the typeface of choice for the corporate world (SEE FIGURE 6.15) and to use it was to resurrect associations with big business: anonymous and ubiquitous companies that lacked the individual character of small, privately owned enterprises with their own histories and cultures; and

6.14   HELVETICA TYPE DESIGN, 1957
Max Miedinger (1910–1980)

Aer Lingus	Evian	Motorola
AGFA	Fendi	Muji
Amtrak	General Motors	National Car Rental
American Airlines	Georgia Pacific	Nationwide Insurance
American Apparel	Greyhound	Navistar
AT&T	Hanes	Nestle
Bank of America	Harley-Davidson	Norelco
Bank One	Hoover	The North Face
Bayer	Husqvarna	Oral-B
Bell Atlantic	Intel	Olympus
Blaupunkt	JCPenney	Pan Am
British Gas	Jeep	Panasonic
BSAF	Kawasaki	Post-it
BMW	Kimberly Clark	Scotch
Caterpillar	Knoll	Sears
Conair	Lufthansa	Skype
Crate and Barrel	Magic Chef	Staples
Digital	Manpower	Target
Dole	Mattel	3-M
Ducati	Met Life	Tupperware
Energizer	Microsoft	Toyota

6.15   CORPORATIONS THAT USE HELVETICA IN THEIR LOGOTYPES

POST-MODERNISM

rules-based systems for layout that came with the corporate identities of the mid- and late twentieth century. By the 1980s, many designers made not-so-positive references to Helvetica and the typeface fell out of favor.

With the advent of computers, the meaning of Helvetica was again recast as a **DEFAULT** among many possible fonts. It was frequently one of only several system fonts supplied in software and it stood for the absence of a deliberate choice, for neutrality and ubiquity, but less for corporate identity. Designers again deployed it in projects that intentionally avoided style, work that spoke with the voice of "non-design." Nothing about the design of the typeface had been altered across these decades, but the surrounding social practices and contexts shifted how readers interpreted its use. The meaning of the typeface changed—we now had, as part of our interpretive experiences, all the instances in which Helvetica stood for something more than a good, legible typeface.

So, when the architect Robert Venturi refers to ambiguous, unclear meanings in his "gentle manifesto," it is to this concept of writerly text that he alludes. If meaning depends on context, time, and the past experiences of viewers or readers, then it cannot be closed, fixed, and the same for everyone. The modernist's enterprise of developing universal form therefore appears to be a wild-goose chase.

ONE VERSUS MANY

At the core of post-structuralism is a concern for multiple meanings, for a lack of resolution about the meaning of something. Early structuralist theory sought meaning in the relationships among things, not in the things themselves. It asked questions about whether meaning resides in the object or in its relationship to other objects and its context. Post-structuralism addresses the same questions but acknowledges that they will never be answered, because meaning is inherently unstable.

Roland Barthes takes on the issue of unresolved meaning in his essay "From Work To Text" (1977), when he suggests that literature may be viewed either as a **WORK** or as a **TEXT**. He defines a work as classic, as occupying a section of the library and a place in history, as being held physically in the hand.[17] For example, *The Adventures of Huckleberry Finn* (1884) is a classic work of American literature. We know the story and we understand who its author, Mark Twain, was and the status he holds among American authors. Other authors refer to the work and it is required reading for most students in the United States.

A text, on the other hand, is an activity of production, is experienced, and is held in language.[18] As a text, *The Adventures of Huckleberry Finn* is open to many interpretations. From our position in the twenty-first century—with all the benefits of the civil rights movement and 100 years of scholarship on Mark Twain—we can debate whether the depiction of the runaway slave Jim is a racist characterization, or Twain's attempt to satirize nineteenth-century racism in the American South, or the humanization of a black man. All interpretations are possible, change with the times and our own repeated readings of the book, and arise from expanding commentary outside the text itself. In other

DEFAULT

A pre-selected option (e.g. one adopted by a computer program) that involves no conscious judgment of quality or function by the user.

WORK

Roland Barthes's term for writing that is classic, that occupies a place in the library and history, and that is held physically in the hand.

TEXT

Roland Barthes's term for an activity of language production and interpretation, which is experienced in the moment. Many interpretations of the text are possible and change with the times.

words, the meaning of *The Adventures of Huckleberry Finn* as a text evolves, is negotiated, and constantly undergoes production, just as language does.

One of the characteristics of a text, therefore, is a plurality of meaning or what Barthes defines not simply as many meanings coexisting at the same time, but as "a passage, an overcrossing."[19] Barthes refers to interwoven signifiers—to references to things outside the text itself—that are called up by the unique combinations of words, or in a design sense, by particular forms. In this way, according to Barthes, the text "quotes without [quotation marks]."[20] It recalls for us all the things to which it could refer, as well as the obvious things present in the text (or design) itself.

For example, in the image in FIGURE 6.16 we see a pair of shoes. They are not just any shoes, but Christian Louboutin high heels. For many—thanks in part to the television show and movies *Sex and the City*—these shoes have strong associations with high fashion and sexy, wealthy, world-wise women. When paired with the words "hot mama," we tease these meanings out of the shoes in ways that we would not, had the high heels been with many others in a catalog.

But the image also includes a toaster and a child's hand, references to a home environment that destabilize the first meaning of the shoes and text. "Hot Mama" could easily be a child's exclamation when reaching for the toaster. And the domesticity called forth in this second reading of the image raises questions about the concepts invoked by the high heels. We do not typically think of mothers in the kitchen as sexy or worldly. Neither do we imagine women who can afford a thousand-dollar pair of shoes as making breakfast for their toddlers. So the phrase "hot mama" has multiple meanings in relation to the objects in the poster.

In terms of Barthes's idea of overcrossing signifiers, this composition is a visual example of pluralism. The plural meanings within the poster are not just any reader's random impression of what he or she thinks this combination of elements could mean. There is, rather, a deliberately designed interplay between meanings of the words and the objects that is drawn from our cultural experience and that resides below the surface of the obvious, denotative significance of the objects alone. In this way, shoes and a toaster can speak volumes about social class and gender roles.

By making reference to class and gender, the poster invites people to consider their own identities, as well as the institutionalized concept of "mother." This framing of context as a means for thinking about our own position in relation to a larger social narrative—such as the notion that mothers are defined as women only in their relationship to children or that wealthy people do not do domestic chores—is characteristic of post-modern work. Modernism assumes that there are **METANARRATIVES** that explain how the world works and that they are natural, true, and not the product of ideology.[21] Such metanarratives, say

6.16   HOT MAMA!

METANARRATIVE

An overarching concept or story that provides a comprehensive explanation for historical or cultural experience.

POST-MODERNISM

the modernists, may be found in science, religion, and other social institutions. Post-modernism, on the other hand, questions these narratives and reveals their underlying value systems and biases.

METAPHOR AND METONYMY

In the same essay, Barthes goes on to discuss the difference between **METAPHOR** and **METONYMY** with respect to the text. The dictionary definition of metaphor concerns analogy, or one thing representing something else. A figure climbing a ladder, for instance, may be seen as a metaphor for working one's way up in business. Metonymy, on the other hand, is when a single attribute or another object suggests the thing for which something stands in a less direct way. For example, we often refer to military or police officers as "brass" or say someone "sets a good table" when we really mean that he or she serves good food.

The aim of metaphor is to close down meaning—something is like something else in very specific ways, and is therefore not like other things. In the film-series poster by Josef Müller-Brockmann (SEE FIGURE 6.17), for example, the "der film" typography is a visual metaphor for the physical characteristics of film. It refers to time through overlapping letterforms, rather than having each typographic character hold its own space as it does in print, and alludes to the transparency of celluloid and watching images of light in a dark room. Nothing about the content of the particular films, the process of filmmaking, watching with others in movie theaters, or any other aspect of cinema is revealed through this typographic metaphor. Neither is there an attempt to make film stand for something more complex, such as a movie made by a tragic celebrity standing for her real life, or film as a contemporary form of philosophy. Instead, Müller-Brockmann refers only to the limited inventory of physical characteristics that separate film from other media. To use Barthes's analysis, the symbolism "runs out," "comes to a halt."[22] This is characteristic of what he calls a *work*.

Metonymy, by contrast, opens up meaning and defers our resolution of understanding about its intention. In the poster in FIGURE 6.16, the relationship between the words "Hot Mama" and the Louboutin shoes is called into question by the very different relationship of "Hot Mama" to the toaster and the child's hand. The elements of the poster are all symbolic (as is the type in

6.17   *DER FILM* POSTER, 1960
Josef Müller-Brockmann (1914–1996)
Museum für Gestaltung, Zürich,
Graphics Collection

Müller-Brockmann's film-series poster uses the visual metaphor of overlapping typography to refer to the frames of a movie projected over time in a dark room. Modernism frequently used a metaphorical approach, in which one thing is like something else, often in a physical sense. Post-modern criticism claims that metaphor closes down meaning by limiting the interpretation only to the ways in which the two things are alike.

Müller-Brockmann's film-series poster) but they are constantly in play with each other, keeping the significance of each element slightly off center and without closure as to the actual meaning. And the elements of the "Hot Mama" poster talk about a person who is not there—the woman who wears these shoes and who is the mother of a child. In this way, they refer to attributes and behaviors that stand for the woman. They are metonymic. If she is a sexy party-girl of considerable wealth, why is she making toast? And if she is making toast for a child, how can she be like the carefree singles of *Sex in the City*? Again, this interplay of signifiers defers meaning and resists closure. In Barthes's terms, this is a *text*, and we actively engage in the production of meaning through the symbols in the poster.

CULTURAL POSITION

The post-modern interest in plural meanings also hints at another overriding theme: recognition that we, as designers, frame a view of the world through the artifacts and representations we produce, and that this worldview will be formed and interpreted differently on the basis of cultural experience.

Modernism was grounded in the concept of "good taste" as something that could be learned through education and contact with "high" culture—ultimately, the aesthetics preferred by white, mostly European, progressive intellectuals. The role of design therefore was to transcend very different cultural experiences and to inculcate, across a broad public, good taste through exposure to examples of good form. The language for accomplishing this transcendence was typically abstraction, which, by definition, separated the artifacts and environments of modernism from those of other cultural experiences, and which was often presumed to be universal and irreducible in its meaning.

Post-modernism, on the other hand, acknowledges that we all have **CULTURAL POSITIONS**, certain identities and subjectivities that frame our interpretations of the world. It further recognizes that a dominant culture—through its social practices, economic influence, and values—marginalizes "others." Post-modernism views gender, race, class, and ethnicity as social constructions that are privileged (or not privileged), circulated, and maintained through the representations and practices of the dominant culture. Such representations frequently seek to perpetuate the status quo or to exoticize "others," thereby framing them only in terms of their obvious differences from the dominant society. In this sense, for example, "black" becomes "not white," "poor" becomes "not educated," and "Middle Eastern" becomes "not Christian." Further, post-modern theories acknowledge that as designers we do not stand apart from culture—we are part of it, both as consumers and as producers of its representations. Our own worldview is shaped by our personal experiences within a culture and we, in turn, shape the perspectives of others by what we contribute to the culture as makers of representations.

It is therefore the contention of post-modern theory that we can never be entirely "innocent" or free from the inherent biases of our own positions within culture. So the post-modern dilemma for the designer is a bit like that of the goldfish asked to describe the nature of water—instead of describing water, it

CULTURAL POSITION

The post-modern concept that we all hold identities and subjectivities that determine our particular interpretation of the world. According to this concept, we can never overcome these biases completely.

recites the characteristics of the living-room on the other side of the glass bowl. We are blind to many aspects of the culture in which we live and, at the same time, our understanding of another culture will always be that of an outsider, filtered through our own cultural experiences.

We can see the awkwardness of this position in examples of recent design: the stock photography that shows one employee of each racial minority in a typical office setting, or the deliberate accessorizing of a home-interiors magazine with African or Mexican artifacts as a message to specific readers that they, too, are valued as customers. The very concept of globalization is complicated in this respect. Is it truly an attempt to be more inclusive in our cultural references and to highlight the aspects of life that we have in common, regardless of cultural context? Or is the term simply a euphemism for selling the products and representations of post-industrial society in developing countries, thus displacing the production of indigenous cultures? If the latter is true, does denying access to the benefits of post-industrial society to developing nations guarantee that they will remain forever "developing"? And just where do the aspects of cultural authenticity actually reside?

Elizabeth (Dori) Tunstall, a design anthropologist, provides a useful framework for thinking about these matters.[23] *Historical consciousness*, according to Tunstall, is people's understanding of where they come from, who they are, and where they are going. *Life goals* embody what matters most to the members of the community. *Community structure* addresses how the collective makes decisions and how individuals fit in and contribute. *Relationships* are the means through which people gain understanding of common values and establish trust. And *agency* is the degree of the individual's control or influence over the things that matter to the community and themselves. In this sense, community—or the larger notion of groups that share some cultural experience—is not restricted to people living within geographic or political boundaries. For example, we can talk about a community of people who are committed to the slow-food movement or a culture of computer gamers.

It is easy to see under this definition of community that people often hold membership in multiple groups with cultural experiences, behaviors, and values that are distinctive to each group. Any of the elements of community may influence members' interpretations of meaning and their cultural positions, even in contradiction to the perspectives of their broader affiliations of race, gender, and ethnicity. Tunstall's analytical framework therefore encourages a much deeper understanding of shared motivations and practices than is suggested by the simple search for visual motifs so frequently used to represent cultural authenticity and position in design.

VERNACULAR, APPROPRIATED, AND DEFAULT FORMS

This dilemma of authenticity is not to say that the visual symbols of culture are irrelevant to post-modern design. If modernism was about abstraction and the "high" culture of fine art, post-modernism is often about the iconic forms of popular culture and the "low" art of advertising. The modernist belief in universal form meant that ornamentation and specific cultural references were to be avoided at all costs. For many avant-garde movements, embedded within style was all that was parochial, sentimental, and tainted by a socially conservative bourgeoisie. But by the second half of the twentieth century, what began as a social movement dedicated to such projects as worker housing, radical political literature, and rebuilding the visual identity of nations decimated by war had become the formal language of big business and the wealthy. Sleek skyscrapers filled urban centers as monuments to corporate function, often replacing eclectic neighborhoods that were evidence of a city's history. Product design of the 1970s often hid the mechanics of how objects worked under smooth geometric forms that fit well in functionalist interiors.

The International Typographic Style dominated graphic design from the 1950s through the 1970s (see pp. 157–58). A system of typographic rules for the arrangement of text and images, it encouraged the use of a limited palette of typefaces, arranged according to a grid of ideal proportions. The modernist rules governing typographic layout were supported by a limited number of "acceptable" typefaces. The method and cost of producing and distributing fonts left the design of typefaces to a small cadre of experienced professionals who drew heavily on historical precedents.

Further reinforcing the use of classical typefaces were such textbooks as James Craig's *Designing with Type* (1971), which featured five families of type as representatives of various historical classifications. Craig's selections, often replicated in subsequent books under different authors, predetermined some degree of success in combining typefaces within the same work; the modern Bodoni was well-matched to the sans serif Helvetica or Univers. The self-published book by the Basle design professor Wolfgang Weingart, *How One Can Make Swiss Typography* (1976), and Rolf Rehe's *Typography: How to Make It Most Legible* of 1974 [SEE FIGURE 6.18] extolled the virtues of modern form and reinforced the rules necessary to achieve clarity and harmony.

By the 1980s and early 1990s, however, there was a feeling among some designers that graphic design had lost its expressive role in communication, beyond that of describing the rules system itself. Such unrest was fueled in 1984 by the introduction of Apple's Macintosh computer, followed by a range of layout- and type-design software programs that allowed anyone to create typefaces by applying formal characteristics by digital program across the twenty-six letters of the alphabet. No longer did a few large type foundries control the aesthetics of type design, nor did technology constrain the formal possibilities of layout, much to the chagrin of the old guard, who saw the expanded repertoire of form as a challenge to modernist standards. The book designer

Rolf F. Rehe
Typography: how to make it most legible

6.18   *TYPOGRAPHY: HOW TO MAKE IT MOST LEGIBLE*, 1974
Rolf F. Rehe (b. 1935)

Rehe's book provides a general description of rules for "good form." Such rules are consistent with the systematic development and application of late modernist principles.

Lorraine Wild, in a controversial article in 1992 for *ID* magazine, "On Overcoming Modernism," described the impact of digital technology on typographic form:

Those who are not terrified by the new typographic technologies are using them in all sorts of ways, as an opportunity to reinvent type aesthetics in response to the technology itself. Unfamiliar forms of work produced in response to major changes in technology are often classified as evidence of aesthetic malfeasance, the obliteration of standards, and practices of craft. It is a functional Modernist impulse to submit aesthetics to the demands of the machine, but in this case the subject of the technology is dematerialized, infinitely variable; the resulting aesthetic mirrors those same qualities and the Modernists are confused![24]

At the root of this debate, which continues today, is the altered definition of craft brought about by new technologies and post-modern challenges to the modernist sources of inspiration for creating good form. In *The Culture of Craft* (1997), the writer and critic Peter Dormer described a separation of design from craft—a distinction between "having ideas" and "making objects"—that took place in the late twentieth century.[25] If craft is only about the "making" side of the equation, then vernacular form appears crude and unsophisticated—the work of "amateurs." Further, digitally produced typography distances the maker from the object through such functions as typing, clicking, and dragging, so traditional notions of craftsmanship as requiring manual skill are lost. On the other hand, if craft is also about ideas, then the appropriation of forms from popular culture and their technological manipulation are not the opposite of good craft.

Critical writing on typography also accompanied the broadening of stylistic options and reconfigured definitions of craft. *Emigre* magazine (SEE FIGURE 6.19), under the Dutch art director Rudy VanderLans, published its first issue in 1984 and went on to interrogate the continuing relevance of typographic conventions throughout the next two decades (SEE FIGURE 6.20). In the production of its own fonts, Emigre became known as a foundry with particular interest in forms that spoke of their cultural positions and origins. A number of young type designers joined Emigre's Zuzana Licko (SEE FIGURE 6.21) in designing fonts that expanded both the breadth and depth of expressive opportunities in the world of new digital technology.

Cranbrook Academy alumnus Jeffrey Keedy, for example, created typefaces that reflected the post-modern value of subjectivity and were often designed for particular clients and contexts before they became available commercially. Although at first glance Keedy's fonts appear to break with tradition, many borrow elements and attitudes from traditional typefaces. Keedy Sans, for example, owes much to Helvetica. Keedy's Neo Theo was a reference to the work of the de Stijl designer Theo van Doesburg (see pp. 151–52). Hard Times was a derivation of Times Roman (SEE FIGURE 6.22). In an interview in 1996 with *Folio: The Magazine of Magazine Management*, Keedy justified this referencing of previous work by saying:

Nowadays a lot of people who are fooling around with type design do it by sampling; they open up the outline and keep whole chunks of type intact, but they'll add a few things. Personally, I'm pro-sampling .... If the designer is dead, he obviously isn't

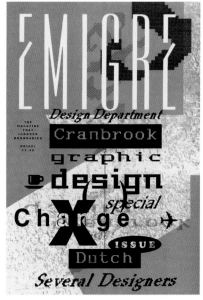

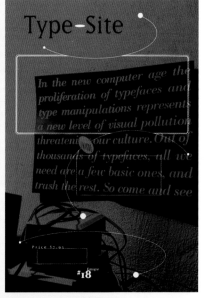

6.19 *EMIGRE* MAGAZINE COVERS,
SELECTED ISSUES 1985–94
Rudy VanderLans (b. 1955) and Zuzana
Licko (b. 1961)

Published between 1984 and 2005, *Emigre*
became the major site for contemporary
discourse on new typographic form.
The magazine's designers, who studied
together at the University of California
at Berkeley, experimented with new
font designs that drew inspiration from
historical and vernacular form, created
layouts that departed radically from
traditional magazine formats, and
commissioned essays that talked about
typography in terms of emerging theories
about culture and design.

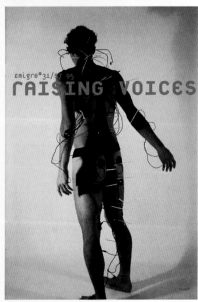

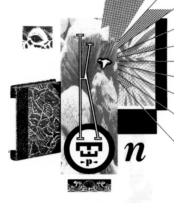

COLD WATER CANYON

Indigenous Shrubs of Santa Monica

PLANOGRAPHIC

YUMMY YUCCA CALCULATOR

PRINTING

sliding aluminum doors

KITCHENETTE

environmentally sound recycled paper

Bakersfield, California

QUALITY

Yosemite National Park

AMERICAN

Chromolithography

CALIFORNIA

APPALACHIAN BLUE GRASS

Environmental

PARKING

Sliding Aluminum Doors

CUCAMONGA

COLD WATER CANYON

flyin' crows

6.20 *EMIGRE* MAGAZINE
SPREADS, SELECTED ISSUES 1992–95
Rudy VanderLans (b. 1955)

6.21 EMIGRE FONTS:
DOGMA, 1994 (*top right*) AND MRS. EAVES,
1996 (*above right*)
Zuzana Licko (b. 1961)

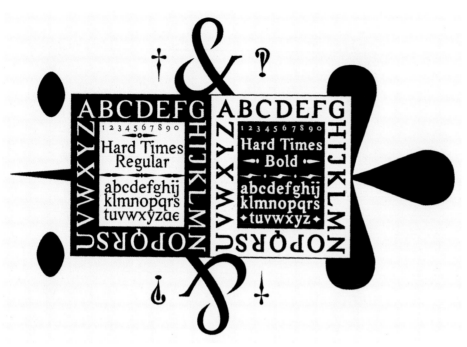

getting a dime for his work anyway, so I don't see a problem. At a certain point, a typeface becomes public domain. But for myself, I draw the line at sampling the work of living designers and encroaching on their intellectual property.[26]

The graphic designer Neville Brody, one of the founding members of London's Fontworks, referred to photographic technology in his font FF Blur of 1992 [SEE FIGURE 6.23] and to jazz history in his font FF Harlem of 1993. His design of the Industria font (1989) for the magazine *The Face* borrows from art deco. The Dead History font by the American graphic designer P. Scott Makela makes reference to the lineage of typeface design, combining serif and sans-serif elements in the same characters [SEE FIGURE 6.24]. The graphic designer Ed Fella was educated first in the advertising agencies of Detroit and later at Cranbrook, and his sophisticated but eclectic approach to typography is informed by those experiences [SEE FIGURE 6.25].

The diversity of these typefaces and layouts reinforced earlier notions that typography and the designer could have a voice, over and above that of the author; that type could speak about something other than its literal verbal meaning and even reflect on its own history. Under the instructional leadership of Wild, Fella, and Keedy, students from California Institute of the Arts pushed the vernacular agenda. Work of this period was frequently for the institution and free from the constraints of commercial clients. Alumni of the California Institute of the Arts (CalArts) and Cranbrook, however, went on to explore similar ideas in professional practice, often for clients who appreciated the intellectual enterprise of work

FF Blur

Dead History

POST-MODERNISM

6.25 *BUY GONE* AND *THIS WORK THAT SERVES NO CAUSE*
Ed Fella (b. 1938)
Prismacolor pencil on paper

Fella's illustrated typography from his sketchbook alludes to his years in advertising. His palette of fanciful forms has the sophistication of an experienced designer, but it is also easy to detect his sources of inspiration in the commercial landscapes of Detroit and Los Angeles.

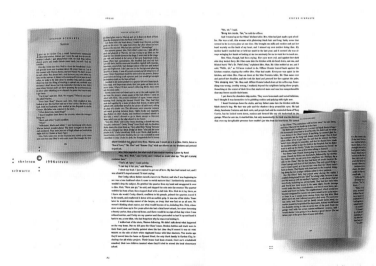

6.26 SPREAD FROM *SPEAK* MAGAZINE, ISSUE 5, 1997
Martin Venezky (b. 1957)
"Skeleton" by Steven Schwartz

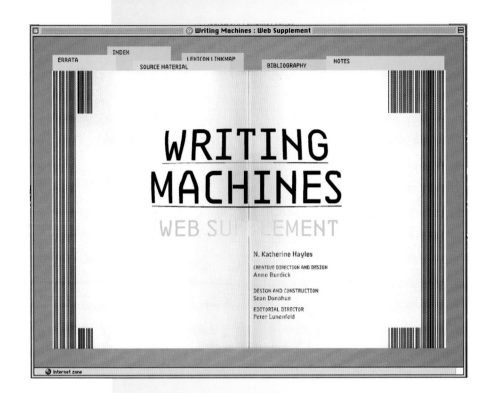

6.27 *WRITING MACHINES*, 2002–3
(left, above, and below)
Anne Burdick (b. 1962)
Text by Katherine Hayles. Produced for the Mediawork pamphlet series by Peter Lunenfeld, MIT Press.

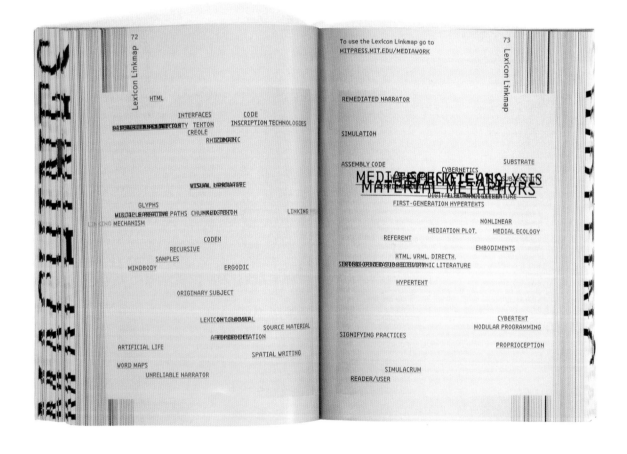

Within the image:

"This visual-verbal dichotomy can be understood through a simple diagram which charts the process (in the Western humanist tradition) of the acquisition of meaning. Seeing and reading are two modes through which we traditionally think of receiving messages. Image and text are two carriers of those messages.

Typically, we think of the process connected with...

This process is... simultaneous...

Upon encountering... fire, a viewer m... heat with little... associations ga... influence this p... experiential on... related to the philosoph... theories of phenomenology.

we see a painting.

On the other hand, the process of reading is typically connected with the verbal process of decoding text's written language signs – letters. To do this, one must know the code. One must have learned to read the particular language of the message. This process is cerebral, rational, deliberate, and linear. If one does not carefully link the proper sequence of signs, one cannot decode the message."
— Katherine McCoy

SEEING

IMAGE   TEXT

6.28   *TYPOGRAPHY AS DISCOURSE*, 1991
Andrew Blauvelt (b. 1964), James Sholly
(b. 1965), and Laura Lacy-Sholly (1965–1999)

that commented on its own roots while solving the immediate communication problem (SEE FIGURES 6.26-6.28).

Other post-modern designers chose typefaces and images that deliberately avoided obvious style in an effort to distance themselves from associations with the high culture of professional design. The Guerrilla Girls, a group of radical feminist artists and designers from the United States, infiltrated mainstream media with messages challenging the patriarchy of the art world and gender discrimination. Their low-budget graphics appeared on the sides of New York buses, on billboards, and in newspapers (SEE FIGURES 6.29-6.30) throughout the 1980s and 1990s. The design recalled the work of anonymous printers who produce volumes of work without the assistance of designers, a fitting approach for a group that does not reveal the identities of its members and takes political action to the streets. In FIGURE 6.30, the "default" form, unlike the rules-based neutrality of late modern typography, is not lacking in cultural character or significance. Quite the contrary. Its meaning depends on our cultural under-standing of the ubiquitous, under-designed form that turns its back on frivolous things and gets straight to the message. It is an intentional use of unpretentious language and low production values in support of political subversion.

Similarly, the work of the American graphic designer Art Chantry draws its inspiration from industrial catalogs, work by self-taught designers, and form created by low-tech and hand processes (SEE FIGURES 6.31-6.32). Often working for

vernacular, appropriated, and default forms

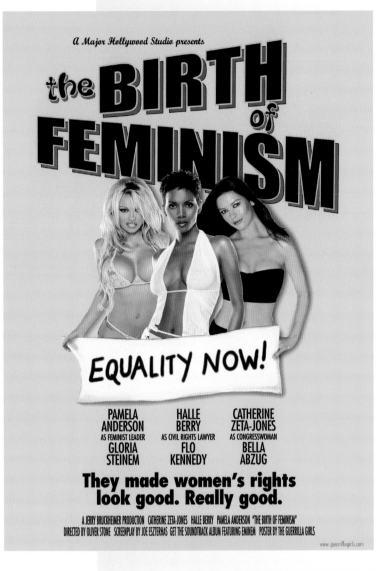

6.29   *THE BIRTH OF FEMINISM*, 2001–5
Guerrilla Girls
Copyright © Guerrilla Girls
Courtesy www.guerrillagirls.com

6.30   *RELAX, SENATOR HELMS*, 1989
Guerrilla Girls
Copyright © Guerrilla Girls
Courtesy www.guerrillagirls.com

6.31   *DESTROY ALL MONSTERS*, 2000
Art Chantry (b. 1954)
Poster for Center on Contemporary Art

Style is more than an arbitrary aesthetic choice; it amplifies meaning. The Guerrilla Girls' vernacular poster style and use of standard typography in newspaper ads and billboards make political statements about the anonymity of women in the gendered world of art. Similarly, members of the group have borrowed the names of famous female artists from history to protect their identity. Chantry also makes references to "undesigned" work in B-movie posters and workplace safety information.

the punk and grunge clients of the rock music industry, his forms are irreverent clashes of design and popular culture—tool catalogs, overly sweet commercial illustrations from the 1950s, science-fiction B-movies, industrial engravings, and vernacular typography undergo the same technological distress of photocopying, tearing, and printing-registration errors. Chantry's compositions speak of simple, physical means of assembly in a digital world of otherwise seamlessly constructed images.

In all of these examples, it is important to understand that the use of vernacular, **APPROPRIATED**, or default form is an intentional repurposing, an entirely self-conscious reassignment of the signification of form from one context to another. In this way, the post-modern use of borrowed form differs from the meaning of these same forms in their original settings or as one-to-one illustrations of subject matter, such as an image of a 1959 Cadillac used to advertise a retro diner with a 1950s theme. The designer is therefore dislocated in a cultural sense—he or she comments from outside the represented culture, choosing these references as a second-level signification or value achieved by their reuse in a new context. The repurposed cultural form may contradict or make ambiguous the meaning of its new context, as in Chantry's use of a tool catalog and "poor" printing to advertise a high-end museum gala (SEE FIGURE 3.10), which forces us to consider the elitism of museums and their audiences. Or it may extend the connotations already suggested by the context, as in the Guerrilla Girls' headline-driven, in-your-face political statement in the daily newspaper, which slips into the prevailing print-media format to assault us with a political message as "tabloid news" and "scandal." In both cases, from a truly post-modern ethos, these images appear to be something they are not.

6.32 *PENIS COP*, 1995
Art Chantry (b. 1954)
Poster promoting condom use, produced for Washington State Department of Social and Health Services

HYPERREALITY AND LIVING IN THE IMAGE

The semiotic and structural analyses of language, and by extension modernism, were frequently criticized as inappropriately "scientific" and as ignoring the subjective aspects of meaning-making and material form. Cultural studies emerged as a way of describing the post-modern relationships between everyday objects, institutions that produce them, and social groups that use them. These studies frequently focus on mass media and often address the issues of class and political or social control.

The Italian philosopher Umberto Eco (b. 1932) addresses the cultural production and exchange of meanings in the relationships among producers, objects, and users. He says we can consider an object in any of five ways: as a physical object; as something that performs a function; as something that has an exchange value; as a sign of some social status; and as a cultural unit that can enter into a discourse with other cultural units.[27] Not only does this describe how objects and images can have multiple meanings that are gained through social interaction and the codes associated with the interacting units, but it also introduces the notion that they signify value beyond their functional use.

For example, an automobile is a physical object that performs the function of moving us from point A to point B. In many cultures it has significant monetary value and the make and model of a car are often associated with a certain social status. A new Mercedes sedan may cost more than a Jeep, but in some social groups it is less desirable. If you are an American teenage male, owning a less expensive, less comfortable Jeep may enhance your personal reputation with peers more than driving your father's Mercedes. And if you customize the Jeep and take it off-road over rough terrain, your status may improve even more. The meaning of the Jeep is more than that of transportation and is shaped by the intersection of various codes that include what are "male," "hot," and "American." The sign-value of the vehicle is therefore a function of its use in social interaction.

Advertising and popular media are the means by which producers influence this cultural transformation from functional product to sign value. Judith Williamson, a British writer and broadcaster on culture and politics, is the author of the seminal work *Decoding Advertisements: Ideology and Meaning in Advertising* (1978). Using examples from magazines, she described how advertising creates a correlation between the product being advertised and another system.[28] Perfume is correlated with a famous model's life, expensive jewelry with romantic love, clothing with athleticism. The external system and the product coexist in the same image. In other words, the meaning of something in an external system (beauty, romance, or physical prowess) is transferred to the product (perfume, jewelry, or clothing) through this coexistence in the image. There is nothing about a man and a woman sharing a kiss that has anything inherently to do with precious metals. According to Williamson we transfer that romantic significance to jewelry through the visual devices of layout, style, and color that connect the couple with the trinkets.

Further, the particular characteristics of the couple are significant—the meaning is different if the people are middle-aged, married, and sitting together on a porch swing than if they are twenty years old, wearing faded jeans, and strolling barefoot on the beach. In each case, the depiction of the couple is an already understood system of meaning, but each gains its particular

6.33   CELEBRATION, FLORIDA
(above and opposite)

The town was founded in 1994 by the Walt Disney Corporation. Disney's project resembles a nineteenth-century American town but has no past and none of the social traditions of places that grow over time. Baudrillard calls this hyperreality, an image of reality that is constructed through the values of advertising but that does not really exist.

significance by not being the other. The sense of comfort with each other and having overcome life's trials together is part of the concept of love associated with the older couple, whereas the younger pair evokes the excitement of new love.

Williamson went on to say that the interchange between the product and another system, through advertising, makes the product and the external system equal in value.[29] And if advertising establishes an equivalence between a line of clothing and all the personal qualities of a sports celebrity, for example, then buying that clothing makes the owner more manly, more successful, more cool, more like the wealthy, or more of any other attribute associated with the celebrity. The clothing is "currency" for acquiring those qualities. In Williamson's terms, it allows us to buy things that could otherwise not be bought and sold.[30]

Eventually, the product can stand as a sign for the attributes of the external system without the images of the external system being present.[31] We read meaning in the surface of the image, not in its substance. An expensive car can stand for an entire world of luxury, and a running shoe or a cell phone can stand for everything that is cool.

The role of style and image is therefore central to post-modern culture, even when it is an inaccurate representation of reality. In *Simulation and Simulacra* (1981), the French theorist Jean Baudrillard (see p. 98) attempted to define post-modern culture as one of simulation, as a copy without an original.[32] Equating the image with sorcery, Baudrillard used Disneyland as the ultimate example of illusion. This imaginary world is constructed to promote a representation of American life, but it does so with the tacit assumption that the real world lacks these very qualities. If these qualities were present in our own lives, why would we pay Disney to experience them? And we are taught by this image to think about an ideal life in these terms. Disney's Main Street is the hometown we all want.

Fifteen years after Baudrillard's discussion, Disney took the simulation a step further in creating Celebration, Florida, a real, planned community built to resemble Disney's image of the perfect American town (SEE FIGURE 6.33). Much like the film *The Truman Show* (1998), in which the actor Jim Carrey breaks down after discovering his life is nothing but image, a stage-set for television viewers that seems real only to him, Celebration is the embodiment of a simple, smalltown America that does not really exist—one with no trash, no crime, no political strife. An article in *Slate*, the online culture magazine, reported:

Celebration was the company's vision of the future, a vision that drew more on Norman Rockwell than Buck Rogers: Think wired bungalows. It was also a social experiment that attempted to provide a variety of housing for a variety of people.... The idea of the inventors of Mickey Mouse making a place for real people—rather than cartoon characters—was tailor-made for ridicule from those who disliked the company's conservative futurism....The truth is that despite its best efforts, the populist Disney Co. has produced an elitist product.[33]

In Baudrillard's view, all cultural forms, all language, have been absorbed into the expressive character of advertising. Here he was not talking literally about advertisements, but about the forms used by advertising: instantaneous, visceral, but easily forgotten messages with no past and no future.[34] The social has collapsed into a commodity to be bought and sold. Celebration, Florida, looks like an idyllic version of nineteenth-century America but it has no real history of its own, no natural evolution that we associate with other cities. Its values are expressed by a corporation, not by the people who live and work there.

Similarly, media teach us the "look" of environmental consciousness, a healthy lifestyle, ethnic diversity, and what it is to have "arrived" socially. These images need not be accurate or rooted in any real cultural traditions. For example, according to CNN, the average wedding in the United States in 2005 cost $30,000.[35] Brides are persuaded to spend by magazines, movies, and other media that reshape public perceptions about what should happen when two people exchange marital vows. These perceptions are in marked contrast to centuries of social practice and a diversity of options, but they ensure the consumption of goods and services for a $125 billion industry.

Many of the more recent images that shape our social identity openly acknowledge the importance of style to the point of being about nothing but style. Nike ads rarely show the shoe. Commercials for the Apple iPod say nothing about the product itself but show dancing figures on a colorful background wearing white ear buds. We recognize that we live in a world of simulation and that style, rather than the functional importance of these objects, drives our consumption.

It is easy to see that design is complicit in creating these simulations. As image-makers in the service of advertising and a capitalist system that encourages consumption, designers are responsible for creating what Baudrillard calls "a map preceding a territory,"[36] visual documentation of a reality that doesn't exist but that guides people's behavior and attitudes. The important point here is not just that the image of the perfect wedding sells goods and services, but that any future bride—financially able or not—begins imagining her nuptials in these terms (or explicitly in opposition to these terms). Just as hundreds of images of the Eiffel Tower shape people's notions of Paris, these simulations frame our dominant perception of "wedding."

Further, designers contribute not only to the content of these images but also to people's ways of processing them. We seduce by surface representations, by images that hide less attractive aspects or consequences, or that are empty of any profound reality. The diversity-indifferent company makes sure that its publicity includes an African-American, an Asian, an Hispanic, and a woman because this is now a coded image for what diversity responsiveness looks like in the corporate world—not to do so would raise questions, even though the coded image may be inaccurate. Audiences have been taught to accept such images as reality or to ignore them completely. We discourage critical thinking about the **HYPERREALITY** such images represent, thereby de-skilling audiences from making judgments about the ideologies behind them. Baudrillard described the engaging quality of such images as "sites of [the] disappearance of meaning and representation"[37] that make it impossible for us to hold a critical viewpoint.

What Baudrillard's post-modern critique illustrates most clearly, however, is that the act of designing is essentially one of social production, and that the images we create produce the society in which we live, over and above any short-term goal to sell or persuade.

SUMMARY

Post-modern design challenged the prevailing assumptions of modernism, including the desire for unity and harmony; a belief in universal form and rational systems; and optimism that design could accomplish the goals of social progress. Such assumptions were undermined by new concepts of the reader; by the formative and illustrative roles assigned to popular culture; by skepticism regarding truth and the possibility of singular meanings; and by the workings of contemporary media on cultural perceptions and values.

While the post-modern ideas discussed in this chapter still shape contemporary design criticism and thinking about the role of design in culture, many designers find them difficult to deploy as generative strategies, as suggesting the kind of form we should make to address the concerns of contemporary society. Contrary to modernist beliefs, design alone could not solve the problems of social class or capitalist economies. And while many designers refocus their efforts toward greater social responsibility and broader notions of who design is for, the fact remains that free enterprise creates most of the clients for design practice.

Further, the stylistic translations of post-modern ideas in the last half of the twentieth century frequently resulted in what some described as overly ambiguous form. Many designers questioned social commentary as a role for client-based projects and argued that designers should be stronger advocates for audience-centered issues. Some felt that the critical discourse embedded in such form was understood only by a small group of design professionals and academics; that it was lost on the public audience at the very center of its concerns. And in many cases, post-modern design had descended into a style without its initial inspiration, into a collection of visual tropes that lacked any true connection to the theoretical bases for such form or any allegiance to texts.

Nevertheless, the discourse of post-modern theory—and its counterpart in the evolving discipline of design history—heightened our understanding of graphic design as a values-driven practice with repercussions in culture. Designers are more aware that the choices they make about form and message belong to a long trajectory of ideas about representation and have consequences that reach well beyond the individual consumer. We now understand that design is a form of cultural and social production. And our concept of the audiences for design and their contribution to the making of meaning continues to expand and deepen.

HYPERREALITY

Jean Baudrillard's term for the simulations created by post-modern culture in which all cultural forms and language have taken on the expressive character of advertising. Baudrillard describes images as being in the service of capitalism, ensuring ongoing consumption by visually representing a view of reality that does not actually exist (e.g. Disneyland has created the "main street" that everyone wants but that will never be found elsewhere in America).

a new paradigm

designing experiences, not object

7

At the same time as post-modern ideas presented interesting challenges to the dominant modernist paradigm, the digital revolution of the late 1980s and the 1990s distracted designers with more practical concerns about how they did their work. Computer technology collapsed the previously separate activities of typesetting, design, photographic processing, retouching, and, eventually, some printing under the responsibilities of the designer. Instead of passing off to specialists the various mechanical tasks necessary to bring art to print, the designer gained complete authority over the technical and formal creation of published work through design and photographic software. The designer took on the traditional role of tradesman, in addition to those of artist and communication strategist.

As software developed, it became possible to create and output accurate facsimiles of printed work in a fraction of the time spent in hand-generated processes and to produce images and typographic form never before attainable by mechanical means. Images could be layered, ghosted, silhouetted, and integrated with text in totally new ways. Glyphs and graphic elements could be set within type and with all the variant specifications of size and weight, as though they were simply additional characters in the alphabet. Text could be arranged along vertical and curved paths and in perspective; it could be converted to outlines, sized, and stretched at will.

The combined freedoms of unlimited form—no longer restrained by the "guilt" of late modernist beliefs in neutrality—and absolute control over most aspects of the production process were exhilarating for designers. It is little wonder that the last decade of the twentieth century was characterized by exuberant visual compositions and the increasing presence of the designer's visual voice in communication.

Likewise, technology left its mark on the audience's interpretation of images. "Photoshop" went from being the name of a software program to a verb referring to the digital alteration of images. Audiences that once viewed photography as the denotative documentation of fact, now see it as an eternally malleable fiction. The cut-and-paste lines, previously visible on the covers of supermarket tabloids, disappear in a seamless representation of a virtual world. Design form therefore now speaks as much about how it is made and distributed as about its subject matter.

With the democratization of the means of technical production, the average person knows about fonts and the significance of publishing has been altered forever. No longer are capital, approval, and production time necessary to distribute content. Everyone is, in some sense, a writer, designer, and publisher.

Although these circumstances expanded the available information, they did not always promote greater understanding or assign deeper credibility. If the imprimatur of a publisher, company, or institutional sponsor was no longer required to produce and distribute content, neither was any other process that ascertained the veracity, quality, or usefulness of information.

Stripped of the role as gatekeepers to technical production, designers looked for new ways to bring value to clients. Design strategy and branding emerged as significant areas of professional practice. Approaching design as an essential business operation, strategists focus not only on how products look and are advertised, but also on what products and services a company provides, how they are delivered, and what contributions they make to the overall relationship with consumers.

The expansion of the Internet, originally designed as communication technology for research scientists and the military, also opened the door to entirely new areas of design practice. The online environment engages users with, and as content producers in, a transformative design opportunity. While in the early days of networked technology designers struggled with the transition from page to screen, it quickly became apparent that interactive media held the potential for bigger and better things than simply replicating the attributes of a static, paper world. Although we still retain some protocols of a print-based culture, many of our communication expectations are now framed in terms of time as well as space, system as well as object, and experience as well as artifact.

THE INSIGHT OF MARSHALL MCLUHAN

The history of writing about electronic media predates the web, the contemporary practice of interaction design, and our current definitions of users. The media theorist Marshall McLuhan (see pp. 27–28, 87–88) was responsible for some of the earliest discourse about media culture and its impact on society, and many of his ideas are still provocative today. Although McLuhan fell out of fashion near the time of his death in 1980, his observations regarding the technological environment have come under new scrutiny in the digital age. McLuhan's former colleague Paul Levinson, in his book *Digital McLuhan* (1999), writes about many of McLuhan's ideas within the context of the networked environment, including:

> → the medium is the message
> → hot and cool media
> → acoustical space
> → the global village

"The medium is the message" is one of McLuhan's most famous aphorisms, and is so evident in all aspects of contemporary media that it is difficult to dispute. This phrase first appeared in McLuhan's *Report on Project in Understanding New Media* (1960) and refers to how media change the world around them by effects that supersede the very content they seek to communicate.[1] The impact of television on how we see the world, said McLuhan, is bigger than the content of any single program.

For example, much has been written about our perceptions of war in the age of television. The first Gulf War (1990–91) was the first time in history that people could watch the bombing of military targets as it happened. CNN broadcast live from the Al-Rashid Hotel in Baghdad as missile strikes took place in the dark of night. A decade later we watched as planes hit the World Trade Center and saw the twin towers collapse in New York City. In the early hours of each story, and only through the power of television, we were "there"—a collective viewing, feeling, and forming of our own impressions of the immediate acts of war taking place from the safety of our homes. Before the end of the first day, however, broadcast networks had names and logos for their coverage and endlessly replayed the iconic footage that came to stand for the events. For many people, their recollections of these events are those of the packaged television experience, not of scenes from their own original viewing (SEE FIGURE 7.1).

McLuhan warned that content distracts us from media effects and that we may not be as critical as we need to be about the real message, the medium itself. He went on to say that such effects intensify as a medium develops by taking on older media and users as its content.[2] Social networking sites, such as Facebook, incorporate the older media of writing and photography and turn participants into content. Any individual's page is less significant than the fact that millions of people are willing to broadcast personal information to strangers, that letters and the telephone are no longer satisfying as the only ways to stay connected to friends at a distance, and that online relationships may be formed more quickly and with fewer social constraints than those made in person. The author and Massachusetts Institute of Technology professor Sherry Turkle, in writing about ubiquitous technology in her book *Alone Together*, says we used to telephone someone to share feelings we already had. Today, many use the cell phone to *get* feelings, to incite emotions that are otherwise absent in our daily lives.

One of McLuhan's most controversial ideas was his description of *hot and cool media*, which refers to our sensory experiences with differing levels of message definition under various technologies. He described radio and film as hot media because they were clearer and more information-rich than other media of his time (they had high-quality sound, clear visuals, and so on). They therefore required little sensory participation by the listener or viewer for completion of the message.[3] Political cartoons and television, according to McLuhan, are low-definition and cool because they require more of our involvement. We are invited to fill in the missing details of the cartoon, and the range and clarity of sound and images on television were, in McLuhan's time, less complete than those of radio and movies. The lack of interactivity in television impressed McLuhan as one of its most important effects. Viewers were encouraged to participate—to fill in detail and depth—by a medium that did not facilitate two-way communication.[4] They were seduced, but with no promise or possibility of fulfillment.

7.1   *DAILY TELEGRAPH*, SEPTEMBER 12, 2001

For many, memories of the 9/11 attack on the World Trade Center in New York are less about any reporting at the moment of the attack and more about the iconic images that were replayed in the media for days after the event.

This hot versus cool aspect of McLuhan's theories suffered a good deal of criticism. At any rate, advancements in technology overcame many of the information deficits cited by him—high-definition color television with stereo sound, for example, may no longer meet his definition of a cool medium—so we rarely hear references to this discussion, except in an historical context.

McLuhan's description of *acoustical space* refers to pre-literate, oral traditions in communication. In the days when information was disseminated orally, by a town crier or in storytelling, everyone within hearing distance had equal access to the same messages at the same time. Sound surrounds all of us simultaneously. McLuhan indicated that, by contrast, we edit vision into figure–ground relationships or frame a field of attention, focusing on things that matter to us and minimizing everything else.[5] In other words, there is less mediation with hearing than with sight, less filtering of information that reaches our consciousness. He suggested that the development of printing changed the world from an acoustical to a visual culture and that the solitary, sequential activity of reading caused us to see the world in fragments and allowed us to detach easily from the fullness of the communication experience.[6]

Television, and by extension computers, reasserted the acoustical storytelling space. It is therefore little wonder that current interaction design favors storytelling as a metaphor for the design of interactive experiences. The computer integrates the shared listening experience of earlier times with the added benefit of visual information and the asynchronous access (on demand, at any time) that we previously associated only with books.

The *global village* is probably one of McLuhan's best-known concepts, although he died before the significance of the term was fully realized in the widespread use of the Internet. The idea of the global village, introduced in a chapter of his book *The Gutenberg Galaxy* (1962), was that electronic media gave people equal access to public information and re-established the simultaneity of the pre-literate acoustical culture—everyone could watch the news on television at the same time, even if they could not talk back. McLuhan went on to discuss the power of media to change how nations practice democracy and business. He famously commented that Richard Nixon's loss of the 1960 presidential election to John F. Kennedy was because the villagers saw too much. Nixon's rumpled, sweaty appearance, in contrast to the cool, composed Kennedy, did not inspire confidence in his possible performance when under the pressures of the presidency.[7]

McLuhan posed four questions that we should ask about any medium in order to understand its effects. He called these the "tetrad" or laws of media:

→ Amplification: What aspect of society or human life does the medium enhance or amplify?

→ Obsolescence: What aspect of earlier media does it eclipse or obsolesce?

→ Retrieval: What does the medium retrieve or pull back into center stage from the shadows of obsolescence?

→ Reversal: What does the medium reverse or flip into when it has run its course or been developed to its fullest potential?[8]

We can think about the cell phone in these terms. It amplified our desire for connectedness over other communication media—for communication with people and for information any time, anywhere. Its wireless technology eclipses landlines and, if fully outfitted, the cell phone provides many of the same functions as our personal computers and televisions. It reinstated the concept of real-time conversation in an e-mail-dominated society, and from an earlier oral society that was made obsolete by print. It also collapsed into one device a phone, camera, computer, and television: media within the medium of the cell phone. The next generation of mobile communication technology integrates computing with the body, clothing, buildings, and the environment, eliminating the need for handheld devices.

What is remarkable about this cyclical process in contemporary times is its velocity. The rapidity with which new technologies obsolesce, retrieve, and reverse old ones is accelerating. Levinson tells us that, in many cases, new media seek to remedy the problems of previous technologies: the personal computer and the Internet facilitate interaction that is not present in television; GPS technology overcomes the physical clumsiness, inaccuracy, and complexity of printed maps; text messaging and voicemail address the problem of on-demand availability for phone conversations.[9]

While McLuhan's ideas suggest little about how to design, they nevertheless provide a framework for understanding the role of technology in defining the challenges for design. At a time when it is tempting to debate the merits of "features and functions" of electronic media, this expanded view is a reminder that technology is not just a tool but also a means of social and cultural production.

A CONVERGENCE OF MEDIA

McLuhan's ideas predate many of our contemporary media but they do reflect awareness that technological change brings about its own results over and above those of any particular affordance introduced by a new medium (see p. 89). The collision and **CONVERGENCE** of old and new produce outcomes that often define particular periods in our technological history.

In the introduction to their anthology *Rethinking Media Change* (2004), the media professors David Thorburn and Henry Jenkins argue the need for "a sensible middle ground between the euphoria and panic surrounding new media" and dispute the idea that "new technologies displace older systems with decisive suddenness."[10] Their book focuses on technological transitions, cautioning us that media convergences occur regularly and constitute an evolutionary process, not a fixed point in time when one medium instantly displaces another.

Thorburn and Jenkins suggest that periods of media change are usually accompanied by heightened reflection as the culture comes to grips with the challenges and opportunities introduced by the new technology. For example, in the 1980s the graphic design press was completely preoccupied with debates concerning the loss of traditional craft and designer control represented by the introduction of the Macintosh, design software, and the democratization of design through desktop publishing. A recurring feature of design conferences during this period was the heated debate between a revered designer from the

CONVERGENCE

Henry Jenkins uses this term to refer to a move from media-specific content to content that flows across multiple media channels. Convergence describes the interdependence of media systems.

modernist tradition and an early adopter of new technology. Their arguments centered on whether those values at the heart of the discipline would survive under the onslaught of changing tools. And design educators still ponder the efficacy of pedagogical strategies that introduce students to the computer in their earliest design experiences, rather than focusing on more conventional strategies of making as prerequisites for digital design (such as drawing and wet darkroom photography).

The authors also explain that these moments of transition and convergence frequently spawn some of the most productive experimentation in the lifespan of that technology.[11] This was certainly the case in the last half of the twentieth century, when digital software expanded the repertoire of formal possibilities of typography and layout. And later, through animation software and digital video, time and motion were added to the repertoire of graphic designers, with results that differed radically from those of traditional animators and videographers.

In contrast, say Thorburn and Jenkins, emerging media also carry the burden of past assumptions and practices. "Inherited forms and traditions limit and inhibit, at least at the start, a full understanding of the intrinsic or unique potential of emerging technologies."[12] The personal computer entered the world in the convergent form of older media (namely, a typewriter and a television). It took nearly two decades before ubiquitous computing embedded similar technology invisibly in objects and surfaces throughout our lives, something the American design consultant Adam Greenfield calls *everyware*. In the early days of the web, screen-based communication looked much like that of print and interaction was defined as page flipping and linking to other sites that also had print as their visual metaphor. Unfortunately, much of this approach still remains in many commercial sites.

REMEDIATION is the process through which the characteristics and approaches of competing media are imitated, altered, and critiqued in a new medium—the representation of one medium in another. The media professors Jay David Bolter and Richard Grusin argue that emerging media gain cultural standing by "paying homage to or rivaling" their predecessors.[13] In some cases, say the authors, these remediations obviously foreground the differences between old and new. Online reference material, for example, adds sound, motion, and search functions to the older technology of books. In other instances, remediation maintains a sense of what Bolter and Grusin call **HYPERMEDIACY**—bits and pieces of other media assembled as fragments within the context of the new medium—or completely subsumes older media so that they are no longer recognizable. YouTube integrates broadcast video with the computer, and online search engines have replaced the library card catalog. Thorburn and Jenkins conclude that "we must resist notions of media purity, recognizing that each medium is touched by and in turn touches its neighbors and rivals."[14]

At a conference in Boston in 2008, Hugh Dubberly (a design strategist and former Apple Computer designer and Netscape/AOL vice-president) suggested that the convergence of different media into single and smaller devices would expand technological mobility. He predicted that the broader application of sensors in the environment will transform the practice of design in more extreme ways than the previous changes that were brought about by the

REMEDIATION

Jay David Bolter and Richard Grusin's term for the process through which the characteristics and approaches of competing media are imitated, altered, and critiqued in a new medium—the representation of one medium in another (e.g. the first personal computer imitated a typewriter and a television).

HYPERMEDIACY

Bolter and Grusin's term for bits and pieces of other media assembled as fragments within the context of a new medium.

7.2 GOOGLE NEWSMAP, 2004
Marcos Weskamp (b. 1977)

Newsmap displays the information gathered by an aggregator in recognizable bands, demonstrating relationships in data as clusters of stories with similar content.

personal computer and design software.[15] We can already see the shifting notion of what constitutes an interface in experimental work by artists and designers, as well as in the concepts developed by commercial companies (SEE FIGURES 7.2–7.6).

Historically, graphic design practice has often focused on constructing visual representations of subject matter (text and image) in books and on signs and screens. In other words, it has focused on the communicative arrangement of form in the space defined by physical artifacts. But new technologies shift our attention from the arrangement of content to the facilitation of behaviors and mediation of experiences in the environment itself, often without users' conscious awareness of the mediation. Greenfield describes this as "information processing dissolving into behavior."[16] "Our interactions with information become transparent: the physical token disappears from the transaction."[17]

Greenfield asserts that this distribution of technological capability throughout the environment (rather than in a CPU and accessed through a keyboard) demands a new set of interface modes and a fundamental change in the paradigm for design. Gestures, for example (as in the finger movements used to scale images on an iPhone), may offer a more intuitive means for interacting with information than the highly conscious interfaces of point-and-click computers. Greenfield argues that the new landscape of information "acts at the scale of the body," in terms both of where we locate technology and how we access it in the environment.[18] In this sense, we can see the importance of establishing a knowledge base for design that is different from the traditional, humanities-based sources—for example, Mark Johnson's work in bodily schemas, as discussed in chapter 3.

7.3 ILLUMINATED MANUSCRIPT, 2002
David Small (b. 1965)
Documenta 11, Kassel, Germany

This project explores the communicative possibilities of spatialized language. Projected typography appears on the physical book. Sensors tell the computer when the user turns the page and sonar sensors allow the user to disrupt and manipulate the text on the page.

A NEW PARADIGM

7.4   TALMUD PROJECT, 1999
David Small (b. 1965)
Cooper Hewitt National Design
Museum, New York

The interface of this exhibit allows
museum visitors to manipulate texts
from the Torah and the Talmud in
French and English. They can trace an
idea from one text to another.

**7.5   CHURCHILL LIFELINE
TABLE, 2005**
David Small (b. 1965)
Churchill Museum, London, England
Designed in consultation with Casson
Mann, UNA Design, and Electrosonic

The 50-foot projection table contains
6000 documents and photographs,
explored through touch strips along
the table edge.

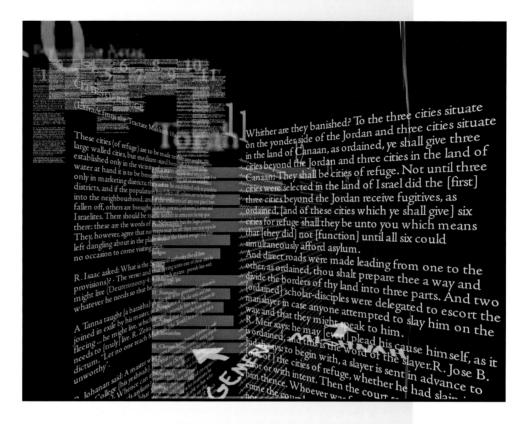

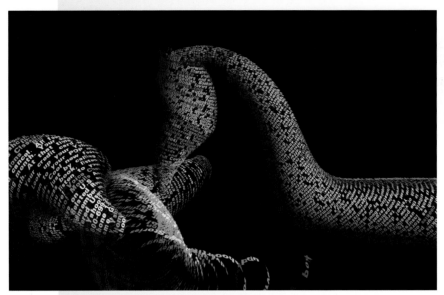

7.6   TENDRIL, 2000
Ben Fry (b. 1975)

Tendril is a web browser that constructs
typographic sculptures from the text
content of web pages. The first page of
a site is rendered as a column of text.
Links in the text are colored, and when
clicked, the text for the linked page
grows from the location of the link.

WHAT IS A SYSTEM?

Graphic designers tend to define systems as something they
make: a graphic identity system; a packaging system for a
family of related products; or a typographic system for the
layout of magazines. In these cases, the designer determines
rules for how visual/spatial components relate to each
other in a variety of applications. Such systems are efficient
because they reduce the number of decisions that have to be
made for each individual application; the rules tell designers
how to deal with recurring conditions.

The complexity of contemporary design problems,
however, argues for a much broader understanding of
systems and system behavior than we find in visual systems.
Instead of thinking of systems only as things we make, we
need to think of them as things that are affected by what
we make. In other words, we need to consider design as
an element or force that produces some kind of change
within other systems that are included in the definition
of the problem. For example, the design of packaging affects
the frequency of damage as products travel to market, the
placement of products in stores, and the impact of waste on
the environment when the package is discarded. How the
product is depicted on the package may determine whether
customers can serve themselves or need expert assistance.

In *Thinking in Systems* (2008), the environmental
scientist and Pulitzer Prize-nominated columnist Donella
Meadows described a system as "a set of things—people,
cells, molecules, or whatever—interconnected in such a way
that they produce their own pattern of behavior over time."[19]
Systems may be affected by outside forces, but they always
respond in ways that are characteristic to the system itself.
If the same force were to affect a different system, the result
would be different, even though the force is the same.
Meadows says that all systems are comprised of three
things: elements, interconnections, and a function or
purpose.[20] A communication system, for example, is
made up of content producers, technologies for the mass
production of messages, physical or virtual artifacts,
channels and policies through which messages circulate,
feedback mechanisms, audiences, and the cultural
environments that shape our interpretations of meaning.
The general function of communication can be specified
further as informative, persuasive, regulatory, and so on.
And interconnections (the relationships that hold elements
together) range from the impact on resources required for
producing communication, to the consequences of that
impact on social identity, economic prosperity, and cultural
literacy. Systems are often big and complex, and while it
is tempting to focus only on the way things look, designers
must understand the larger effects of design action within
the system and on other systems. As Meadows reminded
us, a system is more than the sum of its parts.

In the recent history of graphic design, work that was
once the domain of designers has been increasingly
offloaded to software. The participatory culture, in which
users expect some control over design, has further reduced

The new focus of design in a world of media convergence is on designing tools and systems through which people relate to information, context, and experience, rather than on configuring specific content within physical or even virtual artifacts (see box: "What is a System?").

COMPLEXITY AND EXPERIENCE

As discussed earlier (p. 59), the design methodologist J. Christopher Jones suggested that the problems of post-industrial society reside at the levels of systems and communities (interacting systems). Implicit in design work or the technological mediation of experience at these levels is the idea of **COMPLEXITY**, of an increasingly intricate web of interactions among people, objects, and settings. The chart in FIGURE 7.7 shows accelerating complexity in the nature of the problems tackled by emerging design practices. The horizontal axis represents a continuum of design outcomes, ranging from the design of single

COMPLEXITY

The degree to which design problems increasingly involve interdependent systems: action aimed at one part or aspect of the problem causes change in another part or aspect.

the responsibility of designers for content and how things look. Yet there is significant research to be done by designers in determining how these technological and user-centered systems work. There are a variety of concerns when thinking in systems:

HOW THE ELEMENTS OF THE SYSTEM INTERCONNECT Although it is important to determine what components make up any system, they are often less critical to outcomes than how they interact. A good corporate identity, for example, is useless if customer service is not satisfying. For this reason, designers are now responsible for more than the graphic elements of the brand experience and they often participate in determining the rules for how the system operates.

HOW THE NATURE OF THE SYSTEM IS REPRESENTED TO THE USER The user's conception of what elements are included in the system and what rules guide how elements behave and interact depends on the representations that the system presents to the user. For example, if a website presents itself as offering the user choices, but all choices end at exactly the same destination, then the design misrepresents the system. Or if software grays out certain functions in a navigation system but the user has no idea what caused those functions to become inactive, something in the representation of the system is at odds with the user's idea of how things work.

HOW SYSTEMS AND THEIR USE ARE REGULATED BY FEEDBACK Producers and users of systems depend on feedback to understand the status of the system. Such feedback regulates the system by changing the relationship between things coming in and going out. For example, the battery symbol on a laptop computer tells us how close we are to running out of stored energy. It causes us to adjust our behavior (saving a current document to avoid data loss, recharging, or shutting down to save energy). We interact with the system in specific ways to preserve its functionality. A wayfinding system that provides a map at the front of a building, but no additional signage along the path to a destination is likely to create some anxiety in the traveler. Unlike systems that provide "just in time" instructions at key decision-making points on the route, systems that rely solely on memory do not allow the traveler to process other kinds of information or confirm progress along the correct path. In this example, inputs and outputs are not in sync.

HOW REDUNDANCY AND DIVERSITY IN THE SYSTEM MAKE IT MORE STABLE AND LESS VULNERABLE TO DISRUPTION If there are multiple pathways to accomplishing an end goal, then the failure of any single pathway has fewer negative consequences for the user. The company that allows customers to purchase online, by phone, and through a printed catalog may be more likely to gain market share than the company that sells only through retail stores. And the company website that allows users to search by category, brand, price, size, and sale items may deliver a more satisfying customer experience than the one that limits the customer to any single strategy.

objects to the design of the much broader conditions for people's experiences, which may or may not involve physical objects. The vertical axis represents a continuum of design problems, ranging from simple to complex, defined primarily in terms of the scale at which the problem must be addressed, not in terms of how the design looks.

We can locate traditional and new project types on this matrix, recognizing that the contemporary context argues for work at problem scales of increasing complexity and the engagement of people in experiences. We now understand, for example, that logos have little value if not nested within a larger branding strategy. Whereas corporate identity organized elements, such as logos, typefaces, color palettes, and formats into a cohesive graphic system, branding deals with the larger values of a company, perhaps expressed through the products they make as well as how they are sold. Service design focuses on a still broader range of consumer experiences. For example, Zipcar is the largest urban car-sharing company in the world. As an alternative to ownership, Zipcar members reserve cars on their cell phones or computers. They locate the nearest car via online maps, hold the membership card to the windshield, and unlock the door; the car recognizes the member and the registration time. Gas, reserved parking, and insurance are included in annual plans that start at less than the average cost of a one-day car rental from a conventional rental agency. Drivers return the car to the reserved spot. The company recognized that many urban dwellers and university students do not need to drive every day and do not want the responsibilities of ownership. The service offers fuel-efficient cars that appeal to the social consciousness of its members and uses technology to facilitate the anytime/anywhere registration process for busy members. Zipcar is a designed service experience, and illustrates the fact that the focus of design need not be object-driven.

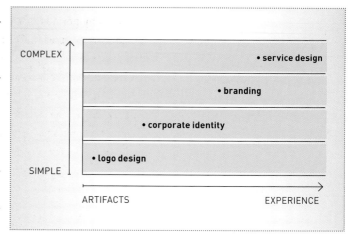

7.7   COMPLEXITY DIAGRAM

Contemporary design problems are increasingly complex and defined in terms of experiences rather than objects.

the nature of experience

The American philosopher John Dewey (1859–1952) wrote in the 1930s that there are conditions that qualify "an experience" from other events in life. First, an experience must have a beginning and an end; we know when it starts and when it finishes. Dewey referred to this as "material running its course to fulfillment."[21] He provided the examples of "a piece of work finished in a satisfactory way" and "a situation . . . [such as] a conversation . . . that is so rounded out that its close is a consummation and not a cessation."[22] In other words, we can bookend an experience in ways that we cannot demarcate other passages of time.

Second, an experience is composed of parts that are distinct but that flow from one to another without interruption. We can remember its moments, but we recall them within a continuous whole. Dewey described this as "the enduring whole . . . diversified by successive phases that are emphases of its varied colors."[23] For example, the experience of a whitewater rafting trip is marked by different levels of challenge and risk in negotiating the rapids, as well as by periods of rest when the raft is simply left to drift with the currents of the stream. Collectively, these sequential events constitute the experience of the trip, yet each episode is marked by its own distinctive physical and emotional demands.

Third, says Dewey, an experience may be described in terms of a quality or unity by which we name it, and thus recall it long after it has happened. We talk about "that baseball game" or "that partnership" as distinct from all other games and collaborations in our past.[24] In some cases, we may even be able to label the quality of the experience: "that once-in-a-lifetime vacation" or "that catastrophic blind date."

Finally, an experience has a pattern and a structure of alternating between *doing* and *undergoing*. "Doing" is the physical or sensory interaction with our environment that we associate with the experience, while "undergoing" is the mental reflection or emotion necessary to interpret the doing—an action and a consequence linked in perception.[25] In doing, we paddle furiously in parts of the whitewater trip, but the undergoing lies in having been challenged by the river and won. Dewey tells us that this relationship is what gives the experience its meaning. The significance of something (and therefore its memorability) depends on the range and content of the relationship between doing and undergoing, as well as on our past experience.

For example, in 1981 the American comedian Steve Martin starred in the musical film *Pennies from Heaven* (adapted from the British television mini-series of the same name), set in the Depression of the mid-1930s. For many viewers it was a forgettable film that did little to promote the actor's dramatic ability. But for anyone with more experience in viewing historical works of art, it was evident that some scenes in the film were based on famous photographs and paintings (by Walker Evans, Reginald Marsh, and Edward Hopper—most notably, Hopper's *Nighthawks*). For these viewers, the experience of watching the film had greater depth, interest, and relevance than it would have had for those who were unaware of these *tableaux vivants*, or "living pictures". Their experience of the film would have been defined, in part, by watching out for and guessing the art-historical connections—in other words, it would have followed a very different pattern of doing and undergoing from the experience of the less culturally aware moviegoer.

In some experiences there may be an excess of doing or an excess of undergoing; things may be out of balance and therefore less satisfying than other experiences.[26] For example, a well-known online travel site requires users to move through a series of sequential pages to reach price information for the purchase of plane tickets. If a particular fare is too high, the user must back out of the site, page by page, to return to the information on dates and times or to check another airline. This excess of doing, in order to compare various options for travel, diminishes the experience of planning a trip. In contrast, a signage system that uses vertical arrows to mean both "forward" and "up" may cause an excess of undergoing—if confronted by both a concourse and an escalator, visitors may pause for longer than necessary before deciding on the appropriate path. When designing the conditions for experience, we must determine the kind of engagement we hope will take place.

It is also important to understand that, as designers, we cannot design someone else's experience. As Dewey pointed out, the doing and undergoing are personal. But we can design the conditions in and through which someone constructs his or her own experience. Thinking about these issues is important as the role of design shifts and expands to include experience-related issues.

evenson's experience model

The design strategist Shelley Evenson offers an experience design model (SEE FIGURE 7.8) that captures both Dewey's concepts of doing and undergoing.[27] She often uses the "Starbucks experience" to explain the model. The customer is *attracted* to Starbucks by an inviting exterior and the smell of good coffee. People appear to be seated comfortably in casual furniture (rather than on the hard surfaces found in fast-food restaurants or standing in seatless convenience stores) and are often reading or engaged in conversation. When customers enter the store they are *oriented* to the appropriate behavior: the design of the store makes clear where they should queue up to place an order and where they can relax, chat with friends, or check their e-mail on the cafe's Internet. Those who have never been in a Starbucks before (are there any of those people left in the world?) are oriented to what the system expects by watching and listening to other customers in the line ahead. The *interaction* with store employees is compelling. The customer does not simply order a small, medium, or large but asks for a tall, grande, or venti. The exotic names of the various coffees reverberate throughout the store as the clerk calls the selection to the barista. The ability to customize the order appears unlimited. All aspects of the environment are considered and the overall experience is *memorable* and positive. The customer leaves the store spreading the social reputation of Starbucks. In this case, the company has designed the conditions for experience—these issues are not left to chance and the conditions are identical in every store.

Evenson's work also addresses the emerging practice of *service design*. While objects and physical environments play important roles in supporting user experiences, service also plays a key role and is something that can be designed. Apple Computer provides an excellent example of a service-based design. We are attracted to the store by its distinctive architecture and/or signage. Machines are not locked in glass cases or stacked in boxes, but are there to touch and interact with. If we have a technical problem with an existing computer, we can register online or in the store for a session at the "Genius Bar," where experts troubleshoot or determine whether the machine should be sent out for repair. If we are looking for parts, such as an adapter or a power cord, the design of Apple packaging—which illustrates the component in a black-and-white photograph on the outside of the box—allows us to find it without assistance from the sales clerk. To make our purchase, we simply locate a clerk by his or her T-shirt and conduct the transaction anywhere in the store. There is no need to wait at a cash register. The clerk either prints a receipt for the sale from a hand-held device or e-mails it to our address. The general atmosphere of the store, therefore, is one of activity and interaction—an innovative service experience that seems consistent with the Apple brand.

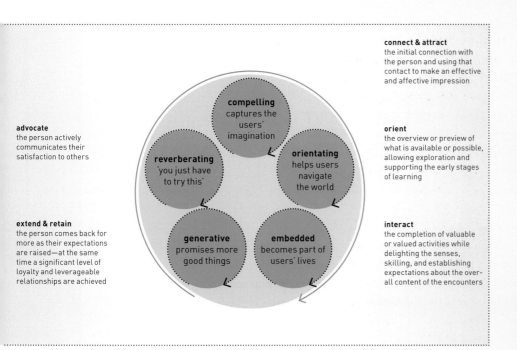

connect & attract
the initial connection with the person and using that contact to make an effective and affective impression

orient
the overview or preview of what is available or possible, allowing exploration and supporting the early stages of learning

interact
the completion of valuable or valued activities while delighting the senses, skilling, and establishing expectations about the over-all content of the encounters

compelling
captures the users' imagination

orientating
helps users navigate the world

reverberating
'you just have to try this'

embedded
becomes part of users' lives

generative
promises more good things

advocate
the person actively communicates their satisfaction to others

extend & retain
the person comes back for more as their expectations are raised—at the same time a significant level of loyalty and leverageable relationships are achieved

7.8   EXPERIENCE DESIGN MODEL, 1980s
Shelley Evenson, John Rheinfrank, et al. Developed at Xerox PARC

designing for an increasingly complex world

It is important to understand that in the chart on accelerating complexity [SEE FIGURE 7.7], work at the "experience" end of the continuum is not just that of big business and is not void of artifacts. Even the socially driven projects that comprise so much of designers' discourse require this level of engagement. At the professional conference of the American Institute of Graphic Arts (AIGA) in 2005, graphic designer Milton Glaser and technologist Nicholas Negroponte shared the stage, commemorating their pairing twenty years earlier at the first AIGA conference. Glaser distributed copies of his most recent poster design for ONE.org, which carried the typographic line, "We Are All African" [SEE FIGURE 7.9]. Negroponte shared his first stories of MIT's $100 laptop, which brought the information world of the Internet to children living in poverty in developing countries [SEE FIGURE 7.10]. What was apparent in this juxtaposition was that graphic design had made such little progress in extending its transformative power across the preceding decades in comparison to technology. In a visual sense, these were equally economical and elegant design solutions, but their basic perceptions of the problems of poverty and what part design could play in addressing them were fundamentally different.

Glaser's poster projected the issue of poverty as a problem to be attacked through a reductivist artifact (as something complicated that the designer simplifies in a compelling phrase and image), not as an enormously complex web of social and physical forces that must be understood before taking action. Negroponte, on the other hand, viewed the complex issues of poverty as something to be managed and made meaningful. He responded with tools and systems, based on an understanding that limited education and access to information have something to do with the reason that people stay poor.

It should be noted that Glaser is not alone in the kind of response he presented. Any beautiful artifact with a similar approach would suffice as an example, and it is fair to say that this poster is linked to a website for the

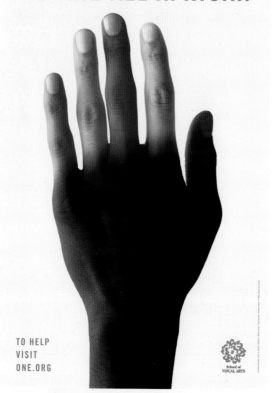

WE ARE ALL AFRICAN

TO HELP
VISIT
ONE.ORG

School of
VISUAL ARTS

one laptop per child

7.9   *WE ARE ALL AFRICAN*, 2005
Milton Glaser (b. 1929)
Designed for one.org

7.10   *ONE LAPTOP PER CHILD*, 2005
Nicholas Negroponte (b. 1943)

A modernist view of complexity was that it was something to be *simplified*. Today, many designers accept that complexity must be *managed*; that the role of design is not to ignore the intricate web of interacting forces but to address problems at the level of systems. The One Laptop Per Child initiative attempted to address poverty in the developing world through a $100 computer that brought learning technology to poor children.

organization, which encourages people in a very general way to lobby their local politicians on the issues of poverty. But the point is that graphic design can do more than provide a simplistic message in explaining to people the complexity of their world and in building the systems necessary to bring about and manage real change.

FIGURE 7.11 shows some of the systems within which any designed object may be nested. Connecting the nodes in the diagram are descriptions of the many relationships that must be taken into account when designing the object. A book has physical qualities that enable or constrain various kinds of thought. It is linear, rather than self-ordered as is information on the Internet. It is reserved as a format for certain categories of content, holds a specific place in the value system of possessions, and is used to advance ideas within particular social institutions, such as education and religion. The printing of books across history changed levels of literacy. In other words, we understand such objects as relating to our thoughts and actions within complex cognitive, physical, social, cultural, technological, and economic contexts.

Moreover, objects change the systems within which they reside. The economic model for the iPod (distributing music through iTunes), for example, is responsible for its success over other MP3 players, but it also changed the recording industry. We no longer feel compelled to buy entire albums and some artists, like the band Radiohead, have bypassed standard sales systems

A NEW PARADIGM

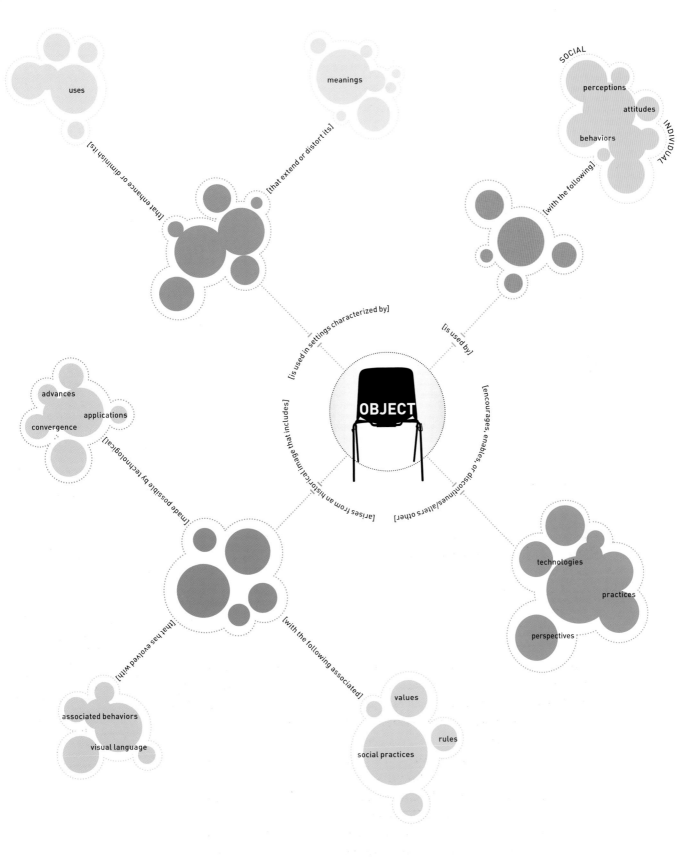

uses

meanings

SOCIAL

perceptions

attitudes

behaviors

INDIVIDUAL

[that enhance or diminish its]

[that extend or distort its]

[with the following]

[is used in settings characterized by]

[is used by]

advances

applications

convergence

OBJECT

[encourages, enables or discontinues/alters other]

[made possible by technological]

[arises from an historical] [image that includes]

technologies

practices

perspectives

[that has evolved with]

[with the following associated]

associated behaviors

visual language

values

rules

social practices

7.11   CONCEPT MAP OF OBJECT CONTEXT

altogether. The cell phone has single-handedly rewritten the rules of etiquette in public spaces and Google, not libraries and newspapers, is the first source for young researchers and newshounds.

Designed objects, tools, and systems therefore serve as mediating devices within intricate networks of people, activities, and settings. If we understand artifacts as mediating between people and something they want to accomplish, not just as physical objects with their own closed system of attributes, then how they look is a consequence of how we want them to perform within a complex system.

THE CHANGING NOTION OF AUDIENCE

In a print-based world it was easy to think of the people for whom we designed as consumers, as the somewhat passive beneficiaries of the designer's expertise. Under modernist ideologies, the designer presumed to judge what kinds of form "worked best" for people (see chapter 5). Under post-modernist frameworks, the designer was also a critic, intervening on the audience's behalf to point out the character of the social landscape: its plurality of meanings, its relationships of power, and the shifting value of its signs (see chapter 6).

Under such communication missions, the designer's concept of audience was shaped largely by personal experience and longstanding cultural conventions governing the presentation of printed information. While marketing studies sliced and diced the audience in terms of demographics and their implications for message approach, clients paid little attention to the audience's actual physical or cognitive engagement with the printed artifact—such interactions were thought to be under the designer's control and embedded within the formal structure of the work itself. A book or brochure, for example, organized information in a linear unfolding of content and maintained a fixed position with respect to the reader, regardless of who he or she was.

But things changed when graphic designers found themselves in the digital world of interactive and networked communication. It was not that printed objects had ever been any less interactive (SEE FIGURE 7.12), but that audience engagement with content became more visible and recordable when people accessed it through computers. The once-absent consumer of information, whose encounter with print-based artifacts usually took place well out of the designer's view, could now be observed. His or her behavior could be studied through methods and software that documented how people ordered information experiences, which features they used, how fluently they used them, and how long they spent with specific content. The consumer became a user and the distinction between products and information was blurred.

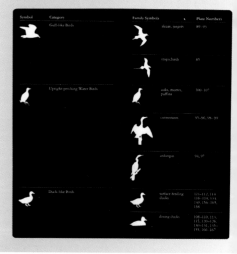

How we communicate with the operating system of a computer, program a DVD player, or text message from a cell phone involves both our physical

7.12 *NATIONAL AUDUBON SOCIETY FIELD GUIDE TO BIRDS*, 1977
Massimo Vignelli (b. 1931)

The field guide is a print example of a database. Readers can access information about birds through location, bird classification, color images, or silhouette.

interaction with an object and our mental interpretation of the graphic language that expresses its underlying system. In times when products were mechanical, not digital, how they worked was apparent to the user: we could, for example, see and hear what happened when a phonograph needle touched the LP record. But the operating systems of digital products are not comprehensible to the user without some kind of interface. We use buttons and icons to interact with the chips and code that drive contemporary products. It is almost impossible, in many cases, to demarcate where the physical interface ends and our interpretive experience begins. This technological collapsing of distinctions between products and communication, brought about by the digital revolution, reinforced the notion of users in graphic design. We could no longer conceive of the people for whom we design simply as consumers of messages—they had to point, click, drag, roll over, save, and delete content in self-directed paths through information.

Human factors—the study of human capabilities (both physical and cognitive)—was a well-established partner in the world of product design but had little influence in communication design prior to digital media. But now that user behavior can be observed, communication designers find themselves accountable for their decisions in new ways and under increasingly social-scientific methods. Intuition and experience are not enough to justify visual strategies in a user-centered context. And the scope of designer responsibility expands well beyond visual aesthetics. Information architecture, the structure and expression of an organizing system for content, frequently falls under the designer's duties, as do the strategies for navigating that structure. In a user-centered design framework the goal is to create the conditions for use and experience, to mediate between people, activities, and the surrounding environment.

scenarios, concept maps, and personas

Among the techniques used by interaction designers to gain a better understanding of users are **SCENARIOS**, **CONCEPT MAPS**, and **PERSONAS**. Scenarios are stories or scripts for projected action. They break down the activities of users into narrative episodes that describe what a user is trying to achieve and the conditions and sequence of steps under which he or she is likely to achieve it. To use a very simple example from the print world, imagine a diner in a restaurant approaching the task of ordering from a menu. Price may be the first consideration: the diner quickly eliminates all entrees that exceed his or her budget. Then personal eating habits may be significant: the diner may not eat red meat or be in the mood for fish. This further limits the viable options on the menu. And finally, the way in which the food is prepared could be relevant: the grilled chicken may be preferable to the fried, or the cooking of a well-done steak is likely take longer than a previously prepared roast. In this way, the act of ordering food is understood as a sequence of decisions, a story, and the typographic design of the menu can be constructed to support that

SCENARIO

A script for an action or a story that is used to understand how a future plan may unfold. A design scenario embeds the components and qualities of the problem in stories that describe both the context and the projected use of designed artifacts or services.

CONCEPT MAP

A diagram showing the relationships among ideas, objects, actions, people, and/or settings. A concept map is a tool for organizing and representing such knowledge.

PERSONA

A social role or character. Personas may be actual or fictional people who represent users. They are useful in understanding the motivations, behavior patterns, and capabilities of those who use goods and services.

experience. Burying the price of entrees typographically within narrative text that describes how the food is prepared ignores, intentionally or otherwise, the diner's need to compare prices.

Concept maps illustrate how actions or events may be sequenced in larger systems. The designer Hugh Dubberly uses such maps to understand a problem in all its complexity before recommending design changes [SEE FIGURE 7.13]. Using a strategy from the education professors Joseph Novak and Bob Gowin, Dubberly connects nodes with propositional statements that describe specific relationships among elements of the diagram. Such maps allow the designer to select a problem area in which to work without losing sight of the larger system or to identify leverage points for design intervention that are likely to produce change.

Personas are descriptions of actual or invented people with particular social roles that allow the designer to think of user interactions in terms of specific goals and behaviors. The motivations of a secretary in word processing, for example, may be very different from those of a fiction writer, a high-school student, or even a designer. By imagining design solutions as used by a range of people, the designer accounts for a wider array of perceptions than his or her own.

The basic premise behind the use of scenarios and personas in design is that they encapsulate a richer understanding of tasks and activities than a simple mechanical description of how the system works—we understand more about a situation and people through stories than through lists and flow charts.

When the design task is the use of a complex computer program or the repositioning of a product in people's busy lives, stories of use can be much more diverse and less predictable than the menu example. In these cases, scenarios and personas are informed by **ETHNOGRAPHIC** research, methods that use observations and interviews with people—in a variety of settings, doing everyday activities—to identify key behaviors and attitudes. Ethnographic research presumes that people are better understood in a holistic sense than through laboratory tests or focus groups that separate the studied activity from the larger context of everyday life. This research is interested in what people say and do, as well as the differences and similarities between the content of the two reporting strategies. IDEO designer Fred Dust explained, for example, that a woman who claimed to have no engagement with "luxury" products or services in interviews was observed having her nails done every week. When questioned about this activity she said she saw it as "essential to life," not as a luxury. In this example, observation provided something that surveys did not.

The cognitive psychologist Elizabeth Sanders is also interested in what people make.[28] Sanders pioneered research methods that ask users to create objects as ways of expressing functions and desires that do not arise from interactions with existing artifacts. In an adaptation of Sanders's methods [SEE FIGURE 7.14], graduate student Michele Wong Kung Fong asked middle-school science students to design a remote-control device for interacting with a computer program on the anatomy of the heart. She discovered through this activity that middle-school students wanted to view the behavior of the human organ under different conditions, such as heavy exertion or a heart attack, and to compare

ETHNOGRAPHY

A research strategy that uses observation, interviews, and questionnaires to gain an understanding of what people do, how they do it, and what meaning it holds for them and their culture. Ethnography is based on the premise that people are best understood holistically and that observing their actions in the fullest possible context will provide the most insight.

7.13 *MODEL OF A BRAND* CONCEPT MAP, 2001 Hugh Dubberly (b. 1958)

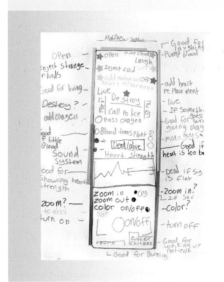
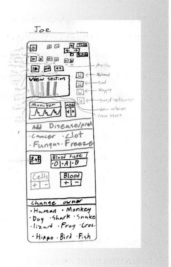

7.14   STUDENT FEEDBACK, 2008
Michele Wong Kung Fong (b. 1983)

Wong's research method asked middle-
school students to design a remote control
for interacting with an online tutorial on
the human heart. The method produced
more detailed responses than if she had
simply asked students what they thought
about the online system. Instead, she
gained information on what students
wanted to know that was not represented
in the prototype.

it to the anatomy of other species. Such revelations would have been unlikely
had she simply asked the students to tell her what they did and did not like
about the software prototype. But it was the opportunity to invent a means for
controlling the program that revealed interest in alternate content. Sanders
describes this as designing *with* people rather than *for* people, as thinking of
people as participants and co-creators in the design process.[29] This position is
consistent with the nature of our participatory media culture.

emergent behavior

Networked media continue to create communities of users who share interests,
knowledge, values, and behaviors. Unlike the isolated readers of print, these
users are self-organizing and they build emergent, adaptive systems from the
ground up. Initially their systems have few rules, but through interactions
with each other, their members develop highly sophisticated communities of
practice with social capital.

In his book *Emergence* (2001), the American technology writer Steven
Johnson describes the history of Slashdot, an online bulletin board and precursor to the blog that began as a way for college student Rob Malda and his
friends to discuss topics of common interest. Before long, he found himself
overwhelmed by participation outside the initial group and unable to screen
comments for usefulness before posting them.[30] He assigned the role of critic
to an elite group of participants who rated comments on a scale of 1 to 5; those
with 3 or above made it to the public site. When the scale of the review task
again exceeded the work force, Malda decided to make everyone a critic, and
published a simple set of rules to guide their critical behavior. In this example,
the system arose from the bottom up, not from designer prediction about how
a site would and should be used.

We can find parallels to this participatory culture in eBay, Facebook, Flickr,
Delicious, and a myriad of other social networking sites. Second Life offers the
opportunity for participants not only to control the interaction with the system,
but also to build a parallel universe with its own social rules and structures. The

role of the designer in these instances is as a facilitator, as someone who builds the tools and systems through which others will invent experiences. The values driving the design are those of the participants as they collaborate, modify, and extend adaptive platforms.

activity theory

Activity theory, as discussed in *Acting with Technology* (2006) by Victor Kaptelinin and Bonnie Nardi, provides a useful model for thinking about design in a participatory culture. Based on the work of Russian psychologists in the 1920s and 1930s, activity theory suggests that wanting to interact with and influence our environment through **ACTIVITIES** is fundamental to human nature. We have motivations and goals, and activities are the means by which we accomplish them.[31] Objects mediate this relationship between people and their environment and, in this sense, all design is interaction design.

Activities can be broken down into their components (SEE FIGURE 7.15). Goals lead to **ACTIONS**, ordered sequences of smaller events within the activity. Under the right circumstances, actions become **OPERATIONS**.[32] Kaptelinin and Nardi use the example of driving. There are some actions, such as looking in the rear-view mirror before changing lanes or using the turn signal, of which we are no longer conscious after we learn to drive. These are operations that were once actions, and they contribute to the larger activity of traveling by car to a destination. Operations can become actions once again if circumstances change—for example, a near miss when pulling out into the passing lane could make us very conscious of using the turn signal immediately after the dangerous encounter.[33]

Kaptelinin and Nardi tell us that the short history of interaction design has been framed in terms of designing and testing actions, not the larger activities they serve.[34] This approach has consequences for design. Think about software manuals that explain how to use features and functions, rather than addressing what it is we really want to accomplish by using them. Human-factors experts tend to test the ability of users to perform actions, to accomplish component tasks; they seat users at computers and watch their behavior. Activity theory argues that this approach misses the point of why the user comes to the computer in the first place and that significant information is lost in focusing only on the physical interaction of an individual with a mediating tool. Activity theorists therefore recommend that design should be tested in real-life use, not in the laboratory or in focus groups.

The designer Jamie Gray provides examples of thinking in terms of larger motives and activities (SEE FIGURE 7.16). Observing the behavior of her family and friends with digital files (photographs, articles, music, movie clips, and so on), she questioned the desktop logic of operating systems as a metaphor for cataloguing personal collections of data. Like collectors in the analog world, her digital collectors search for, sort, and share files in far more idiosyncratic ways than suggested by folders and alphabetical menus. Just as flea-market scavengers and vinyl-record connoisseurs cluster and classify objects by their eccentric properties or personal meanings, so digital collectors group files according to very individual significance. Gray's design of digital collecting

ACTIVITY THEORY

A theory with roots in the early twentieth-century work of Russian psychologist Lev Vygotsky. Activity theory focuses on the analysis of activities as goal-oriented interactions of people with their environment, through the use of physical and psychological tools.

ACTIVITIES

The means through which people, motivated to interact with their environment, accomplish something.

ACTIONS

Components of activities; ordered sequences of smaller events that constitute the complete activity,

OPERATIONS

Actions that become routine through repetition and that are processed less consciously than other actions.

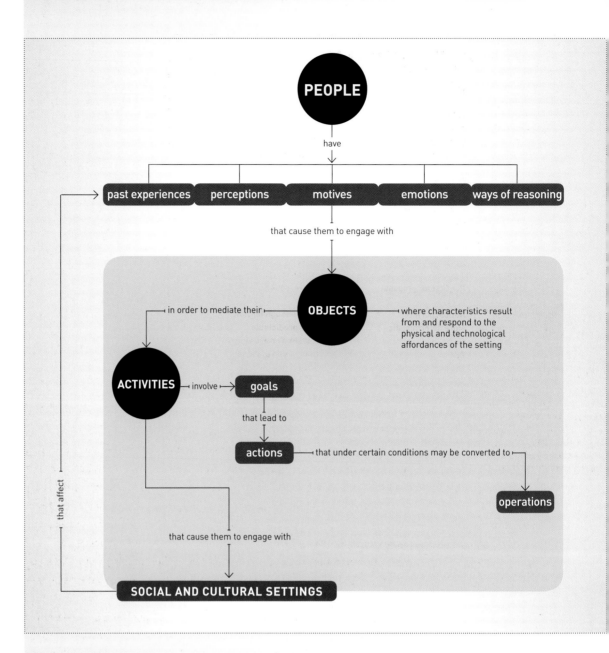

PEOPLE

have

| past experiences | perceptions | motives | emotions | ways of reasoning |

that cause them to engage with

OBJECTS — where characteristics result from and respond to the physical and technological affordances of the setting

in order to mediate their

ACTIVITIES — involve → goals

that lead to

actions — that under certain conditions may be converted to → operations

that cause them to engage with

SOCIAL AND CULTURAL SETTINGS

that affect

7.15   ACTIVITY THEORY
Based on discussion in *Acting with Technology* by Victor Kaptelinin and Bonnie Nardi.

7.16   CURSOR DESIGN, 2006
Jamie Gray (b. 1977)

The cursor moves through a field of photographic images that have been tagged with descriptive keywords. The cursor attracts images that correspond to the selected keywords and repels those that do not match. The user then arranges the selected images according to various organizing principles.

PRINCIPLES OF ORGANIZATION		
	MECHANICAL OBJECT	ORGANIC SYSTEM
ECONOMIC ERA	Industrial age	Information age
PARADIGM AUTHOR	Newton	Darwin
METAPHOR	Clockwork	Ecologies
VALUES	Seek simplicity	Embrace complexity
CONTROL	Top down	Bottom up
DEVELOPMENT	From outside	From inside
	Externally assembled	Self-organizing
	Made	Grown
DESIGNER AS	Author	Facilitator
DESIGNER'S ROLE	Deciding	Building agreement
CLIENT AS	Owner	Steward
RELATIONSHIP	Request for proposal	Conversation
STOPPING CONDITION	Almost perfect	Good enough for now
RESULT	More deterministic	Less predictable
END-STATE	Completed	Adapting or evolving
TEMPO	Editions	Continuous updating

7.17 PRINCIPLES OF ORGANIZATION, 2008
Hugh Dubberly (b. 1958) and Paul Pangaro (b. 1951)
Originally published in *Interactions* magazine, September 2008

tools allows users to tag, sort and re-sort, and display holdings by visual characteristics or private meanings, in the same way as analog collectors.

Activity theory therefore situates our interaction with designed objects and communication within the context of larger motivations to influence the social and physical environment. It extends the scope of study beyond the object itself and examines the concepts of *agency,* our desire and ability to act in the sense of producing effects or outcomes in our world; *transparency,* the ability to turn actions into operations and to render the mediation invisible; and *affordance,* the attributes or capabilities of the technology or design that integrate our capacity for physical responses with our perceptual experiences in culture (see p. 89).[35]

This change in attitude about the people *for* and *with* whom we design is part of a much longer trajectory of technological innovation, beginning with graphical user interfaces, which eliminated the need for users to understand code, and software that moved some control over how something looks from designers to users. It raises questions about the continuing role of the designer and the need to consider new ways of thinking about professional practice.

A NEW PARADIGM

The design strategist Hugh Dubberly, with the technologist Paul Pangaro, argues that these shifts in the focus of design are substantive. In an article for the magazine *Interactions,* Dubberly describes the guiding principles of organization under a new design paradigm (SEE FIGURE 7.17).[36] Under an object-centered, mechanical definition of design practice, the designer is seen as an expert who decides on the attributes of a finished product, which is delivered to management to solve a problem. Under an organic, systems-oriented definition of practice, opportunities and insights emerge from anywhere within the organization or system. The designer steps into this context as a facilitator who builds consensus around ideas that continue to evolve under changing conditions—solutions are "good enough" for the current state of things but "adaptable" to new, unpredictable circumstances.

The latter model, according to Dubberly, is about designing extendable platforms that can respond to change without requiring the redesign of the entire system. He goes on to describe the questions that we must ask when designing a system:[37]

→ For this situation, what is the system?

→ What is the environment?

→ What goal does the system have in relation to its environment?

→ What is the feedback loop by which the system corrects its actions?

→ How does the system measure whether it has achieved its goal?

→ Who defines the system, environment, goal, etc., and monitors it?

→ What resources does the system have for maintaining the relationship it desires?

→ Are its resources sufficient to meet its purpose?

A comparison of designobserver.com or core77.com and the current cadre of glossy design magazines illustrates the differences between an adaptable and a fixed framework. The purpose of these websites and magazines is to feature writing on design and to include articles from contributing authors and editors, comments from readers, recommended reading and resources, and job listings. Both deploy standardized visual systems in their construction. And both have the goals to be timely and critical. But the editorial, copyright, and production protocols of printed magazines limit the ability of these publications to respond quickly to news in the field, whereas the websites can simply link to content generated by other producers. Neither can magazines reconfigure their information hierarchies or expand their content at some point during the period of initial publication, nor can they supplement visual content with sound, video, annotation, and reader-generated content. The archiving capability of online systems also allows content to be repurposed within the system. The magazines, on the other hand, can undergo a redesign but their potential is still limited by technology, editorial infrastructure, and the economic context in which magazines exist.

At the same time, both the magazines and the websites are tied to the conventions of publishing. They have editors, make clear distinctions between experts and readers, and divide content into conventional categories. Neither is prepared to become something else if the social, technological, or economic forces argue for change or expanded roles; to provide in-store design commentary at the time of purchases; to link to, rank, and sort electronic databases of design literature; or to curate a virtual museum of design. In other words, both the magazines and the websites have been designed as frameworks, not as extendable systems.

A NEW PARADIGM

It is clear that a new paradigm for design practice requires new information, not just expanded technological capabilities or the application of old knowledge to a new context. This demand argues favorably for the expansion of the research culture in design and the development of methods of inquiry that respond to the particular concerns of designers, as well as to the interests of other disciplinary experts. In a poll of design professionals conducted in 2005 by *Metropolis* magazine, 81 percent said their firms engage in research that is essential to their business but few share results outside their offices. This suggests that most private practices view the generation of new knowledge as proprietary, as "trade secrets." It is therefore incumbent upon the field to support the development of research in colleges and universities, where the expectation is that knowledge will be disseminated widely. Without such efforts, design will continue to yield increasing intellectual territory to disciplines in which concern for the human condition is a much lower priority.

SUMMARY

Digital technology restructured the work of graphic designers and opened new formal opportunities that were not possible under previous methods for generating type and image. More importantly, it challenged traditional definitions of the relationship between designers and audiences, first recasting the people to whom we communicate as *users*, and more recently, as *participants* in the generation of content and form. Under new forms of design practice, the framing of design as mediation between people and activities through which they influence their environment encourages the development of new methods that surpass the mere testing of features and functions.

Marshall McLuhan laid the groundwork for media theory in the 1960s and many of his predictions were fully realized with the introduction of networked technology. Henry Jenkins and others have written about media convergence in which older media forms collapse into single devices, sometimes with visible residue of past technologies and at other times with no evidence of what preceded the current medium.

McLuhan warned that the introduction of technology changes the scale of everything around it, as is evident in the increasing complexity of problems for design. The shift from designing simple objects to designing for experiences refocuses designers' attention on interactions and behaviors, with the goal of making complexity manageable and meaningful. The philosopher John Dewey provides insight into the nature of experience, describing aesthetic experiences as those in which there is a balance of doing and undergoing, of action and reflection.

Adam Greenfield and Hugh Dubberly describe a progression of technology that will again reconfigure what designers do. Greenfield describes ubiquitous computing as "everyware"—sensors in the environment that do not require conscious experience of an interface with information. Dubberly argues that the design task will be to develop systems and extendable platforms under an organic ethos that is in marked contrast to the mechanical, object-oriented design processes of the past.

It is clear from this limited compilation of ideas that there is no single, unified theory of graphic design. Even more apparent is that the discipline constantly re-evaluates its focus and its field of knowledge as its context shifts.

What began as a trade arising out of printing and typesetting is now both a profession and a discipline. Trades do not worry about theory. Professions and disciplines do, as theory both underlies practice and guides scholarship. As a profession, the contemporary practice of graphic design shows all the requisite behaviors of more mature fields. It has a documented history, standards of fair practice, interest in methodology, and the beginnings of a research culture. As a discipline, however, graphic design—or whatever name we assign to its contemporary iteration—is still exploring the extent of its domain.

Such exploration is difficult when the boundaries are permeable. What we think is important or relevant is always subject to modulations in the culture and the environment. Furthermore, defining the limits of graphic design presents particular problems because it is inherently interdisciplinary: it concerns itself with issues of the humanities and social sciences, of objects and experiences, of people and messages. And as the distinctions between disciplines blur, what truly defines our expertise as designers is often best understood through example, rather than through an inventory of skills and knowledge.

What is not up for debate, however, is that the study and practice of design demand more than a good eye and technical skill. Whether the field will meet its contemporary challenges by borrowing from other disciplines or by constructing its own paradigms and theoretical knowledge remains to be seen.

We live in interesting times.

conclusion

	1800	**1825**	**1850**	**1875**

RENAISSANCE, c. 1300–1600

ENLIGHTENMENT, c. 1650–1800

INDUSTRIAL REVOLUTION, c. 1760–1830

Eadweard Muybridge studies locomotion 1877

GOTHIC REVIVAL ARCHITECTURE POPULAR, 1740s–20th century

NEOCLASSICAL ARCHITECTURE POPULAR, 1750–1950

DAGUERREOTYPE POPULAR, 1830s–50s

Crystal Palace 1851

WORLD WAR I, 1914–18

RUSSIAN REVOLUTION, 1917

WORLD WAR II, 1939–45

ELLIS ISLAND PROCESSES IMMIGRANTS TO THE U.S., 1892–1954

F. W. Taylor publishes *Principles of Scientific Management* for the evaluation of factory productivity 1911

Dorothea Lange begins work for the Farm Security Administration 1935

Lewis Hine begins work for the National Child Labor Commission 1908

The first commercially successful method for producing photographic halftones is patented by Frederic Ives 1881

Paris Exhibition 1900　　Shannon/Weaver model of communication 1949

Sinclair's *The Jungle* 1906

MODERNISM, 1880s–present

ARTS AND CRAFTS MOVEMENT, 1880–1910

Introduction of the Macintosh computer 1984

FUTURISM, 1909–early 1940s

Launch of World Wide Web on the Internet 1991

DADA, 1916–early 1920s

DE STIJL, 1917–31　　*STRUCTURALISM, 1950s–present*

Saussure's *Course on General Linguistics* 1906–1911

SUPREMATISM, 1915–34　　*POST-MODERNISM, 1960s–present*

Barthes's *S/Z* with post-structuralist discussion of readerly and writerly texts 1970

CUBISM, 1907–21　　*POST-STRUCTURALISM, 1960s–present*

Baudrillard's *Simulacra and Simulation* 1981

RUSSIAN CONSTRUCTIVISM, 1917–32

McLuhan's *Understanding Media* 1964

Eisenstein's *Battleship Potemkin* 1925　　Venturi's *Complexity and Contradiction in Architecture* 1966

Loos's *Ornament and Crime* 1929　　Venturi's *Learning from Las Vegas* 1972

Levittown 1947

Miedinger's Helvetica typeface 1957

Neurath's International Picture Language, 1936

GEORGE EASTMAN PATENTS PHOTOGRAPHIC FILM, LAUNCHING THE MODERN AGE OF PHOTOGRAPHY, 1884

Sullivan proclaims "Form follows function" 1896

BAUHAUS, 1919–32

Frutiger's Univers typeface 1954

ADVERTISERS DISCOVER THE ROLE OF ART, 1920–present

Tschichold's *The New Typography* 1928

Cook and Shanosky's pictogram system for AIGA 1974

INTERNATIONAL TYPOGRAPHIC STYLE, 1920s–65

TYPOGRAPHIC EXPERIMENTATION AT CRANBROOK AND CALARTS, 1980–90

EMIGRE *MAGAZINE PUBLISHES POST-MODERN DISCOURSE ON TYPOGRAPHY, 1984–2005*

NOTES

CHAPTER 1

1   Claude Shannon, "A Mathematical Theory of Communication," *Bell System Technical Journal 27* (1948): 379–423, 623–56. Diagram adapted from the original.

2   Philip Emmert and William Donaghy, *Human Communication: Elements and Context*, New York, 1981, p. 40. Diagram redrawn from Figure 2.3.

3   Naomi Klein, *No Space, No Choice, No Jobs, No Logo: Taking Aim at the Brand Bullies*, New York, 2000, p. 28.

4   Ibid., p. 28.

5   Ibid., p. 29.

6   Gerhard Fischer, "Beyond Couch Potatoes: From Consumers and Designers to Active Contributors," *First Monday*, 7(12), 2002 (http://www.firstmonday.org/Issues/issue7_12/fischer/).

7   Ibid.

8   David Berlo, *The Process of Communication: An Introduction to Theory and Practice*, New York, 1960, p. 72. Diagram redrawn from the original.

9   Jean Baudrillard, *The System of Objects*, New York, 2002, pp. 73–84.

10   Ibid., pp. 73–84.

11   Thomas Starr, interview on National Public Radio Talk of the Nation, July 3, 2003, http://www.backspace.com/notes/2006/02/type-and-nation-3.php.

12   Marshall McLuhan, *Understanding Media: The Extensions of Man*, Cambridge, MA, 1994, p. 7.

13   Richard Saul Wurman, *Information Anxiety*, New York, 1989, p. 34.

14   Larry Keeley, "Tailoring: A Design Strategy for the 1990s," paper presented at the American Center for Design conference "Design Strategies in a Changing World," Chicago, October 1990.

CHAPTER 2

1   Gunther Kress and Theo van Leeuwen, *Reading Images: The Grammar of Visual Design*, New York, 2005, p. 6.

2   Imogen Foulkes, "Red Cross mulls 'neutral' emblem," BBC News, December 5, 2005 (http://news.bbc.co.uk/2/hi/europe/4497840.stm).

3   Ibid.

4   Donald Norman, *Things That Make Us Smart: Defending Human Attributes in the Age of the Machine*, New York, 1993, p. 19.

5   Stuart Hall, *Representation: Cultural Representations and Signifying Practices*, London, 1997, p. 24.

6   Ibid., p. 24.

7   Ibid., p. 25.

8   Ibid., p. 25.

9   Steven Heller, *The Swastika: Symbol Beyond Redemption*, New York, 2000.

10   Stuart Hall, *Doing Cultural Studies: The Story of the Sony Walkman*, London, 1997, p. 15.

11   Martha Augoustinos and Iain Walker, *Social Cognition*, London, 1996, p. 34.

12   Ibid., p. 34.

13   George Lakoff, *Women, Fire, and Dangerous Things*, Chicago, 1987, p. 8.

14   Ibid., p. 8.

15   Ibid., p. 8.

16   Eleanor Rosch and Carolyn Mervis, "Family Resemblances: Studies in the Internal Structures of Categories," in *Rethinking Intuition: The Psychology of Intuition and Its Role in Philosophical Inquiry*, ed. Michael DePaul, Lanham, MD, 1998, p. 30.

17   Ibid., p. 30.

18   Ibid., p. 30.

19   Eugenia Picado, graduate student at North Carolina State University, contributed to the analysis of this series of images.

20   Roland Barthes, *Image Music Text*, trans. Stephen Heath, New York, 1977, p. 17.

21   Kress and van Leeuwen, *Reading Images*, p. 46.

22   Ibid., p. 56.

23   Ibid., p. 56.

24   Ibid., p. 66.

25   Stuart Ewen, *All-Consuming Images: The Politics of Style in Contemporary Culture*, New York, 1988, p. 87.

26   Ibid., p. 89.

27   Barthes, *Image Music Text*, p. 25.

28   Ibid., p. 26.

29   American Institute of Architects, *The Architect's Handbook of Professional Practice*, New York, 2001 (13th edn), p. 12.

30   Norman, *Things That Make Us Smart*, pp. 63–65.

31   Matt T. Rosenburg, "Peters Projection vs. Mercator Projection," http://geography.about.com/library/weekly/aa030201a.htm.

CHAPTER 3

1   Christopher Alexander, *Notes on the Synthesis of Form*, Cambridge, MA, 1964, p. 15.

2   Ibid., p. 17.

3   Herbert Simon, *The Sciences of the Artificial*, Cambridge, MA, 1969, p. 55.

4   J. Christopher Jones, *Design Methods*, New York, 1970, p. 31.

5   Ibid., p. 32.

6   Ewen, *All-Consuming Images*, p. 159.

7   Ibid., p. 161.

8   Ann Marie Seward Barry, *Visual Intelligence: Perception, Image, and Manipulation in Visual Communication*, Albany, 1997, p. 42.

9   Ibid., p. 44.

10   Kathryn T. Spoehr and Stephen T. Lehmkuhle, *Visual Information Processing*, San Francisco, 1982, p. 174.

11   Ibid., p. 166.

12   Ibid., p. 166.

13   Ibid., pp. 164–65.

14   Ibid., pp. 174–75.

15   Reported following a study of the Smithsonian's Bicentennial Exhibition in 1976. Source unknown.

16   John H. Falk and Lynn D. Dierking, *The Museum Experience*, Washington, D.C., 1998, pp. 141–42.

17 Spoehr and Lehmkuhle, *Visual Information Processing*, p. 182.

18 Ibid., pp. 182–83.

19 Donald Norman, *Emotional Design: Why We Love (or Hate) Everyday Things*, New York, 2004, p. 11.

20 Ibid., p. 32.

21 Ibid., p. 29.

22 Ibid., pp. 17–20.

23 Ibid., p. 23.

24 Mihaly Csikszentmihalyi, *Flow: The Psychology of Optimal Experience*, New York, 1990, pp. 71–74.

25 Donald Norman, *The Design of Everyday Things*, New York, 1990, pp. 38–39.

26 Norman, *Emotional Design*, p. 38.

27 Ibid., p. 38.

28 William Hubbard, *Complicity and Conviction: Toward an Architecture of Convention*, Cambridge, MA, 1980, pp. 67–85.

29 Jonathan Barnbrook, "Design Anarchy," *Adbusters*, 37, 2001.

30 Norman, *Things That Make Us Smart*, pp. 70–71.

31 Ibid., p. 245.

32 Norman, *Emotional Design*, p. 25.

33 Bernice McCarthy, *The 4MAT System: Teaching to Learning Styles with Right/Left Mode Techniques*, Barrington, IL, 1987, pp. 3–23. (Based on work by David Kolb.)

34 Ibid., pp. 3–23.

35 Ibid., pp. 3–23.

36 Hall, *Doing Cultural Studies*, p. 11 (quoting Raymond Williams from *Keywords*, 1976).

37 Ibid., p. 11.

38 Ibid., p. 12 (quoting Raymond Williams from *The Long Revolution*, 1961).

39 Ibid., p.12.

40 Penny Sparke, *Introduction to Design and Culture: 1900 to the Present*, London, 2004 (2nd edn), p. 4.

41 Ibid., p. 4.

42 Martha Augoustinos et al., *Social Cognition: An Integrated Introduction*, London, 2006 (2nd edn), p. 69.

43 Ibid., pp. 70–71.

44 Ibid., pp. 85–87.

45 Christopher Alexander, *A Pattern Language*, New York, 1977, p. 613.

46 Steven Heller, "Exploiting Stereotypes: When Bad Is Not Good", http://www.aiga.org/interior.aspx?pageid=3080&id=1916, December 13, 2005.

47 Ibid.

48 Ibid.

49 Augoustinos et al., *Social Cognition: An Integrated Introduction*, p. 209.

50 Michael Joyce, *Of Two Minds: Hypertext Pedagogy and Poetics*, Ann Arbor, p. 23 (discussing work with J. David Bolter and Storyspace).

51 Paul Levinson, *Digital McLuhan: A Guide to the Information Millennium*, London, 1999, pp. 95–96.

52 McLuhan, *Understanding Media*, p. 313.

53 Levinson, *Digital McLuhan*, pp. 101–2.

54 http://www.webhustlers.com/nest/about/

55 McLuhan, *Understanding Media*, p. 7.

56 Dennis Puhalla, "Color as Cognitive Artifact: A Means of Communication, Language and Message," doctoral dissertation, North Carolina State University, 2005.

57 Kevin Lynch, *The Image of the City*, Cambridge, MA, 1960, pp. 46–82.

58 Mark Johnson, *The Body in the Mind: The Bodily Basis of Meaning, Imagination and Reason*, Chicago, 1987, pp. 18–40.

59 Richard Florida, "The World is Spiky," *Atlantic Monthly*, October 2005, pp. 48–51.

60 Ewen, *All-Consuming Images*, pp. 153–84.

61 Jean Baudrillard, *The Consumer Society: Myths and Structures*, 1970, trans. Chris Turner, London, 1998, p. 49.

62 Wurman, *Information Anxiety*, p. 33.

63 Ibid., p. 33.

CHAPTER 4

1 Terence Hawkes, *Structuralism and Semiotics*, Berkeley, 1977, p. 20.

2 Ibid., p. 20.

3 Ferdinand de Saussure, *Course in General Linguistics*, trans. Wade Baskin, New York, 1959, pp. 11–12.

4 Johanna Drucker, *The Visible Word: Experimental Typography and Modern Art, 1909–1923*, Chicago, 1994, p. 13.

5 Ibid., p. 15.

6 Saussure, *Course in General Linguistics*, pp. 11–12.

7 Ibid., pp. 25–26.

8 Ibid., p. 25.

9 Drucker, *The Visible Word*, p. 17.

10 Saussure, *Course in General Linguistics*, pp. 122–27.

11 Keith Smith, *Structure of the Visual Book*, Rochester, NY, 2003, p. 327.

12 Ibid., pp. 284–87.

13 Scott McCloud, *Understanding Comics*, Northampton, MA, 1993, p. 94.

14 Drucker, *The Visible Word*, p. 11.

15 Ibid., p. 105.

16 Ibid., p. 107.

17 Katherine McCoy with David Frej, "Typography as Discourse," *ID*, March/April 1988, pp. 34–37.

18 Saussure, *Course in General Linguistics*, pp. 122–27.

19 James Liszka, *A General Introduction to the Semeiotic of Charles Sanders Peirce*, Bloomington, 1996, p. 18.

20 Ibid., p. 18.

21 Ibid., p. 18.

22 Ibid., p. 19.

23 Mark Gottdiener, *Postmodern Semiotics: Material Culture and the Forms of Postmodern Life*, Cambridge, MA, 1995, p. 10.

24 Hawkes, *Structuralism and Semiotics*, p. 129.

25   Ellen Lupton and J. Abbott Miller, *Design Writing Research*, New York, 1996, p. 42.

26   Hawkes, *Structuralism and Semiotics*, pp. 107–8.

27   Michael Moriarty, *Roland Barthes*, Stanford, 1991, p. 25.

28   Ibid., p. 25.

29   Hawkes, *Structuralism and Semiotics*, p. 110.

30   Roland Barthes, *Elements of Semiology*, trans. Annette Lavers and Colin Smith, New York, 1990, p. 26.

31   Roland Barthes, *The Fashion System*, trans. Matthew Ward and Richard Howard, New York, 1983, p. 5.

32   Ibid., p. 9.

33   Ibid., p. 15.

34   Ibid., p. 17.

CHAPTER 5

1   J. M. Roberts, *The New Penguin History of the World*, New York, 2002, p. 716.

2   Ibid., p. 713.

3   Ibid., pp. 866–67.

4   Ibid., p. 716.

5   Sparke, *An Introduction to Design and Culture*, p. 81.

6   Original caption by Lewis Hine to figure 5.1. Source: http://www.historyplace.com/unitedstates/childlabor/.

7   Christopher Phillips, "Introduction" in Maud Lavin et al., *Montage and Modern Life: 1919–1942*, Cambridge, MA, 1992, p. 31.

8   Ibid., p. 35.

9   Liz Heron and Val Williams, *Illuminations: Women Writing on Photography from the 1850s to the Present*, Durham, NC, 1996, p. 68.

10   Ibid., pp. 64–65.

11   Ibid., p. 65.

12   Ibid., p. 66.

13   Ranier Crone and David Moos, *Kazimir Malevich: The Climax of Disclosure*, Chicago, 1991, p. 140.

14   Richard Hollis, *Swiss Graphic Design: The Origins and Growth of an International Style, 1920–1965*, New Haven, 2006, p. 37.

15   Jan Tschichold, *The New Typography: A Handbook for Modern Designers*, Berkeley, 1995 (originally 1928), p. 45.

16   Hawkes, *Structuralism and Semiotics*, p. 51.

17   Ibid., p. 44.

18   David Galenson, *Artistic Capital*, New York, 2006, p. 223.

19   Christopher Crouch, *Modernism in Art, Design, and Architecture*, London, 1999, p. 56.

20   Paul Overy, *De Stijl*, London, 1991, p. 32.

21   Jeannine Fiedler, *Bauhaus*, Cologne, 2000, pp. 20-21.

22   Crouch, *Modernism in Art, Design, and Architecture*, p. 47.

23   Otto Neurath, *International Picture Language: The First Rules of ISOTYPE*, London, 1936, p. 18.

24   Ibid., p. 33.

25   Jae Young Lee, "Otto Neurath's ISOTYPE and the Rhetoric of Neutrality," *Visible Language*, 42(2), 2008, p. 162.

26   Ibid., p. 165.

27   Richard Lanham, *The Economics of Attention: Style and Substance in the Age of Information*, Chicago, 2006, pp. 162–65.

28   Hollis, *Swiss Graphic Design*, pp. 38–42.

29   Ewen, *All-Consuming Images*, p. 27.

30   Ibid., p. 32.

31   Pierre Bourdieu, *Distinction: A Social Critique of the Judgement of Taste*, 1979, trans. Richard Nice, Cambridge, MA, 1984, p. 231.

32   Ibid., p. 231.

33   Ewen, *All-Consuming Images*, p. 32.

34   Crouch, *Modernism in Art, Design, and Architecture*, p. 23.

35   Marita Sturken and Lisa Cartwright, *Practices of Looking: An Introduction to Visual Culture*, New York, 2001, p. 196.

36   Sigfried Giedion, *Space, Time, and Architecture: The Growth of a New Tradition*, Cambridge, MA, 1982 (5th edn), p. 204.

37   Ibid., p. 181.

38   Louis Sullivan, "The Tall Office Building Artistically Considered," *Lippincott's Magazine*, 57, March 1896, pp. 403–9.

39   Ulrich Conrads, "Adolf Loos: Ornament and Crime, 1908," *Programs and Manifestoes on 20th-Century Architecture*, Cambridge, MA, 1986, p. 20.

40   Robin Kinross, *Modern Typography: An Essay in Critical History*, London, 2004, p. 107.

41   Jan Tschichold, *The New Typography: A Handbook for Modern Designers*, Berkeley, 2006 (originally 1928), p. 69.

42   Frederic Goudy, *Typologia: Studies in Type Design and Type Making*, Berkeley, 1977, p. 148.

43   Crouch, *Modernism in Art, Design, and Architecture*, p. 30.

44   Isabelle Anscombe, "The Search for Visual Democracy," *Journal of Decorative and Propaganda Arts*, 4, Spring 1987, p. 12.

45   Crouch, *Modernism in Art, Design, and Architecture*, p. 42.

46   Anscombe, "The Search for Visual Democracy," p. 13.

47   Ibid., p. 13.

48   Frederic J. Schwartz, *The Werkbund: Design Theory and Mass Culture before the First World War*, New Haven, 1996, p. 189.

49   Ibid., p. 189.

50   Ibid., p. 189.

51   Daniel Boorstin, *The Americans: The Democratic Experience*, New York, 1976, pp. 89–145.

52   Daniel Pope, *The Making of Modern Advertising*, New York, 1983, p. 30.

53   William Leiss et al., *Social Communication in Advertising: Persons, Products and Images of Well-Being*, London, 1997, p. 59.

54   Ibid., pp. 65–68.

55   Ibid., p. 65.

56   Ibid., p. 65.

57   Ibid., p. 82.

58   Ibid., p. 83.

CHAPTER 6

1   Dick Hebdige, *Hiding in the Light*, London, 1988, p. 195.

2   Margaret Rose, *The Post-Modern and the Post-Industrial: A Critical Analysis*, New York, 1991, p. 102.

3   Robert Venturi, *Complexity and Contradiction in Architecture*, New York, 1966, p. 23.

4   Robert Venturi et al., *Learning from Las Vegas*, Cambridge, MA, 1977 (rev. edn), p. 3.

5   Ibid., p. 7.

6   Ibid., pp. 6–13.

7   Charles Jencks, *The Language of Post-Modern Architecture*, New York, 1977, pp. 6–7.

8   Rose, *The Post-Modern and the Post-Industrial*, p. 103.

9   Jencks, *The Language of Post-Modern Architecture*, pp. 90–96.

10   Ibid., pp. 122–23.

11   Hugh Aldersey-Williams et al., *Cranbrook: The New Discourse*, New York, 1990, pp. 32–33.

12   Barthes, *Image Music Text*, pp. 160–1.

13   Bernard Tschumi, *Architecture and Disjunction*, Cambridge, MA, 1996, p. 5.

14   Barthes, *Image Music Text*, pp. 160–1.

15   Stuart and Elizabeth Ewen, *Typecasting: On the Arts and Sciences of Human Inequality: A History of Dominant Ideas*, New York, 2006, p. 195.

16   *Helvetica*, dir. Gary Hustwit, 2007.

17   Barthes, *Image Music Text*, p. 155.

18   Ibid., p. 157.

19   Ibid., p. 159.

20   Ibid., p. 160.

21   John Storey, *Cultural Theory and Popular Culture: An Introduction*, Athens, Georgia, 2006 (4th edn), p. 132.

22   Barthes, *Image Music Text*, p. 158.

23   Elizabeth Tunstall, presentation at North Carolina State University, Raleigh, January 11, 2008.

24   Lorraine Wild, "On Overcoming Modernism," *ID*, September/October 1992, pp. 74–77.

25   Peter Dormer, *The Culture of Craft*, Manchester, 1997, pp. 147–57.

26   Ken Coupland, "The Many Faces of Mr. Keedy," *Folio: The Magazine for Magazine Management*, May 1996

27   Gottdiener, *Postmodern Semiotics*, pp. 177–78.

28   Judith Williamson, *Decoding Advertisements: Ideology and Meaning in Advertising*, New York, 1978, pp. 29–31.

29   Ibid., p. 38.

30   Ibid., p. 38.

31   Ibid., pp. 36–38.

32   Jean Baudrillard, *Simulation and Simulacra*, trans. Jean Glaser, Ann Arbor, 2004, pp. 12–14.

33   http://www.slate.com/id/2113107/slideshow/2113258/fs/0//entry/2113259/.

34   Baudrillard, *Simulation and Simulacra*, p. 87.

35   http://money.cnn.com/2005/05/20/pf/weddings/

36   Baudrillard, *Simulation and Simulacra*, p. 1.

37   Jean Baudrillard, "The Evil Demon of Images and the Precession of Simulacra," in *Postmodernism: A Reader*, ed. Thomas Docherty, New York, 1993, p. 194.

CHAPTER 7

1   Levinson, *Digital McLuhan*, p. 35.

2   Ibid., p.37.

3   McLuhan, *Understanding Media*, pp. 22–25.

4   Levinson, *Digital McLuhan*, pp. 9–11.

5   Ibid., p. 6.

6   Ibid., p. 6.

7   Ibid., pp. 68–69.

8   Ibid., p. 16.

9   Ibid., p. 190.

10   David Thorburn and Henry Jenkins, *Rethinking Media Change: The Aesthetics of Transition*, Cambridge, MA, 2004, p. 2.

11   Ibid., p. 6.

12   Ibid., p. 10.

13   Jay David Bolter and Richard Grusin, *Remediation: Understanding New Media*, Cambridge, MA, 1999, p. 49.

14   Thorburn and Jenkins, *Rethinking Media Change*, p. 11.

15   Hugh Dubberly, presentation at AIGA "Massaging Media 2" Conference, Boston, April 5, 2008.

16   Adam Greenfield, *Everyware: The Dawning Age of Ubiquitous Computing*, Berkeley, 2006, p. 26.

17   Ibid., p. 27.

18   Ibid., p. 48.

19   Donella Meadows and Diana Wright, eds, *Thinking in Systems: A Primer*, White River Junction, VT, 2008, p. 2.

20   Ibid., p. 11.

21   John Dewey, *Art as Experience*, New York, 1934, rev. 1980, p. 35.

22   Ibid., p. 35.

23   Ibid., p. 38.

24   Ibid., p. 36.

25   Ibid., pp. 43–44.

26   Ibid., p. 44.

27   Shelley Evenson and Hugh Dubberly, "On Modeling: The Experience Cycle," *Interactions*, 15(3), 2008, pp. 11–15.

28   Elizabeth Sanders, "Scaffolds for Building Everyday Creativity," in *Designing Effective Communications: Creating Contexts for Clarity and Meaning*, ed. Jorge Frascara, New York, 2006, pp. 67–71. (See also http://www.maketools.com/.)

29   Ibid., p. 67.

30   Steven Johnson, *Emergence: The Connected Lives of Ants, Brains, Cities, and Software*, New York, 2001, pp. 152–55.

31   Victor Kaptelinin and Bonnie Nardi, *Acting with Technology: Activity Theory and Interaction Design*, Cambridge, MA, 2006, pp. 59–62.

32   Ibid., p. 62.

33   Ibid., p. 62.

34   Ibid., p. 34.

35   Ibid., pp. 32, 79–80.

36   Hugh Dubberly, "Design in the Age of Biology: Shifting from a Mechanical-Object Ethos to an Organic-Systems Ethos," *Interactions* 15(5), 2008, p. 36.

37   Hugh Dubberly, presentation at the AIGA National Conference, Denver, October 2007.

FURTHER READING

Aldersey-Williams, Hugh, et al., *Cranbrook Design: The New Discourse*, New York, 1990

Alexander, Christopher, *Notes on the Synthesis of Form*, Cambridge, MA, 1964

Alexander, Christopher, *A Pattern Language*, New York, 1977

Armstrong, Helen, *Graphic Design Theory: Readings from the Field*, New York, 2009

Augoustinos, Martha and Iain Walker, *Social Cognition*, London, 1996

Banham, Reyner, *Theory and Design in the First Machine Age*, 1960, rev. edn Cambridge, MA, 1980

Barry, Ann, *Visual Intelligence: Perception, Image, and Manipulation in Visual Communication*, Albany, 1997

Barry, Peter, *Beginning Theory: An Introduction to Literary and Cultural Theory*, Manchester, 1995

Barthes, Roland, *Elements of Semiology*, trans. Annette Lavers and Colin Smith, New York, 1964

——, *The Fashion System*, trans. Matthew Ward and Richard Howard, New York, 1983

——, *Image Music Text*, trans. Stephen Heath, New York, 1977

——, *The Language of Fashion*, trans. Andy Stafford, New York, 2004

Bartram, Alan, *Futurist Typography and the Liberated Text*, New Haven, 2005

Baudrillard, Jean, *The Consumer Society: Myths and Structures*, London, 1998

——, *Simulation and Simulacra*, trans. Sheila Glaser, Ann Arbor, 2004

——, *The System of Objects*, New York, 2002

Berlo, David, *The Process of Communication: An Introduction to Theory and Practice*, New York, 1960

Bierut, Michael et al., *Looking Closer: Critical Writings on Graphic Design*, vols 1–5, New York, 1994–2007

Bolter, Jay David and Richard Grusin, *Remediation: Understanding New Media*, Cambridge, MA, 1999

Bolton, Richard, *The Contest of Meaning: Critical Histories of Photography*, Cambridge, MA, 1990

Bourdieu, Pierre, *Distinction: A Social Critique of the Judgement of Taste*, trans. Richard Nice, Cambridge, MA, 1984

Bury, Stephen, ed., *Breaking the Rules: The Printed Face of the European Avant Garde 1900–1937*, London, 2007

Clark, Hazel and David Brody, eds., *Design Studies: A Reader*, New York, 2009

Conrads, Ulrich, *Programs and Manifestoes on 20th-Century Architecture*, Cambridge, MA, 1986

Crouch, Christopher, *Modernism in Art, Design, and Architecture*, New York, 1999

Csikszentmihalyi, Mihaly, *Finding Flow: The Psychology of Engagement with Everyday Life*, New York, 1997

——, *Flow: The Psychology of Optimal Experience*, New York, 1990

Design Issues. Published since 1984, the journal is currently headquartered at Weatherhead School of Management at Case Western Reserve University in Cleveland, Ohio

Dewey, John, *Art as Experience*, New York, 1934

Docherty, Thomas, *Postmodernism: A Reader*, New York, 1993

Dormer, Peter, *The Culture of Craft*, New York, 1997

Drucker, Johanna, *The Visible Word: Experimental Typography and Modern Art, 1909–1923*, Chicago, 1994

Emmert, William and Philip Donaghy, *Human Communication: Elements and Context*, New York, 1981

Emigre. The magazine was published 1984–2005 and may still be found in some libraries. A selection of essays appears on the Web at: http://www.emigre.com/.

Erlhoff, Michael and Tim Marshall, *Design Dictionary: Perspectives on Design Terminology*, Boston, 2008

Ewen, Stuart, *All-Consuming Images: The Politics of Style in Contemporary Culture*, New York, 1988

Eye. The magazine has been published since 1990. Information can be found at: http://www.eyemagazine.com/home.php

Fischer, Gerhard, "Beyond Couch Potatoes: From Consumers and Designers to Active Contributors," *First Monday*, 7 (12), December 2002 (http://www.firstmonday.org/htbin/cgiwrap/bin/ojs/index.php/fm/article/view/1010/931)

Frascara, Jorge, *Designing Effective Communications: Creating Contexts for Clarity and Meaning*, New York, 2006

——, *User-Centered Graphic Design: Mass Communications and Social Change*, London, 1997

Gay, Geri and Helene Hembrooke, *Activity-Centered Design: An Ecological Approach to Designing Smart Tools and Usable Systems*, Cambridge, MA, 2004

Glusberg, Jorge, *Deconstruction: A Student Guide*, London, 199

Gottdiener, Mark, *Postmodern Semiotics: Material Culture and Forms of Postmodern Life*, Oxford, 1995

Greenfield, Adam, *Everyware: The Dawning Age of Ubiquitous Computing*, Berkeley, 2006

Hall, Stuart, *Doing Cultural Studies: The Story of the Sony Walkman*, London, 1996

——, *Representation: Cultural Representations and Signifying Practices*, London, 1997

Hawkes, Terence, *Structuralism and Semiotics*, Berkeley, 1977

Hebdige, Dick, *Hiding in the Light*, New York, 1988

Heller, Steven and Elinor Pettit, *Graphic Design Timeline*, New York, 2000

Heller, Steven and Philip Meggs, *Texts on Type: Critical Writings on Typography*, New York, 2001

Heron, Liz and Val Williams, *Illuminations: Women Writing on Photography from the 1850s to the Present*, Durham, NC, 1986

Hollis, Richard, *Swiss Graphic Design: The Origins and Growth of an International Style, 1920–1965*, New Haven, 2006

Hubbard, William, *Complicity and Conviction: Steps Toward an Architecture of Convention*, Cambridge, MA, 1980

Jencks, Charles, *The Language of Post-Modern Architecture*, New York, 1977

Jenkins, Henry, *Convergence Culture*, New York, 2006

Johnson, Mark, *The Body in the Mind: The Bodily Basis of Meaning, Imagination, and Reasoning*, Chicago, 1987

Johnson, Steven, *Emergence: The Connected Lives of Ants, Brains, Cities, and Software*, New York, 2004

Jones, J. Christopher, *Design Methods: Seeds of Human Futures*, New York, 1970

Julier, Guy, *The Culture of Design*, London, 2008

Karp, Ivan and Steven Lavine, eds., *Exhibiting Cultures: The Poetics and Politics of Museum Display.* Washington, D.C., 1991

Kaptelinin, Victor and Bonnie Nardi, *Acting with Technology: Activity Theory and Interaction Design*, Cambridge, MA, 2006

Kinross, Robin, *Modern Typography: An Essay in Critical History*, London, 2004 (2nd edn)

——, *Unjustified Texts: Perspectives on Typography*, London, 2002

Kress, Gunther, *Literacy in the New Media Age*, New York, 2003

Kress, Gunther and Theo van Leeuwen, *Reading Images: The Grammar of Visual Design*, New York, 2005

Lakoff, George and Mark Johnson, *Metaphors We Live By*, Chicago, 1980

Lanham, Richard, *The Economics of Attention: Style and Substance in the Age of Information*, Chicago, 2006

——, *The Electronic Word: Democracy, Technology, and the Arts*, Chicago, 1993

Laurel, Brenda, *Computers as Theatre*, Reading, MA, 1991

Leiss, William et al., *Social Communication in Advertising: Persons, Products, and Images of Well-Being*, London, 1997

Levinson, Paul, *Digital McLuhan: A Guide to the Information Millennium*, London, 2004

Levinson, Paul, *New New Media*, Boston, MA, 2009

Liszka, James, *A General Introduction to the Semeiotic of Charles Sanders Peirce*, Bloomington, 1996

Lupton, Ellen and J. Abbott Miller, *Design Writing Research*, New York, 1996

Lynch, Kevin, *The Image of the City*, Cambridge, MA, 1960

Mandler, Jean Matter, *Stories, Scripts, and Scenes: Aspects of Schema Theory*, New York, 1984

Manovich, Lev, *The Language of New Media*, Cambridge, MA, 2001

Margolin, Victor, *Design Discourse: History, Theory, Criticism*, Chicago, 1989

Margolin, Victor and Richard Buchanan, *The Idea of Design: A Design Issues Reader*, Cambridge, MA, 1998

McLuhan, Eric and Frank Zingrone, *Essential McLuhan*, New York, 1995

McLuhan, Marshall, *The Gutenberg Galaxy*, Toronto, 1962

——, *The Medium is the Message: An Inventory of Effects*, New York, 1967

——, *Understanding Media: The Extensions of Man*, Cambridge, MA, 1994

McLuhan, Marshall and Bruce Powers, *The Global Village.* New York, 1989

Meadows, Donella, *Thinking in Systems*, White River Junction, 2008

Moggeridge, Bill, *Designing Interactions*, Cambridge, MA, 2007

Norman, Donald, *The Design of Everyday Things*, New York, 1990

——, *Emotional Design: Why We Love (or Hate) Everyday Things*, New York, 2005

——, *Things That Make Us Smart: Defending Human Attributes in the Age of the Machine*, New York, 1993

Novak, Joseph and Bob Gowin, *Learning How to Learn*, New York, 1984

Poynor, Rick, *No More Rules: Graphic Design and Postmodernism*, New Haven, 2003

Rose, Margaret, *The Post-Modern and the Post-Industrial*, New York, 1991

Saussure, Ferdinand de, *Course in General Linguistics*, trans. Wade Baskin, New York, 1959

Schwartz, Frederic, *The Werkbund: Design Theory and Mass Culture before the First World War*, New Haven, 1996

Simon, Herbert, *The Sciences of the Artificial*, Cambridge, MA, 1969

Sparke, Penny, *Introduction to Design and Culture: 1900 to the Present*, London, 2004

Spoehr, Kathryn and Stephen Lehmkuhle, *Visual Information Processing*, San Francisco, 1982

Stafford, Barbara Maria, *Good Looking: Essays on the Virtue of Images*, Cambridge, MA, 1997

Sturken, Marita and Lisa Cartwright, *Practices of Looking: An Introduction to Visual Culture*, New York, 2009

Teitlbaum, Matthew, ed., *Montage and Modern Life: 1919–1942*, Cambridge, MA, 1992

Thackara, John, *Design After Modernism*, London, 1988

Thorburn, David and Henry Jenkins, *Rethinking Media Change: The Aesthetics of Transition*, Cambridge, MA, 2004

Tschichold, Jan, *The Form of the Book: Essays on the Morality of Good Design*, trans. Hajo Hadeler, Point Roberts, WA, 1991

Tschichold, Jan, *The New Typography: A Handbook for Modern Designers*, trans. Ruari McLean, Berkeley, 1995

Van Leeuwen, Theo and Carey Jewitt, *Handbook of Visual Analysis*, London, 2001

Venturi, Robert, *Complexity and Contradiction in Architecture*, New York, 1966

Venturi, Robert et al., *Learning from Las Vegas*, Cambridge, MA, 1972

Visible Language. Founded in 1967 as the *Journal of Typographic Research*. Information can be found at: http://visiblelanguagejournal.com/

Williamson, Judith, *Decoding Advertisements: Ideology and Meaning in Advertising*, New York, 1978

Wurman, Richard Saul, *Information Anxiety*, New York, 1989

GLOSSARY

abstract Theoretical, conceptual, apart from the physical world. Denoting an idea, quality, or state.

abstraction A reduction of the *content* or concept of something to its most essential form. Twentieth-century artists and designers used abstraction to free visual language from the illusory conventions of art of the past, such as perspective, and to focus on the pure *perception* of *concrete* visual phenomena.

actions Components of *activities*; ordered sequences of smaller events that constitute the complete activity.

activities The means through which people, motivated to interact with their environment, accomplish something.

activity theory A theory with roots in the early twentieth-century work of Russian psychologist Lev Vygotsky. Activity theory focuses on the analysis of activities as goal-oriented interactions of people with their environment, through the use of physical and psychological tools.

aesthetics A branch of philosophy concerned with the fundamental nature of beauty or taste, not with a specific style or arrangement of form.

affect Donald Norman's term for the experience of feeling or *emotion*, as distinct from other kinds of thought.

affordance James J. Gibson's term for the quality of an object, environment, or technology that allows someone to perform an action. Technology can be enabling or constraining in terms of such "action possibilities."

analogous Roland Barthes's term for a *representation* that is natural or that physically resembles what it stands for. A photographic representation is analogous to the subject being photographed, whereas a gesture drawing may be less so.

appropriated Taken for one's own, usually without permission. "Appropriated form" in design is often taken from another *culture* or another period of history in order to borrow the *connotations* of the original.

arbitrariness Ferdinand de Saussure suggested that the relationship between a *sign* and what it stands for is arbitrary. In visual and verbal language, the correspondence between the sign and its meaning is a matter of cultural agreement, not an inherent property of the sign itself.

audience The *receiver* of designed messages. In this context, design must perform, engage, and elicit a full spectrum of human response. Under some circumstances, audiences move from being receivers to being active *participants* in the design process.

behavioral emotion Donald Norman's term for the satisfaction or pleasure that comes from the use of something or from doing something well.

categorization The act of identifying stimuli in the environment and grouping them in memory as members of a category, similar to others in that category but different from members of other categories. Categorization allows us to think and communicate *metaphorically*. Eleanor Rosch and George Lakoff use the concept of categorization in their work.

channel A *medium* for communication or the passage of information. In mechanical terms, the channel is a circuit used as the path for a signal. More broadly, it is the means for delivering messages: print, digital networks, and projection are channels for visual communication.

co-creator A person who engages actively with a designer to determine the best strategies for design solutions. Through structured *activities*, a co-creator may not only provide information about the useful, usable, and desirable characteristics of products, services, and communication, but may also suggest what to make in the first place.

code A set of conventions or principles governing how the *audience* interacts with the *elements* of a message in various media or formats. The left-to-right, top-to-bottom pattern of reading English, for example, demands a certain pattern of engagement with printed text that is different from the ways in which a photograph is read or a film is watched.

collision montage Sergei Eisenstein's term for the frame-to-frame relationships within a film that are achieved through editing and that are intentionally jarring in order to amplify emotional impact. A break in continuous action or point of view used to heighten the visual contrast for dramatic effect.

community J. Christopher Jones's term for a set of interacting or interdependent *systems* that define the scale of design problems in *post-industrial* society.

complexity The degree to which design problems increasingly involve interdependent *systems*: action aimed at one part or aspect of the problem causes change in another part or aspect.

concept map A diagram showing the relationships among ideas, objects, *actions*, people, and/or settings. A concept map is a *tool* for organizing and representing such knowledge.

concrete Physical, tangible, real. Existing in a material form that can be understood through sensory experience.

connotation An idea or feeling that a *representation* invokes in addition to its literal meaning. Because such meanings are not explicit, objective descriptions of fact, they generally arise from cultural and social experiences in which people, things, places, and events become associated with particular *abstract* ideas, *emotions*, or behaviors. Sometimes referred to as second-level meaning.

constructionism The theory that knowledge and meaning are derived from life experiences in a social world. This is in contrast to the ideas that meaning is inherent in objects or that an individual can assign meaning that will be understood automatically by others without explanation. See also *constructionist approach*.

constructionist approach Stuart Hall's term for a view of *representation* in which the meaning of something is shaped partially by the social practices that surround it. See also *constructionism*.

consumer A person who buys and uses goods and services. In design, consumers are those for whom products, services, and messages are created. Human-factors studies and marketing research are used to determine which characteristics and behaviors the members of the target *audience* have in common.

consumer society A social and economic *system* sustained by developing the desire usually through advertising, to purchase goods in increasing amounts.

consumption The acquisition and use of goods by a *consumer*.

content The subject matter or topic of a message.

context The circumstances and background that form the setting for the communication and interpretation of messages. Context includes the communicators themselves as well as the physical, social, cultural, technological, and economic factors that are characteristic of the setting and that place particular interpretive demands on *audiences*.

convergence Henry Jenkins's term for a move from media-specific *content* to content that flows across multiple media *channels*. Convergence describes the interdependence of media *systems*.

corporate identity The *persona* of a corporation, usually expressed through its name, logo, typefaces, and supporting visual applications, which are guided by a manual of *style*.

craftsmanship The exercise of great skill, usually acquired through training. The mastery of materials and *tools*, combined with knowledge of when to use them to accomplish the best results.

cultural position The *post-modern* concept that we all hold identities that determine our particular interpretation of the world. According to this concept, we can never overcome these biases completely.

culture A particular way of life that expresses certain meanings and values in ordinary behavior. According to Raymond Williams, a culture is "a network of relationships with congruent ways of seeing the world."

daguerreotype A nineteenth-century photographic process that used silver-coated copper plates, which were exposed to light and developed using mercury vapor. These fragile metal images required long exposure times (twenty to thirty minutes) and were susceptible to scratching and oxidation.

default A pre-selected option (e.g. one adopted by a computer program) that involves no conscious judgment of quality or function by the user.

denotation The literal or surface meaning of a *sign*. Denotative meaning is explicit and direct and usually avoids *metaphor*. Sometimes referred to as first-level meaning.

design strategy A segment of design practice that helps companies and organizations to determine what to make and do, how to innovate, and how to implement processes for the benefit of the *consumer* as well as the producer.

diachronic Over time. In writing and speech, one word follows another in time.

double coding Charles Jencks's term for the ability of architecture to convey many meanings simultaneously.

dynamic sensation The futurists' term for the idea that objects and forms are in constant motion and in constantly changing relationships with each other and their environment. This concept reflects the futurists' interest in speed and the machine.

element Any text, image, or graphic component of a visual composition. In design, white space is considered an element because its physical qualities are designed and contribute to meaning, in the same way as positive objects.

embodiment Mark Johnson and George Lakoff's term for the idea that cognition and language are shaped by physical experience, by bodily interactions with a *concrete* world.

emergence Steven Johnson's term for what happens in networked media when relatively simple parts interact in simple ways but the result is a higher-level *structure* that emerges with little or no master planning. Social networking is an example of emergent behavior.

emotion Donald Norman's term for the conscious experience of *affect*, in which it is possible to identify the cause or object of the emotion.

ethnography A research strategy that uses observation, interviews, and questionnaires to gain an understanding of what people do, how they do it, and what meaning it holds for them and their *culture*. Ethnography is based on the premise that people are best understood holistically and that observing their *actions* in the fullest possible *context* will provide the most insight.

event schema Martha Augoustinos and Iain Walker's term for a time-based script for everyday *activities*. A *schema* in which there is a sequential organization of episodes that make up an activity or event.

feedback Information given as a response to a message and that serves as the basis for extending, curtailing, or improving communication. Feedback may take the form of an action, discourse, or observable patterns in behavior or opinion.

fixation The period of time in which the eye is at rest or focused on a single object or element in a visual field.

flâneur A term used by Charles Baudelaire to describe a person who walks the city in order to experience it; someone who wants to see and be seen. From the French word meaning "stroller, saunterer."

formative role Penny Sparke's term for the concept that design shapes the *culture* in which it is produced and is actually a means for constructing the values and ideas that eventually become part of the social environment.

Gestalt theory Principles developed by German psychologists in the early 1900s in an attempt to establish a scientific understanding of the relationship between human *perception* and the physical world. These principles focus on the ability of the human mind to recognize whole figures within a collection of individual elements, based on the self-organizing nature of the human brain. From the German word for "configuration," or "essence or shape of an entity's complete form."

hypermediacy Bolter and Grusin's term for bits and pieces of other media assembled as fragments within the context of a new medium.

hyperreality Jean Baudrillard's term for the simulations created by *post-modern culture* in which all cultural forms and language have taken on the expressive character of advertising. Baudrillard describes images as being in the service of capitalism, ensuring ongoing *consumption* by visually representing a view of reality that does not actually exist (e.g. Disneyland has created the "main street" that everyone wants but that will never be found elsewhere in America).

icon Charles Sanders Peirce's term for a type of *sign* that factually resembles the concept or thing for which it stands.

ideographic writing A *system* in which each word is reduced to a single *sign* that is unrelated to the sound of the word itself.

ideology A set of ideas and beliefs characteristic of a social group. Ideology frequently forms the basis of social, economic, or political theory and, in the case of design, may be expressed through particular aesthetic principles.

illuminated manuscript A handwritten text adorned with decoration (e.g. ornate borders and elaborate initial letters at the start of a paragraph).

illustrative role Penny Sparke's term for the concept that design expresses the *culture* in which it is produced, and illustrates the ideas and values that are already present in the social environment.

index Charles Sanders Peirce's term for a type of *sign* in which the relationship between the sign and what it stands for is habitual or causal (e.g. smoke is an index for fire).

intentional approach Stuart Hall's term for a view of *representation* in which the meaning of something is imposed on the representation by its author or maker.

langue Ferdinand de Saussure's term for the *abstract* system of *signs*, governed by rules for their combination in expressing ideas. According to Saussure, it is the differences between signs that make them meaningful and it is the *system* of grammar that allows people within a cultural group to use them to communicate.

learning preference A preferred way of interacting with, taking in, and *processing* stimuli or information.

legibility The degree to which typographic forms and layouts are decipherable, based on their appearance.

low or popular culture Relating to the *taste* of the general public and the use of forms often associated with contemporary commercial media.

materiality The physical qualities of a *representation* that give it individuality and allow it to be categorized. The specific visual, spatial, auditory, kinesthetic, and temporal characteristics of form.

medium A mode or *system* of communication that extends our ability to exchange meaning. Photography and drawing are media.

metanarrative An overarching concept or story that provides a comprehensive explanation for historical or *cultural* experience.

metaphor An analogy or implicit comparison between two things or concepts. A metaphor asserts that two things are alike in some way.

metonymy A figure of speech in which something is called by the name of another thing with which it is closely associated or in which a single attribute is substituted for the larger concept (e.g. "Washington" stands for the American government). Metonymy calls up a field of associations with the thing or concept, whereas *metaphor* targets a specific meaning and assigns it to something else.

model A mental or physical *structure* that represents experience of and knowledge about the world. In conceptual models, meaning resides in the organization or relationships among ideas or concepts. Physical models describe the arrangement of components and the roles they represent within a larger *system*.

modernism An array of cultural movements in the late nineteenth and twentieth centuries that responded to new economic, social, and political conditions and the growth of industrialization, mostly in Western countries. Modernist ideas can be traced to the Enlightenment, an "age of reason," marked by the rejection of superstition and religion as dominant forces in *culture*.

motivation The reason for doing something or viewing something in a certain way. Motivation activates goal-oriented behavior and can be intrinsic (something essential arising from within the individual) or extrinsic (as a response to something outside the individual).

myth A term used by Roland Barthes to describe how bourgeois society asserts its values. The myth depends on *connotations* that are not factual (*denotative*) descriptions of things, but are values assigned to something (such as an image) as a second-order reading of the object that is made to appear natural. For example, according to Barthes, the image of a young black soldier saluting the French flag that was shown on the cover of an issue of *Paris Match* in 1955 propagated the myth that the colonization of Africa by France was supported by everyone—black and white alike.

narrative Storytelling. An unfolding of connected events or *actions*.

noise Anything that interferes with, interrupts, or distorts the successful transmission of a message from its

origin to its destination. Noise can be physical, psychological, social, cultural, or technological in origin.

objectivity The ability to view something with accuracy and neutrality, as it actually exists.

operations *Actions* that become routine through repetition and that are processed less consciously than other actions.

paradigmatic axis, associative axis Ferdinand de Saussure's term for the menu of possible words with associated meanings that could have been used at a particular point within a sentence but were not. Meaning is assigned to the choice of a particular word in the knowledge that others were available but were not chosen. This relationship is vertical and *synchronic*.

parole Ferdinand de Saussure's term for the individual aspect of language or an individual utterance in a specific *context*.

participant Gunther Kress and Theo van Leeuwen's term for any person, object, or *element* within a visual composition or photograph. A participant is an "actor" in the *narrative*.

pastiche A mixture of visual references that imitate previous *styles* or works in a new *context*, a fragmented experience. *Bricolage* is a related term that refers to the construction of something from a diverse range of things.

perception The ability to see, hear, or become aware of something through the senses. Perception includes both the observation of phenomena and the understanding that comes from such observation. It therefore involves memory and is influenced by perspective or point of view.

persona A social role or character. Personas may be actual or fictional people who represent users. They are useful in understanding the *motivations*, behavior patterns, and capabilities of those who use goods and services.

petite bourgeoisie A French phrase referring to the lower-middle *social classes* (between the working class and the upper class) in the eighteenth and nineteenth centuries. Marxist theorists use the phrase to refer to shopkeepers and professionals who are not engaged in production, but who may employ workers and benefit from their labor. The term is also sometimes used derisively to refer to levels of *taste* and habits of *consumption* that are failed attempts to imitate the upper class.

phonetic writing A *system* in which there is a direct correspondence between *symbols* and sounds.

photogram A photographic image made without a camera by placing objects directly on a photo-sensitive surface and then exposing them to light. Areas covered by the objects appear white, while the exposed background is black.

photomontage A composite picture made up of images from more than one source and from multiple points of view.

place schema Martha Augoustinos and Iain Walker's term for a *schema* in which the *content* and spatial organization of elements arise from experience with place.

plastic universal The futurists' term for a set of mostly geometric forms that embodied modern life and that were to be experienced directly, without the illusionistic conventions of previous artistic approaches.

pluralism A condition in which two or more theories, visual references, principles, meanings, etc., coexist in or are called forth by the same design.

positioning The promotion of goods and services in the marketplace, based not on their inherent attributes but on the lifestyle, status, or other forms of socially acquired identity they make possible for *consumers*. Goods and services are positioned strategically in juxtaposition to all the other meanings held by the group of related goods and services.

post-industrial Relating to an economy that no longer relies on heavy industry or mechanical production.

post-modernism A term the meaning of which is debated in a variety of disciplines but that often refers to the conditions of later capitalism and the media saturation of Western societies. Some identify post-modernism as a rejection of the traditional visual forms of *modernism*, while others focus on its distrust of theories and ideologies associated with how meaning is constructed.

post-structuralism An extension of *structuralism* that emphasizes plural and deferred readings of *text*, as well

as a reluctance to ground the analysis of text in any single theory of meaning-making. Post-structural analyses acknowledge that the reader always has a *cultural position* and that no reading of text can be "innocent" of the values or biases that come with such a position.

processing The human transformation of information (stimuli) into meaning. Processing involves *perception*, *motivation*, and *reasoning*.

propaganda A form of communication aimed at influencing opinion or inciting action, based on a particular, usually political or cause-related, point of view.

prototype Eleanor Rosch's term for the "best example" of a category. A prototype is a member so central to the category that it contains most or all of the characteristics that define the category, unlike other members that might be more peripheral and likely to invoke other categories.

rayograph A photographic image made without a camera by placing objects directly on a photo-sensitive surface, exposing them to light, and then shifting the composition for additional exposures. Objects of different densities record at different values from white to black. Rayographs were developed by the American painter and photographer Man Ray.

readability The degree to which typographic forms and layouts are easy or desirable to read, based on their appearance.

readerly text Roland Barthes's term for the idea that the author imposes a singular meaning on the text. This view is consistent with *intentional approaches* to *representation* and privileges the roles of author and maker in design.

reasoning The process of determining a cause, explanation, or justification for something. Reasoning involves forming judgments logically.

receiver The destination of a message.

reception theory The theory that the meaning of something is not created by the inherent qualities of the communication (or literary text) but by the relationship between the object and the reader.

reflective approach Stuart Hall's term for a view of *representation* in which the

meaning of something is inherent in the person, object, place, or event itself and the representation simply mirrors what is already there.

reflective emotion Donald Norman's term for the type of *emotion* that involves contemplation, memory, and learning.

relational The idea that judgments about how design performs (its *legibility*, *readability*, expressiveness, reproducibility, and so on) depend on the particular combination of formal variables, *audience*, and setting.

remediation Jay David Bolter and Richard Grusin's term for the process through which the characteristics and approaches of competing media are imitated, altered, and critiqued in a new *medium*—the *representation* of one medium in another (e.g. the first personal computer imitated a typewriter and a television).

representation A depiction of something (an idea, concept, quality, person, place, thing, or event) in a form other than the one in which it originated. A process through which such forms are created that is motivated by *context* and intention.

role schema Martha Augoustinos and Iain Walker's term for a type of *schema* that contains the norms and expected behaviors related to people's achieved roles (those acquired through effort or training) and ascribed roles (those assigned by society to age, gender, race, and so on).

saccade Rapid eye movement between periods of rest. Saccades relocate the gaze in a different direction and are usually motivated by a search for what the person feels is the most informative area or element of the visual field.

scenario A script for an action or a story that is used to understand how a future plan may unfold. A design scenario embeds the components and qualities of the problem in stories that describe both the *context* and the projected use of designed artifacts or services.

schema Martha Augoustinos and Iain Walker's term for a mental *structure* that contains general expectations and knowledge about people, social roles, events, and places. These structures tell us what to think and how to behave in certain situations and are formed by experiences in a social world.

semantic network Stuart Hall's term for the field of related meanings or *connotations* that are affiliated with a person, thing, place, or event. It is through such affiliations that objects can be "read culturally."

semiosis The process of meaning-making through the interpretation of *signs*.

semiotics, semiology The study of *signs*, particularly their production and interpretation in the *context* of communication and social interaction. Ferdinand de Saussure and Charles Sanders Peirce, the founders of semiotics, sought to define what constitutes a sign and the laws that govern its use. Later work expanded the focus of the discipline to include all sign *systems*, not just words. Under Roland Barthes, images, gestures, sounds, and fashion were studied in semiotic terms.

sender The origin of a message.

sign The most basic unit of *representation*. According to Ferdinand de Saussure's linguistic model, a sign consists of a *signifier* and a *signified*. According to Charles Sanders Peirce, a sign is something that means something to someone in some respect.

signification Charles Sanders Peirce's term for the *consumption* of *signs*: a mental process in which meaning is actively determined and resides in the mind of the interpreter, not in objects themselves.

signified One of two components (with the *signifier*) of a *sign*. The signified is the concept for which the sign stands.

signifier One of two components (with the *signified*) of a *sign*. The signifier is the sound or image that represents the concept. The relationship between the signifier and the signified is *arbitrary* (i.e. a matter of cultural consensus regarding the correspondence between the two, rather than the result of an inherent natural relationship).

social class The hierarchical arrangement of people in groups according to economic or cultural criteria.

standardization The process of developing and agreeing upon uniform technical specifications, criteria, methods, or practices. The assembly line and mass production required the standardization of components so that work could be accomplished through a division of labor.

stereotype A type of *role schema* in which a number of traits are grouped in the mind and may be called forth by a single visual cue, such as skin color or dress.

streamlining Designing the shape of a vehicle to provide the least resistance to air. Streamlined form was popular from the 1930s to the 1950s and was applied to products other than those related to transportation (e.g. irons and toasters).

structuralism A methodological approach to the interpretation and analysis of human *activities* (including cognition, behavior, language, and *culture*) that focuses on the relationships of contrast among elements within a conceptual *system*, not solely in the elements themselves.

structure The arrangement of and relationships among the parts of something complex. In visual terms, structure is composition and involves not only the organization of *elements* but their relationship to the field of vision (i.e. on a page, on a screen, or in the environment).

style A distinctive form or prevailing mode of expression. Often associated with an era or a *culture*, and having less to do with the subject matter of the communication than with how it is *represented*.

styling The surface application of fashionable forms to otherwise functional objects and environments, usually for the purposes of marketing. In the twentieth century, styling became the method of planned obsolescence in American industrial design. *Consumers* purchased the latest product to signify their participation in the display of the most recent cultural trends, even though older versions of the same object were still serviceable.

sustainability Concern for the ecological implications of the full lifespan of goods. The concept is discussed in William McDonough's book *Cradle to Cradle* (2002), which argues that an industrial *system* "takes, makes, and wastes," rather than generates ecological, economic, and social value.

symbol Charles Sanders Peirce's term for a type of *sign* in which the relationship between the sign and what it stands for must be learned and is governed by a *code* or cultural convention.

synchronic At one point in time.

syntagmatic axis, syntax The horizontal relationship between words in a sentence. The syntax of a sentence is the specific arrangement or ordering of words, according to the rules of grammar within the language *system*. Meaning is established not only by the choice of the word, but also by its position within the sentence. The relationship between words on the syntagmatic axis is *diachronic*.

system J. Christopher Jones's term for a set of interacting or interdependent products that make up an integrated whole. Donella Meadows defines a system as a set of things interconnected in such a way that they produce their own pattern of behavior over time, as interconnected elements with a purpose.

tailoring The design of goods and services to respond to the needs and wants of specific *audiences* and to adapt over time as circumstances change.

taste Stuart Ewen's term for an interpretation informed by experiences related to one's *social class*, cultural background, education, and other aspects of identity.

Taylorism A twentieth-century approach to determining the optimal method for performing a manufacturing task. Developed by the mechanical engineer F. W. Taylor.

text Roland Barthes's term for an activity of language production and interpretation which is experienced in the moment. Many interpretations of the text are possible, and they change with the times.

tool The means by which someone accomplishes a task in a given *medium*.

treatment The subjective contribution to the meaning of a message by its maker or author. In design, these aspects of a *representation* are often referred to as *style*.

universal An unchanging entity or quality that transcends the individual, *culture*, or time. Under *modernism*, it was thought that there were universal *metanarratives*, enduring *abstract* ideas that ordered and explained historical experience and knowledge.

vector The dynamic forces or tensions among *participants* in a visual composition or photograph. A vector may be visible (as in a line) or implied (as in the direction of a person's gaze or the perceived trajectory of a shape in space).

vernacular The everyday language of ordinary people that is characteristic of a region or *culture*. In the context of design, "vernacular form" refers to the visual language produced by people who are not trained in design and contains *connotations* of a particular culture, place, or use.

visceral emotion Donald Norman's term for an instinctive or unreasoned emotional response to something.

work Roland Barthes's term for writing that is classic, that occupies a place in the library and history, and that is held physically in the hand.

writerly text Roland Barthes's term for the idea that the reader constructs or writes meaning as an active *participant* in the communication process. This view is consistent with *constructionist* approaches to *representation* and supports the position that there are many meanings of the same text.

PICTURE CREDITS

INDEX

Page references in *italic* refer to illustrations.